The Text
of Great Britain

The Text
of Great Britain

Theme and Design
in Defoe's *Tour*

Pat Rogers

DELAWARE

Newark: University of Delaware Press
London: Associated University Presses

Associated University Presses
440 Forsgate Drive
Cranbury, NJ 08512

Associated University Presses
16 Barter Street
London WC1A 2AH, England

Associated University Presses
P.O. Box 338, Port Credit
Mississauga, Ontario
Canada L5G 4L8

The paper used in this publication meets the requirements of the American National Standard for Permanence of Paper for Printed Library Materials Z39.48–1984.

Library of Congress Cataloging-in-Publication Data

Rogers, Pat, 1938–
     The text of Great Britain : theme and design in Defoe's Tour / Pat Rogers.
        p.   cm.
     Includes bibliographical references (p.) and index.
     ISBN 0-87413-617-2 (alk. paper)
     1. Defoe, Daniel, 1661?–1731. Tour thro' the whole island of Great Britain.   2. Great Britain—History—18th century—Historiography.   3. Travelers' writings, English—History and criticism.   4. British—Travel—Historiography.   I. Title.
DA620.D31R64   1998
914.104'7—dc21
                                                              97-727
                                                                CIP

for Ilse-Renate Vickers

Was it any wonder that England was the most widely explored country on earth? In a sense, nothing was unknown in England— it was just differently interpreted.
                              —Paul Theroux, *The Kingdom by the Sea*

For Europe is absent. This is an island and therefore Unreal.
                              —W. H. Auden, "Journey to Iceland"

Contents

Abbreviations

The following abbreviations are used in the text:

Backscheider   Paula R. Backscheider, *Daniel Defoe: His Life* (Baltimore: Johns Hopkins University Press, 1989).

Camden   William Camden, *Britannia,* ed. Edmund Gibson (1695; reprint, Newton Abbot, Devon: David & Charles, 1971).

Checklist   J. R. Moore, *A Checklist of the Writings of Daniel Defoe* (Bloomington: Indiana University Press, 1960).

Lee   William Lee, *Daniel Defoe: His Life and Recently Discovered Writings,* 3 vols. (1869; reprint, Hildesheim: Georg Olds, 1968).

Letters   *The Letters of Daniel Defoe,* ed. G. H. Healey (Oxford: Clarendon, 1955).

Tour   Daniel Defoe, *A Tour thro' the Whole Island of Great Britain* (1724–26; reprint in 2 vols., London: Frank Cass; New York: A. M. Kelley, 1968). All references in the text follow this edition.

Preface

Daniel Defoe's *Tour thro' the Whole Island of Great Britain* has long been recognized as a key book of its age. It has been lauded by the most eminent historians as a prime source of understanding for Britain in the eighteenth century (indeed, for understanding the birth of the modern, on a global scale), and remains one of the most-quoted works in general surveys of the period. However, the *Tour* has still not been accorded the detailed treatment by literary scholars that it ought to have enjoyed. This is a pity, since it ranks with *Robinson Crusoe*, *Moll Flanders*, and *Roxana* as one of the richest and most enduring items among Defoe's astonishingly diverse output. A recent abridgment, sumptuously illustrated, has joined earlier editions to give the work renewed currency. But until late years, travel writing was a comparatively neglected genre, and we still do not have a well-established poetics of the form, though studies such as Charles L. Batten's *Pleasurable Instruction: Form and Convention in Eighteenth-Century Travel Literature* (1978) have gone a little way to remedy this deficiency. Nevertheless, we are far from doing critical justice to the *Tour*, or to other classics of eighteenth-century travel writing.

The aim of this book is to provide a basis for reassessment of the work by describing the elements that went into its making. In the introduction I have tried to set out enough of a conceptual framework to make the more detailed chapters that follow fully intelligible. This task involves putting the *Tour* into the historical context of travel writing, and the development of a rhetoric of tourism (an aspect developed in chapter 7). I also seek to locate the book within Defoe's wider oeuvre: although extensive comparisons and links are not developed (beyond a sustained parallelism explored in chapter 6), enough should have been said to indicate how we might apply some of this book's findings to the better-known novels. Other aspects of the *Tour*'s ideology are considered, notably its political bearings and especially its treatment of the South Sea Bubble of 1720, a recent national disaster that had strong personal overtones for Defoe. Finally, I attempt to illuminate the "design" of the work, that is to say its formal structure, along with the intellectual attitudes supporting and supported by that structure.

The main body of this study is divided into three parts, dealing
respectively with "Pre-Text," "Text," and "Context." Three chapters
are grouped in each part. The first group concerns itself with the
actual circumstances of writing—the *production* of the text, in the
sense of when and how the *Tour* came into existence, including the
nature, scope and timing of Defoe's research for the book. Chapter 1
considers in detail the composition of the first volume, while chapter
2 considers that of its two successors. In both cases I wish to show
that the text was based on a more up-to-date sense of the nation than
has generally been allowed, especially for the regions of Britain nearest
to London (with which Defoe was always most familiar and which
occupy much of the first two volumes). Following this, chapter 3
assesses the contribution to the text made by raids on Defoe's predecessor in topographical writing, William Camden, and more specifically on the edition of *Britannia* put out by Edmund Gibson and his
collaborators in 1695. Defoe acknowledges some of his debt to Camden, but occludes his borrowing in many other places. One prolonged
section of plagiarism is discussed in order to illustrate Defoe's habits
at times of greatest stress, that is in the absence of real information
of his own.

Part II deals with issues surrounding the method and content of
the *Tour*. Thus, chapter 4 considers an aspect of the style of the work,
its continual opposition of images of growth and decay, with a view to
understanding Defoe's complex attitudes toward change in the social
landscape around him. This figurative technique serves, in fact, to
express a particular vision of the state of Britain, as it negotiated its
transition from the old semifeudal world into a commercial and "polite" civilization. Next, in chapter 5, a pervasive Virgilian theme in
the work is identified and its contribution to the texture of the writing
is analyzed. Chapter 6 compares the ways in which Defoe describes
progress across land in the *Tour* and in a fictional work, set in a part
of the world he never visited—*Captain Singleton*.

Part III moves into historical and ideological bearings of the *Tour*.
The "context" supplied is variously that of the natural landscape, the
man-made environment, and the general march of the British economy.
Chapter 7 deals with an extensive passage in which Defoe mocks the
conventional panegyrics of the Derbyshire "Peak District," a site of
the emergent tourist industry and a locus of standard touristic rhetoric
in topographical writing. After this, in chapter 8, comes an account
of the way in which Defoe treats architecture, an element in the *Tour*
that has been almost entirely neglected despite extensive coverage in
the text. Finally, chapter 9 assesses Defoe's account of Britain as a
social and economic entity. The *Tour* depicts the nation as a large

organism in the throes of a dynamic urge toward "improvement." Sometimes the system appears to have achieved equilibrium, at others the competing energies of change and stability produce a situation of conflict, which Defoe's narrative and organizational strategies attempt to resolve.

This chapter leads directly into the conclusion, where I summarize Defoe's effort to provide a verbal enactment of the scope of national life, and a literary equivalent of its identity at the start of the Han- overian era. An appendix briefly considers some of the afterlife of the *Tour,* involving the most significant among its later publishers and editors, Samuel Richardson, as well as possible distribution through the chapbook trade. It should not be forgotten that the *Tour* was one of the most popular works of Defoe for several generations (when his novels apart from *Crusoe* were largely forgotten) and survived in revised form into the last quarter of the eighteenth century.

The Text of Great Britain was first conceived twenty-five years ago, and many of the findings have been presented on scattered occasions in the interim. But they have been reexamined for the purposes of this book, the materials checked and mistakes corrected, and conclu- sions have been reevaluated in the light of developing scholarship. Some earlier conjectures have been abandoned for lack of evidence, and new suggestions offered. In chapters 1 and 2, I have deleted some merely corroborative documentation when the facts are sufficiently established without it. Other portions of the book have been planned to round out the coverage of key issues. Chapters 7 and 8, together with the conclusion, are wholly new, as is the majority of the intro- duction and of chapter 9. There are significant additions to every one of these sections.

There is inevitably some overlap between chapters, as the same material is processed from a different angle. Consequently, a few quo- tations from the text appear more than once in this book. I hope this is forgivable, as it is the words of Defoe—and not my own—that are repeated.

Overall, I have sought to unravel some of the threads that went into the complex fabric of the *Tour,* and to reveal its rich literary, as well as historical, interest, as a text expressive of the dynamic state of a nation that it evokes with such particularity and gusto. The term "design" has been used to convey the intellectual ordonnance that governs the entire work. Some of the overtones of this word in English are reinforced in the Italian term *disegno,* current in criticism that was being written in Defoe's youth. It meant an architect's ground plan, but also a plot or fable. Defoe creates in a way a mythic Britain, as selective in some of its emphases as the "fables" or legends of Brut in Geoffrey of Monmouth, and the plot of the three volumes may be said to body forth this myth. In the following chapters, several aspects of design are explored: the shape of the nation as displayed in topographic terms, the social and economic system that fuels the activity of Britain, the literary and antiquarian template on which modern experience is constructed. The *Tour* may be seen as an elaborate work of rhetorical engineering that emplots these separate designs. All combine to form a book of inexhaustible factual information and great imaginative richness.

Acknowledgments

I am grateful to Beth Latshaw for her help in preparing the manuscript for publication, and to Adrienne Condon for careful proofreading. Two anonymous readers for the University of Delaware Press made helpful suggestions that have led to considerable changes and, I hope, many improvements.

Some portions of the book have appeared in a different form as follows:

Parts of the introduction are based on material in my edition of the *Tour* (Harmondsworth: Penguin Books, 1971), as well as an article, "Literary Art in Defoe's *Tour*," *Eighteenth Century Studies*, 6 (1972–73): 153–85. This article is also used in chapter 4.

Chapter 1 is a revised version (shorn of some detail) in *Bulletin of the New York Public Library*, 78 (1975): 431–50; and similarly chapter 2 of an essay in *Prose Studies*: 3 (1980), 109–37.

Chapter 5 draws on an essay in *English Miscellany*, 22 (1971): 93–106. Chapter 6 is a slightly revised version of an article in *Studies in the Literary Imagination*, 15 (1982): 103–13.

Chapter 9 makes use of material in my introduction to editions of the *Tour* published by the Folio Society (London, 1982), and by Webb and Bower (Exeter, 1989).

Appendix A includes information first used in an essay in *Studies in Bibliography*, 28 (1975): 305–7, and one in *The Library*, 6.6 (1984): 275–79.

I am grateful to the publishers and editors for permission to reprint this material in a new context.

It should be added that a version of chapter 7 was given as the plenary address to the Congress of the Canadian Society for Eighteenth-Century Studies, at the Memorial University of Newfoundland, St John's, Newfoundland, in 1992. Thanks are due to Don Nichol for his kind reception and to other participants who made valuable comments in discussion.

The Text
of Great Britain

Diagrammatic Representation of Journeys
The exact course of journeys is not shown in detail

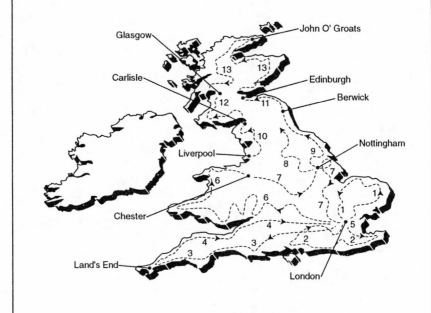

Illustration by Nathan A. Heim

Introduction

DANIEL Defoe produced his *Tour thro' the Whole Island of Great Britain* in three volumes between May 1724 and August 1726. Evidence assembled in chapter 1 below suggests that the actual writing of the first volume was performed in late 1722 and 1723. We do not know the exact date of Defoe's birth, but his biographer, Paula Backscheider, supports the view that it probably took place in the fall of 1660.[1] If so, it was during the composition of the initial volume that Defoe reached his own "grand climacteric." The first part of *Robinson Crusoe* had emerged during his sixtieth year, and *Moll Flanders* in his sixty-third. The *Oxford English Dictionary* explains the term "climacteric" like this: "A critical stage in human life; a point at which a person was supposed to be especially liable to changes in health or fortune. . . . *Grand climacteric* . . . the sixty-third year of life . . . supposed to be specially critical." It was a more or less formal marker for the onset of the status of a senior: modern retirement is only a pale shadow of the notion. So the great works of the 1720s, the final decade of Defoe's life, are the products of one who was considered by others, and must have thought himself, an elderly man.

But Britain itself was passing through a sort of climacteric, as it reached a new access of nationhood. Defoe wrote in the first years of Walpole's long sway, as the Hanoverian dynasty consolidated itself—the *Tour* was written just after the first Jacobite rising, just before the second. More directly, it appeared a very few years after the South Sea Bubble, the traumatic national stock market crash that awakened many memories in Daniel Defoe, a former trader who had twice gone bankrupt and had known the debtor's jail. The country stood on the brink of great imperial expansion (something Defoe half anticipated, though not in the right corners of the globe), and immense commercial and industrial development. Defoe lived in an age that historians have seen as marked by "the growth of political stability" but also by "the financial revolution."[2] In short, Britain was a country poised for transition into the modern world, yet still deeply rooted in traditional practices and institutions. Defoe was the ideal commentator, as a man raised in the seventeenth century, with a morally conservative outlook, but yet one who admired "improvement," growth, and above all the dynamism of trade.

Again and again in the *Tour*, he stresses his aim of describing things as they actually are: "If *Novelty* pleases," we read on the very first page of the work, "here is the *Present State* of the Country, the Improvement, as well in Culture [i.e., husbandry, cultivation], as in Commerce, the Encrease of the People, and Employment for them" (1: 1). This, moreover, in "the most flourishing and opulent Country in the World, so there is a flowing Variety of Materials." We generally perceive in this Defoe the social commentator, but the phrasing equally shows us Defoe the practicing author. The materials of economic progress are also the materials for the book. The *Tour* is a hymn to abundance, sometimes unrealistically so; it celebrates the richness of the expanding nation, and employs its own rich rhetoric to convey this ideological message of Whig advancement.

In the sections that follow, I shall take up a number of the issues already touched on. First, it is necessary to set the *Tour* in the context of Defoe's career, and to relate it to his other literary works of the 1720s. Second, we must pay some attention to the political bearings of the work and in particular the shadow of the South Sea Bubble. Third, we need to look at the context of travel writing, and to see the book as part of a developing rhetoric of tourism. Finally, we shall explore in more detail the design of the book, that is the way in which its outward structure serves to express a particular ideological view of the nation. Defoe, I shall argue, sees the island as a kind of text that he explores in his various imaginative (indeed, often imaginary) "circuits," to produce a literary tour that directly enacts in a literary form the experience of traversing space in the real world.

I

We do not know when Defoe first conceived the idea of compiling a full-scale survey of the nation. He had begun to travel widely around the country in the 1680s, and during the reign of Queen Anne he had kept detailed accounts of his journeys on behalf of Robert Harley, setting up a team of informants in towns and cities in most parts of England. In the *Review* in 1711, he claimed to have explored "every Nook and Corner" of the land. His lifelong interest in geography and exploration (reflected in the contents of his library, sold after his death)[3] had already led him to compose a number of works in this branch of study.

Perhaps the most important work falling squarely into this category would be the *Atlas Maritimus & Commercialis*, to which Defoe made major contributions. It did not appear until 1728, but had been in preparation as early as 1719, when it was trailed in advertisements attached to *The Farther Adventures of Robinson Crusoe*. But by 1724 Defoe had also written much on such matters as the African company, or the voyages of Sir Walter Ralegh, and several of his books came fitted out with maps—almost all his novels could usefully have contained such an aid. Oddly, he had written rather less about the geography of his own country than he had about that of foreign parts. Possibly he found it easier to dilate upon unexplored and undeveloped tracts of the earth than he did about regions loaded with historical associations, which had already become the property of the breed of antiquarian topographers who now seemed to be everywhere in Britain.

If we cannot fix the precise moment when the *Tour* germinated in Defoe's mind, we can at least read his own account of the way he went about equipping himself for the task. This comes in *The Great Law of Subordination Consider'd . . . in Ten Familiar Letters*, a tract on social issues published in April 1724, about seven weeks prior to the first volume of the *Tour*.

> As thus I made myself Master of the History, and *ancient State* of England, I resolv'd in the next Place, to make my self Master of its *Present State* also; and to this Purpose, I travell'd in three or four several Tours, over the whole Island, critically observing, and carefully informing myself of every thing worth observing in all the Towns and Countries [i.e., counties] through which I pass'd.
>
> I took with me an *ancient Gentleman* of my Acquaintance, who I found was thorowly acquainted with almost every Part of *England*, and who was to me as a walking Library or a moveable Map of the Countries and Towns through which we pass'd; and we never failed to enquire of the most proper Persons in every Place where we came, what was to be seen? what Rarities of Nature, Antiquities, ancient Buildings were in the respective Parts? or, in short, every thing worth the Observation of Travellers.

Defoe adds that he invariably took a map and read up on the history of the places he visited. Further, "I had a Book, entitled *Britannia*, written by that very learned Antiquary, Mr. *Camden*, and some other Books too, which treat of the natural History, as well as the Antiquities of each County."[4] Defoe nowhere makes such a direct admission in the *Tour* itself; we have to deduce his reliance on William Camden from his acknowledged references and from many concealed borrowings, as described in chapter 3 below. Plainly such a tour must have postdated 1695, when *Britannia* came out in a new edition by Edmund Gibson (the one Defoe used).The "other Books" certainly included William Dugdale's works on monasticism and antiquarian topics, as well as the county histories that Defoe appears to have consulted, although we may doubt whether he actually carried around these ponderous folios on such trips as he actually made. Moreover, even these latter sources may sometimes have been drawn on via Camden, rather than directly.

In *The Great Law of Subordination,* Defoe goes on to characterize his working method. He tells us that with the help of his learned companion, he made a point of observing the language, manners and customs of the people he encountered, for, he adds, "I meet with very few that take Notice of the common People; how they live, what their general Employment is, and what the particular Employment of them is in the several Counties especially." He further informs us that the original journey was accomplished as far back as 1684 to 1688, and that his companion's father was a great clothier in the West Country: a circumstance that is reflected in the heavy coverage of this aspect of the nation's trade in the published *Tour,* forty years later.[5] Defoe here suppresses his own, largely unsuccessful, career in trade, most relevantly his years as a London hose-factor. Paula Backscheider remarks that "by the end of 1681 Defoe had made his choice: he would become a wholesale hosier."[6] Pertinent to this decision was the rapid growth of the fashion industry in stocking-knitting. Later, he went into a variety of other business speculations; the hosiery venture ended in bankruptcy in 1694. Defoe had plenty of other things on his mind—his marriage, his quixotic support for the Monmouth Rebellion, his ride to Henley to meet the triumphant William III in 1688, leading to a growing connection with the royal court in the new reign, and his links with the Royal African Company. The point for our immediate purposes is that the young Defoe had a finger in many pies, and had many reasons for traveling about the country even if he had never met the learned son of the West Country clothier. From early on, then, Defoe was familiarizing himself with the landscape of the nation, especially its networks of trade and commerce.

The next crucial stage for the man who would ultimately become author of the *Tour* was his spell as an agent for Robert Harley, at first Speaker of the House of Commons, and later Secretary of State. Defoe's serious correspondence begins at the moment when he started to work for Harley around 1703, after the politician had engineered Defoe's release from Newgate prison. Thereafter, the overwhelming majority of his surviving letters were addressed to Harley, right up to the date of the Hanoverian accession. It is well-known that Defoe

performed a variety of tasks for Harley, as political agent, spy, propa-
gandist, and public relations adviser. During the first decade of the
century, he traveled widely on Harley's behalf, a fact that is evident
from his private letters and also sometimes from the pages of his journal, the *Review*. But Defoe also began to work for Sidney Godolphin,
the Lord Treasurer, and for some years had to juggle with these two
balls in the air. It was Harley who sent him to Edinburgh in 1706,
to help prepare the opinion-formers in the Scottish capital for the
forthcoming union of parliaments. During his sojourn in Edinburgh,
which lasted on and off until 1710, Defoe formed the strong impressions of the economic life of Scotland that were to figure in the last
three sections of his *Tour*.

However, it was his earlier travels on behalf of Harley that leave
the most obvious mark on the text of his book. For example, he made
an extensive trip to most parts of England (or at least those of political
or economic importance, as it was then seen) between July and November 1705. He wrote "an Abstract of my Journey" for Harley, in
which he gave a detailed report on "Publick Affaires" in towns
throughout the nation. The following April, he was able to draw up
a list of more than sixty agents in key locations up and down the
country, who would distribute copies of a pamphlet to the faithful.[7]
This network had obviously been set up in part during the long trip
of 1705. The *Tour* could not have been written without the information gained on this occasion: for several portions of the text, it was
clearly the author's most recent sight of the region he was to describe.[8]
It may be added that the journey ended along a route from Bury St.
Edmunds and Sudbury via Colchester and Chelmsford to London, an
exact reversal of the opening sequence of the published *Tour*. As chapters 1 and 2 will reveal, Defoe did not cease to conduct travels on
public and private business after 1714, but he never traversed the
nation so regularly as he did in the years of his association with Harley
and Godolphin.

The immediate spur toward writing the *Tour* may have been literary
as much as biographic. Most galling of all was the success of John
Macky's guidebook, *A Journey through England in Familiar Letters*,
to which we shall return below (pp. 45–46). Here was a Scottish
rapscallion, a mere adventurer (uncomfortably like Defoe in some of
his attributes), a man who had spent many years on the Continent,
and would eventually die at Rotterdam in 1726—here was such a
man, with few pretensions to literary skill, producing a standard guide
to the land that Defoe knew so well. It must have been unbearable.
The *Tour* is apart from all else an attempt to put Macky in his (lowly)
place, as evidenced by many thrusts in the text at Defoe's adversary,

either by name or under a disguise such as "a late author" or "other pretended travelling Writers" (2: 622).

Another possible stimulus to Defoe's pen was the appearance of a new edition of Edmund Gibson's version of *Britannia*, which came before the public in 1722. Defoe continued to use the 1695 edition, which remained in his library at his death.[9] Less widely applicable, but still serviceable, was the new edition of Stow's *Survey of London* which John Strype had issued in 1720; Nathan Bailey produced his *Antiquities of London and Westminster* in 1722, and the same year saw the appearance of John Stevens' *History of Abbeys and Monuments.* Not long before, in 1718, Stevens had produced a translation and abridgment of Dugdale's *Monasticon,* a work Defoe certainly knew. The collaborative survey of the nation called *Magna Britannia* had begun to be published in parts in 1720, avowedly as an update of Camden. Thomas Hearne had issued the first published version of Leland's *Itinerary* only a decade before. This does not exhaust the list of antiquarian and topical works that date from the crucial years leading up to the writing of the *Tour;* we should also recall more specialized books, such as the series of "surveys" of Welsh cathedrals that Browne Willis produced between 1717 and 1721, since Defoe certainly employed these to eke out his slender knowledge of such matters. But the effective cause was most probably Macky, since here Defoe knew he could outdo his rival, something that was not necessarily true in the case of the antiquarians. The new edition of *Britannia* may be regarded as a secondary trigger for Defoe's imagination to begin firing. He was over sixty; he had run into a profitable vein of literary form with *Crusoe* and its fictional successors, and he had a lifetime's preparation behind him.

Of course, not all the earlier experience was reserved for the *Tour.* As we have seen, Defoe had been given an early start on the matter of West Country wool trading; some of this would emerge in *A Plan of the English Commerce* (1728). In the latter work, Defoe gives another detailed account of his plan for a new town to be settled in Hampshire, which he had originally drafted for Godolphin in 1709, and set forth in the *Review* that year. There is an extensive rerun of the proposal in the third letter of the *Tour* (1: 200–6); this differs in several respects from the account provided in the *Plan of the English Commerce,* though it is not apparent whether Defoe had changed his mind on some points or inadvertently altered the figures.[10]

Equally, it is impossible to read *The Complete English Tradesman,* published in 1725–27 as the later sections of the *Tour* were coming out, without being reminded of the parallels between the two works. One obvious link is the description of the arrest of James II at Faversham, which is given in detail both in the *Tradesman* (2: 200–4) and a little more briefly in the *Tour* (1: 111–12). The treatment of the wool trade in the West Country is closely similar in the two books (*Tradesman,* 2: ii, 56–59: *Tour,* 1: 280–86). Defoe's taste for disasters leads him to describe the loss of Admiral Shovel's fleet off the Scilly Islands in both places, although the *Tour* is more detailed. Again, the unhappy fall of apparently prosperous tradesmen, as a result of the South Sea Bubble, is another theme common to the two works. This material is perhaps more integral to the *Tradesman,* a sustained expo-sure of the perils of business life ("No Prosperity in Trade is out of the Reach of Disaster," 2: i, 95), but as we shall see, the topic recurs ominously throughout the *Tour.* In both works Defoe laments the fate of the South Sea directors, "sinking still under the Oppression of their Fortunes, and whose Weight I would be far from endeavouring to make heavier."

To a modern reader, one other parallel may be even more striking. This is the short trip into East Anglia that the heroine makes toward the end of *Moll Flanders.* This involves Moll's visit to her girlhood hometown of Colchester, but in fact her route follows in reverse the first stretch of the *Tour* as published two years later. She goes to Stourbridge Fair in the hope of rich plunder, but finds nothing more than "meer Picking of Pockets": in the *Tour* Defoe spends much longer on the fair, and describes the system of summary justice meted out to wrongdoers, a possible disincentive to Moll (1: 85–86). Then Moll proceeds via Newmarket and Bury to Ipswich and Harwich (cutting out the middle section of the itinerary in the *Tour*), and thence back to London through Colchester.[11] We know from Backscheider's re-searches that Defoe had acquired a large property in Colchester on lease in August 1722:[12] this would of course provide an authentic reason for embarking on his travels in just this direction on "the 3d of *April,* 1722" (1: 5) and might explain, too, the Colchester setting in *Moll Flanders.* There are other stray parallels: Moll's passing refer-ence to Bath as "a Place of Gallantry enough; Expensive, and full of Snares"[13] is amplified in a paragraph of the *Tour:* "The Town is taken up in Raffling, Gameing, Visiting, and in a Word, all sorts of Gal-lantry and Levity" (2: 433). It is no surprise today to find that the materials of Defoe's fiction are often identical with the matter of his nonfictional works written at the same stage of his career. It is worth adding that the author's last novel, *A New Voyage Round the World,* was published in November 1724, six months after the first volume of the *Tour* and seven months before the second. As the title suggests, it is another book reflecting Defoe's pervasive interest in travel and exploration.[14]

Since the *Tour* avowedly aims to evoke for its readers a sense of "the present state" of the nation, we should not be surprised to find that the text glances from time to time at topical issues that Defoe dealt with elsewhere in journalism and pamphleteering. For example, there are a number of references to recent criminal cases. Paula Backscheider observes that "Between 1718 and 1721 Defoe became increasingly concerned and analytical about crime."[15] This new preoc-cupation resulted in several books contemporaneous with the *Tour*, dealing with figures such as Jonathan Wild and Jack Sheppard, as well as (if we accept a possible attribution) a full-scale history of pirates. This of course is to leave out the important strand of criminal-ity in the fictional rogues' lives of Moll, Roxana, Colonel Jacque, and Captain Singleton. In addition, Defoe wrote extensively on allied matters in his work for Applebee's and Mist's newspapers in the early 1720s.

It may be added that some cases addressed in the *Tour* point to the possibility of unrecognized works by Defoe. A very brief reference to the Waltham Blacks (1: 143) serves to remind us of the prominence of this story at the time Defoe was writing, and it is distinctly possible that Defoe was responsible for a pamphlet entitled *The History of the Blacks of Waltham in Hampshire* (1724).[16] A fuller entry is provided for the recent attempted murder of Edmund Crisp by the barrister Arundel Coke (1: 50–51). This was also a very newsworthy item for a short time in 1722. It figures in the newspapers for which Defoe regularly wrote; and further research might well show that Defoe was involved in the pamphlet literature here too.[17] More widely topical matters such as the Atterbury conspiracy come in for passing mention, and in such instances we can naturally refer to other passages in Defoe's writing where the same theme arose. All this means is that the author of the *Tour* was a prolific commentator on diverse aspects of the life around him, and therefore many issues that crop up in the text were dealt with (often more fully) in his other works. And, as we shall see in chapter 4 especially, some of the expressive devices he had developed elsewhere came into play once more within the *Tour*.

Any reader familiar with Defoe's work will find echoes surfacing in the text of the *Tour*. When we reach Edgehill and the narrator discourses on the opening battle of the English Civil War (2: 428–29), we are reminded of an episode in *Memoirs of a Cavalier*, and the same is true at Marston Moor (2: 640–41), where a more protracted description is given of battle tactics. (See also chapter 5, pp. 138–39 below, as well as Appendix C.) There is more than one reference to the Great Storm of 1703 (see for example, 1: 121; 228–29): this was an event that prompted Defoe's collection of disaster stories, *The Storm*

(1704), and it left an image of desolation that never faded from his mind. A different kind of preoccupation is seen in a passage concerning the trade between Glasgow and the American colonies. The narrator observes that one "article" of this trade consists of servants willingly emigrating to the New World: and he praises the Scottish "who go with sober Resolutions, namely, to serve out their Times, and then become diligent Planters for themselves; and this would be a much wiser Course in *England* than to turn to Thieves, and worse, and then be sent over by Force, and as a Pretence of Mercy to save them from the Gallows" (2: 748). Here the author of *Moll Flanders* and *Colonel Jacque* is not well concealed.

A final example will serve to illustrate the long duration of Defoe's pet projects. Literally so, because the source for several ideas in the *Tour* is one of his very first books, that is *An Essay upon Projects* (1697). Several of the ideas that Defoe floated in this book, on topics relating to insurance, trade and banking, turn up in his social pamphlets of the 1720s, and they flit briefly into the *Tour*. But the most interesting point of contact, and one that has not previously been noted, relates to Defoe's section "Of the Highways" in his *Essay*.[18] Here the author deplores the present bad state of English roads, and calls for parliamentary action to improve their condition. He proposes local commissioners to oversee the road building, in a manner close to that of the actual Turnpike Trusts that proliferated in the eighteenth century. The work of these turnpike authorities began just in time for Defoe to herald their appearance in his famous appendix to Volume II of the *Tour* in 1725.

It would not be quite accurate to say that the proposals set out in the *Essay* formed a blueprint for the development of the turnpike movement, and it should be recalled that a hesitant start had been made on making an odd stretch of road into a turnpike as far back as 1663. Nonetheless, the real impetus did not begin until the second and third decades of the eighteenth century. It was greatly to Defoe's credit that he saw the importance, social as well as economic, of the new system of communications that was starting to appear. Hence the deserved renown of his appendix in the *Tour*. But it is in the end more striking that he should so early have perceived the importance of these matters and should have provided in the *Essay* such a clear statement of the need for radical improvements in the road network. Obviously, when he came to write the appendix, Defoe had not forgotten what he set down more than a quarter of a century before. For instance, in the *Essay*, he states, "Nor have the Romans left us any greater tokens of their grandeur and magnificence that the ruins of those causeways and street-ways, which are at this day to be seen in many parts of the kingdom. . . ."[19] In the appendix, the narrator tells us that the memory of the Romans is preserved "in nothing more visible to common Observation, than in the Remains of those noble Causways and Highways, which they made through all parts of the Kingdom" (2: 519). In the *Essay* there is mention of Camden's treatment of the Roman roads, and it can be deduced that the author was already well acquainted with Gibson's edition of *Britannia,* published two years prior to the *Essay.* In 1725 much remained to be done, and Defoe repeats his criticisms of the bad state of highways in the Weald and other parts of Kent and Sussex (2: 529), a complaint he had raised in the *Essay.*

Characteristically, however, the final note is one of optimism in both books. Defoe perceived in 1697 how improved roads would supply "a great help to negoce, and [promote] universal correspondence, without which our inland trade could not be managed." The various parts of the country would, he foresaw, "reap an advantage a hundred to one greater than the charge of it," if his ideas were put into effect.[20] In 1725 he would herald the ongoing march of the turnpike trusts, and specify at length "the Advantage to our Inland Commerce" that would result from extending the process. The state of national commerce was, of course, a prime concern for Defoe first and last; and it thus apt to the central purposes of the *Tour* that it should dilate upon a topic that its author had taken as his own fully twenty-eight years earlier.

II

The *Tour* is not an explicitly political book. That might seem nothing more than the nature of its genre, but Defoe's own caution was also responsible for an element of evasion and temporizing. It would of course be possible to look for a kind of subliminal politics in certain aspects of the treatment of the nation; and a start in this direction has been made by Alistair M. Duckworth, in his analysis of "Whig landscapes" in the *Tour.* (See below, p. 34). However, the overt ideology of the work is deliberately uncontroversial for the most part. Only a handful of passages in the text reveal open commitment on the author's part, and it is these that call for immediate discussion. The largest single event overshadowing the book is, as already stated, the South Sea Bubble, but even here Defoe avoids some of the more sensitive political implications of the episode. It should be added that the *Tour* never openly takes sides on the issues of the English Civil War, when (as often happens) the narrator comes on remnants of that great and divisive struggle.

Despite the great familiarity Defoe had built up with the state of the parties, as he traveled round the country for Robert Harley, he seldom allows this knowledge to obtrude in the *Tour.* Only very rarely does any information surface regarding the local party contentions. At Coleshill he refers slyly to the lord of the manor, Lord Digby, "and as that noble Person is at present a little on the wrong Side as to the Government, not having taken the Oaths to King *George,* so the whole Town are so eminently that Way too, that they told me there was but one Family of *Whigs,* as they call'd them, in the whole Town, and they hoped to drive them out of the Place too very quickly" (2: 481).[21] The following paragraph is equally significant since it contains an open reference to the nonjuror John Kettlewell (1653–95), vicar of Coleshill from 1682 to 1690, when he was deprived for refusing the oaths to William and Mary; and to Thomas Carte (1686–1754), the Jacobite historian, who had concealed himself with the curate of Coleshill after the failure of the rising in 1715. Carte was closely associated with Francis Atterbury, and when the Atterbury plot came to light a proclamation was issued offering a reward for Carte's arrest. This was in 1722, a dating clue mentioned in chapter 2, where the passage is glossed more fully (p. 96).

On the next page, Defoe moves to Coventry, a city with which he had long familiarity—perhaps since 1690. In his report on his travels for Harley in 1705, there is no entry for Coventry, since Defoe was able to refer his employer to a separate account of riots at a recent election, which he had published in the *Review* on 10 May 1705.[22] The coverage in the *Tour* alludes to the same occasion: "It was a very unhappy Time when I first came to this City; for their Heats and Animosities for Election of Members to serve in Parliament, were carry'd to such a Hight, that all Manner of Method being laid aside, the Inhabitants (in short) enraged at one another, met, and fought a pitch'd Battle in the middle of the Street . . ." (2: 482: for the full passage, see the discussion of this episode in chapter 2, pp. 95). A leading informant for the *Review* piece was Edward Owen, a former Alderman and Mayor of Coventry, with whom Defoe was in regular contact.[23] Rather lamely, Defoe adds in the *Tour,* "Nor is the Matter much better among them to this Day, only that the Occasion does not happen so often" (2: 482), possibly an oblique allusion to the new Septennial Act. In the event, there had been further riots at the elections of 1715 and 1722, involving the same forces as before: a strongly Whig corporation opposed by a large number of the two thousand freemen who could vote in this relatively "open" constitu-

ency. In November 1722, just about the time Defoe was at neighboring
Coleshill, parliament declared the election void on account of the
"notorious and outrageous riots, tumults and seditions at the late
election."[24] There was a rerun in the following month. Defoe must
surely have known about all this, but he keeps discreetly silent. This
is despite the fact that a writer in Applebee's *Journal*, almost certainly
Defoe himself, discussed the Coventry election in April 1722.[25] (See
further p. 96 below.) It is noticeable that his updating sections, consist-
ing of small additions in the prefatory or concluding material of each
volume, do not include recent political events.

The narrator remarks near the end of the English sections of his
Tour, "I have not concern'd this Work at all in the Debate among us
in *England*, as to Whig and Tory" (2: 656). Broadly speaking this is
true. He proceeds, "But I must observe of this Town [Northallerton],
that, except for a few Quakers, they boasted that they had not one
Dissenter here, and yet at the same time not one *Tory*, which is what,
I believe, cannot be said of any other Town in *Great Britain*." Defoe
must have registered the presence or otherwise of his own dissenting
kind in the places he visited, and the presence in itself constituted a
major feature of the political map. But his comments, where they
occur, are brief and unrevealing: in Wakefield, for example, "Here is
a very large Church, and well filled it is, for here are very few Dissenters" (2: 593). In Scotland he permits himself a little more freedom in
one or two places, as when he writes of Melrose Abbey, "But the
Reformation has triumph'd over all these things, and the Pomp and
Glory of Popery is sunk now into the primitive Simplicity of the true
Christian Profession" (2: 763), together with a few other swipes at
"*Romanists*" (2: 757).

In general, the treatment of Roman Catholicism is subdued. If we
had only this book to go on, we should be inclined to suppose that
the author exhibited the tolerance he seems to commend at Holywell,
where a number of disguised priests were in evidence: "No Body takes
Notice of them, as to their Profession, tho' they know them well
enough, no not the *Roman* Catholicks themselves; but in private, they
have their proper Oratory's in certain Places, where the Votaries
resort; and good Manners has prevail'd so far, that however the Prot-
estants know who and who's together; no Body takes Notice of it, or
enquires where one another goes, or has been gone" (2: 465).[26] The
odd syntax of this passage reflects Defoe's care in avoiding an unduly
explicit statement on the issue. On less-topical themes, he can be
slightly more open: thus, his preference for Protestant Oxford over
the former Catholic university is not disguised (2: 426), although it
is shrouded in verbosity. The most clear-cut single phrase of all is too

brief and general to be capable of offense: this is the reference at Hadleigh in Suffolk to the state of the nation "if the detestable Conspiracy of the Papists now on Foot, should succeed" (1: 48), that is the Atterbury plot. The Jacobite scare made it possible for Defoe just for a moment to vent his feelings against Catholicism generally.

Overall, the omissions and suppressions are more striking. When Defoe has occasion to mention figures like the Earl of Mar, implicated in the 1715 rising, he shows considerable restraint. Equally, tributes to powerful Whigs such as Walpole (1: 93) or Townshend (1: 73) are curt and deliberately without any fulsome quality. More delicate was the task posed by Lord Barrington, a prominent dissenter who had been MP for Berwick-upon-Tweed from 1715. In February 1723 he was expelled from the House of Commons for his part in the fraudulent Harburg lottery scheme. Defoe sets out his earlier career in some detail, and then concludes, "His Lordship is a Dissenter, and seems to love Retirement. He was a Member of Parliament for the Town of *Berwick* upon *Tweed*" (1: 15). Could there be a grim joke in the phrasing about loving retirement? It seems more likely that the entry was already substantially complete when news reached Defoe of Barrington's disgrace. He was reluctant to lose the commendations he had included, but knew that Barrington had been ditched by his Whig parliamentary colleagues. Barrington, too, represented exactly the kind of self-made tradesman whom Defoe lauded in his own work. There is a certain stoicism in the decision to leave the entry where it stood and brave out the actual facts of the case.

Something analogous can be seen in the case of certain figures who had suffered as a result of the Bubble. This is the single issue on which Defoe felt most embarrassment, and his writing is frequently awkward when he is forced to consider any individual caught up in the crash: "The other House is that of Sir *John Fellows,* late Sub-Governor of the *South-Sea* Company, who having the Misfortune to fall in the General Calamity of the late Directors, lost all his unhappy Wealth, which he had gain'd in the Company, and a good and honestly gotten Estate of his own into the Bargain" (1: 159). It happens that some of the principal sufferers in the fiasco were men of the stamp Defoe had specially admired, and so it is not surprising that his contemporaneous manual on the life of trade should be as much as anything a warning against the potential disasters facing the complete English tradesman. So far as the *Tour* is concerned, it can be stated that Defoe wishes at the same time to erase painful memories of the Bubble and yet to draw attention to this huge portent. So it comes about that he writes of fallen traders with obvious anguish, and yet reverts to their fate

with a surprising punctuality, each time the *Tour* brushes up against
a forfeited estate.

More representative of the methods of the *Tour* as a whole are
passages of general threnody. The best examples occur at the end of
the first and second letters. From the opening letter:

> I shall cover as much as possible the melancholy part of a Story, which
> touches too sensibly, many, if not most of the Great and Flourishing Fami-
> lies in *England*: Pity and matter of Grief is it to think that Families, by
> Estate, able to appear in such a glorious Posture as this, should ever be
> Vulnerable by so mean a Disaster as that of Stock-Jobbing: But the *General
> Infatuation of the Day* is a Plea for it; so that Men are not now blamed
> on that Account: *South-Sea* was a general Possession; and if my Lord
> *Castlemain* was Wounded by that Arrow shot in the Dark, 'twas a Misfor-
> tune: But 'tis so much a Happiness, that it was not a mortal Wound, as
> it was to some Men, who once seem'd as much out of the reach of it; and
> that Blow be it what it will, is not remember'd for joy of the Escape; for
> we see this Noble Family, by Prudence and Management rise out of all
> that Cloud, if it may be allow'd such a Name, and shining in the same
> full Lustre as before.
>
> This cannot be said of some other Families in this County [Essex],
> whose fine Parks and new-built Palaces are fallen under Forfeitures and
> Alienations by the Misfortunes of the Times, and by the Ruin of their
> Masters Fortunes in that *South-Sea* Deluge.
>
> But I desire to throw a Veil over these Things, as they come in my
> way; 'tis enough that we write upon them as was written upon King
> *Harold*'s Tomb at *Waltham-Abbey*, INFAELIX, and let all the rest sleep
> among Things that are the fittest to be forgotten.(1: 90–91)

This is one of the most eloquent stretches of writing in all Defoe's
work. It enlists a number of his deepest concerns, and it ties the
pervading theme of growth and decay beautifully into the ongoing
narrative. A brilliant imaginative touch allows Defoe to hark back to
the tomb of the king at Waltham, mentioned just two pages earlier.
Nothing could be more poignantly expressive of the effects of the
Bubble as the *Tour* seeks to present them.

In the second letter there is a closely comparable passage:

> It would also take up a large Chapter in this Book, to but mention the
> overthrow, and Catastrophe of innumerable Wealthy City Families, who
> after they have thought their Houses establish'd, and have built their
> Magnificent Country Seats, as well as others, have sunk under the Misfor-
> tunes of Business, and the Disasters of Trade, after the World has thought
> them pass'd all possibility of Danger; such as Sir *Joseph Hodges*, Sir *Justus
> Beck*, the Widow *Cock* at *Camberwell,* and many others; besides all the

late *South-Sea* Directors, all which I chuse to have forgotten, as no doubt they desire to be, in Recording the Wealth and Opulence of this Part of *England,* which I doubt not to convince you infinitely out does the whole World. (1: 169)

The *Tour* ostensibly celebrates the "Wealth and Opulence" of Britain, but in practice this demands a more complex rhetoric involving both growth and decay, as described in chapter 4 below. Although such plangent sections as those just quoted are relatively brief and scattered, they are supported by at least a dozen other references to the South Sea catastrophe. Thus, Defoe mentions the appointment of a new sub-governor of the South Sea Company "immediately after the Ruin of the former Sub-Governor and Directors, whose Overthrow makes the History of these Times famous" (1: 37). Most writers in the 1720s, from Pope and Swift downwards, were only too keen to upbraid the former directors for their malfeasance. It took courage for Defoe to allude to them in such restrained terms in 1724. "The Fall of a great Tradesman," he remarked in *The Complete English Tradesman* (2: i, 19), "is a Stroke even to the Trade itself: he sinks every Man about him."

London is the hub of Defoe's Britain, and the fulcrum of the *Tour.* And the very center of that hub was the City of London, around which the nation's trade circulated. Ripples are sent out from the capital into the surrounding countryside, where (as the last passage makes clear) city financiers and merchants had set up their landed estates. It follows that most of the references to the Bubble occur in the sections dealing with the southern counties in Volumes I and II of the *Tour.* But there was also an impact on trade itself, outside the capital, as we learn at Bisham Abbey: "Those Mills went on by the Strength of a good Stock of Money in a Company or Partnership, and with very good Success, 'till at last, they turned it into what they call a *Bubble,* brought it to *Exchange-Alley,* set it a Stock-jobbing in the Days of our *South Sea Madness,* and brought it up to be sold at One hundred Pounds *per* Share, whose intrinsick Worth was perhaps Ten Pounds, 'till, with the Fall of all those Things together, it fell to nothing again" (1: 300). The company treasurer, "a Tradesman in *London,*" collapsed, "having misapply'd about Thirty thousand Pounds of their Money," with the result that "the whole Affair sunk into a Piece of mere Confusion and Loss, which otherwise was certainly a very beneficial Undertaking." It is a parable straight out of *The Complete English Tradesman.*

The place of "our late Calamities of Stocks and Bubbles" (1: 46) in the design of the *Tour* emerges clearly in such episodes. The South

Sea mania was a negation of the gradual accretion of wealth and stability that is hymned on so many occasions. Elsewhere I have argued that *A Journal of the Plague Year* (1722) constitutes a fictional replay of the Bubble experience through the metaphor of the plague.[27] If that is true, then the *Tour* prolongs this line of imagery. The noble seats around London "reflect Beauty, and Magnificence upon the whole Country, and give a kind of Character to the Island of *Great Britain* in general" (1: 167). The shortsighted rage for gain that provoked the Bubble flouted those solid principles of trading that Defoe espouses in all his work. His entire output as a writer may be seen as a quest for security, personal as well as financial. Naturally, the *Tour,* which embodies so many of his recurrent themes, portrays the "one unhappy *Stock Jobbing Year*" (1: 160) as an aberration in the nation's drive towards fulfilment; but Defoe is unable to keep out of his prose the sense that it could all happen again.

No other recent event colors the text to anything like the same degree. In the Scottish sections, Defoe writes as an unabashed proponent of the Union, though he admits that so far only Glasgow has greatly increased its prosperity as a result of this measure (2: 745–46). He carefully sets out the limits of his discussion of the Union in a preface (2: 542). Overall it may be said the *Tour* is a remarkably unpolitical book for one so political by instinct as Defoe; but even this caution was laid aside when a matter so personally fraught as the South Sea affair entered the text.

The most important discussion of the political drift of the *Tour* is that of Alistair M. Duckworth, in his consideration of "Whig" landscapes in the work. Acknowledging that his aim is "not to collapse but reestablish distinctions," Duckworth sees Defoe as portraying "the landscape of Augustan compromise." The book favors "humanized English landscape, rich, fertile, cultivated and populous." In general "Defoe's scenic descriptions distinguish his social and political outlook—his epic vision—from those of a more 'tory' sort, just as they distance his humanism from that of Pope, Swift and Bolingbroke." In more specific areas, the *Tour* witnesses "the virtual eclipse of tory squires and parsons in favor of that of the whig grandees and their trading allies."[28]

There is much that is convincing in this analysis, but it will bear some qualification in my view. The productive *paysages riants* that Duckworth rightly finds in the *Tour* are also those of Virgil and those of Pope in the *Epistle to Burlington*. It is possible to exaggerate the "opposing habits of expression" visible in Defoe as against the Scriblerian group: and the differences that are there may owe something to generic considerations—Pope and Swift did not write surveys of the nation in prose. Again, while it is true that most of Defoe's longest architectual entries concern the mansions of Whig magnates (see chapter 8 below), this need not reflect a strong bias. Defoe was writing in the first years of the Hanoverian age, when Whig dynasts had come out firmly on top. It was they who typically had the power and money to set up great family estates. In their building mania of these years, the imposing new seats were those of Robert Walpole, at Houghton, Sir Josiah Child at Wanstead, and similar exercises in Palladian splendor. The Whigs were the English patrons of the Palladian movement, although fine public buildings in the baroque style continued to be created by James Gibbs. Finally, it is misleading to use landscape in the narrow sense as an index of the full range of Defoe's attitudes. The *Tour,* as we have seen, is a complex feat of literary engineering. Description of scenery is one element, but there are also townscapes, historical excursions, anecdotes, autobiographical recollections, and much else. Insofar as the terms carry any precise weight, the *Tour* may be judged more Whig than Tory in its attitudes, but Defoe strives to appear evenhanded, and to a large degree he succeeds in presenting a rounded picture of the nation. His design embraces old and new, genteel and demotic, "improved" and unregenerate states of the nation.

III

In order to understand the success enjoyed, initially by Defoe's own work, more lastingly by the formula he helped to devise, we must give some thought to the development of travel literature in Britain. There are several accounts: perhaps the most useful for present purposes is a study by Esther Moir, *The Discovery of Britain* (1964).[29] The author divides her material along fairly predictable but well-defined lines: the Tudor antiquarians, seventeenth-century travelers, "Romans and Goths" (antiquarians and proto-archeologists like William Stukeley), picturesque tourists like William Gilpin, students of the land and its husbandry like Arthur Young, seekers for the sublime in industrial landscapes, and so on. Defoe together with Celia Fiennes is the subject of a chapter entitled "A Planted Garden." Fiennes and Defoe come fairly early in the story, but they are central because they embody— Defoe especially—so many of the separate impulses visible elsewhere. It should be added that in Moir's terms Camden "scarcely qualified as a tourist,"[30] since he did not visit most of the places covered, but relied on secondhand information: this may reduce his relevance as a tourist, but scarcely as a travel writer.

Moir makes some useful discriminations between Celia Fiennes and Defoe, although when she says, "Unlike Defoe she was not in anyone's pay,"[31] this could be misleading. Certainly Defoe had made some of the crucial journeys that underlie the *Tour* when he had been working for Harley. But the book itself was written years later as a private literary enterprise, and he had no one to please except the public. There is, after all, not even a dedication to the work. Further, though Moir is right to state that condemnations of old buildings in the two writers would have bewildered Leland or Stukeley,[32] Defoe's professed hostility to "antiquities" masks considerable awareness of the ancient heritage visible in the landscape, as we shall discover (see below pp. 125–28). And Defoe like Fiennes, is unable to resist a curiosity, including the Eskimo fisherman preserved at Hull, actually in Trinity House rather than the "Town-Hall" (2: 653). In fact other visitors such as Sir John Percival were much impressed by this odd relic. Defoe seems to have paraphrased his entry here from the account that John Ray had communicated to Gibson for the new edition of *Britannia* in 1695.[33]

We shall return to Celia Fiennes in her proper historical sequence: she occupies a hinge position in the long-term narrative of travel writing. Without going into the prehistory of the subject, we can see this genre emerging with the great Tudor topographers, John Leland, William Harrison, and William Camden. The scholarly cleric Leland made the journeys on which his *Itinerary* was based during the 1530s: but he died in 1552, with his planned *Britannia* unwritten. It was not until 1710–12 that the Oxford antiquary Thomas Hearne, famous alike for his learning, crustiness, and High Toryism, published the *Itinerary*. Its content remained skeletal—a sort of frozen work in progress, with clipped itemized entries and no running narrative. But the fullness and accuracy of Leland's survey gives it permanent interest, especially as a graphic record of an England still largely medieval in landscape, the visual testimony to a feudal and military past. William Harrison's *Description of Britain* (1577), written as an appendix to Holinshed's chronicle, is more analytical than Leland's, less close to the detailed geography of the country.[34] It supplied nonetheless a vivid picture of the nation, its customs, manners, and occupations, with a hint of the realism of portraiture found in Elizabethan satire and city comedy. Then came Camden, whose *Britannia* (the first of many editions, 1586) displays a formitable antiquarian zeal and a lucid, connected manner of writing.[35] Just as the structure of Defoe's "tour"— the imaginative vehicle of a number of "circuits"—expresses his primary literary intention, so the organization of *Britannia* reveals Camden's attitude to his material and to his rhetorical task. Significantly, the work is set out according to the distribution of the British tribes. Counties are a further subdivision—an afterthought of administrative history.

At the start of the seventeenth century, various tributaries can be see to flow from this main stream of topographic inquiry. Poets as different as Drayton, with his fanciful, anecdotal, and mythopoetic *Poly-olbion* (1612–22), and John Taylor, a kind of ur-McGonigall who produced doggerel accounts of his trips by land and water, can be related to a growing craze for travel books. A flood of county histories, of which Dugdale's *Warwickshire* (1656) is unrepresentative only in its exceptional quality, illustrate another side of this vogue. And as the century went on, the trend continued unabated. "A new discovery of England was in progress," Christopher Morris has said of the Restoration era:

Treatises were written on Stonehenge and poems on 'the Wonders of the Peak.' A new edition of Camden's *Britannia* [1695], brought up to date by Bishop Gibson, seems to have lain on the parlour tables of most of the well-to-do people. . . . A devoted band of antiquaries and topographers were grubbing up the English past. Ogilby's wonderful road-book had appeared in 1675 and there were also surveys, comparable with modern directories and gazetteers, such as . . . Chamberlayne's *Angliae Notitiae* [from 1669]. Statisticians like Gregory King and Sir William Petty were trying to estimate the population. The English were becoming highly immodest about their own political discoveries, their own great men or 'worthies', their own architecture and landscape and, above all, their own prosperity.[36]

Now, this mood of self-discovery has very precise literary analogues. The form apt to a country emerging into a consciousness of its own power and nationhood has traditionally been the epic. And indeed great poets projected a definitive English epic more than once at this time. If the task never quite became the shirt of Nessus that the Great American Novel was to prove until the provident canonization of *Moby Dick*, then that was purely because these poets sublimated their heroic ambitions elsewhere—Milton in *Paradise Lost*, Dryden in satire and elevated tragic writing, Pope in his Homer and ultimately in *The Dunciad*. The pompous sagas on Boadicea and Alfred we do possess will induce no regret that patriotic self-awareness fled from the high literary forms. Against all decorum, it reappeared most feelingly in the tame foothills of Parnassus allotted to the travel book.

Coming nearer Defoe's own time, the best-known journeys today are those of Celia Fiennes, made just before the turn of the century.[37] Defoe was already an experienced traveler by this date, and in any

case he cannot have been influenced by the *Journeys,* since they remained in manuscript until 1888. Celia Fiennes compels admiration
as a person, as she uncomplainingly rides along the ill-made road,
charting an erratic course between the noxious inns and the comfortable homes of her endless relatives. (On one level her progress is like
a conducted tour around *Familiae minorum gentium.*) But as a writer
she lacks Defoe's awareness of a larger reality; her England is all a
microcosm, no macrocosm, and she reveals little sense of history. The
Journeys are perhaps best read as a charming notebook of a picturesque
traveler born before her time. To be sure, her standards of beauty, of
comfort, of emotional intensity, are not those that will be current
when the picturesque moment arrives, almost a century later. But
her headlong impressionistic style converts even the most domestic
sentiments into the accents of sensibility.

In the vein of travels per se, nothing else of this quality anticipated
Defoe's *Tour.* The book that may have set him to work would be
adequate at best as an effective cause, certainly not as a sufficient
inspiration for Defoe so to enhance the status of travel literature. *A
Journey through England, in Familiar Letters* (1714–23: the title of the
third volume is modified to suit the Scottish tour described) is the
work of John Macky. A Scot, with a biography even more checkered
than Defoe's own, Macky assuredly knew his way around Britain
and the Continent. But his journey is shapeless, its itinerary wholly
arbitrary and imaginatively unconvincing. The writer hedgehops from
one town to the next, alighting now and then to "do" a country seat.
We have no real sense of place, none of the buoyancy and movement
Defoe achieves. In fact, the work is little more than an annotated
road-book.

Defoe was certainly aware of Macky's work, and refers to it sneer-
ingly on several occasions. Indeed, J. H. Andrews has suggested that
he borrowed up to five thousand words from the earlier account.[38]
Andrews points out a number of resemblances: some of these may be
chance, others are certainly due to a common source, and others, like
the use of the phrase, "the *Montpelier* of *Suffolk*" (1: 49), incorporate
familiar usages. Nor is it certain that the new bridges and the new
dockyards mentioned in Defoe's updating exercises all proceed from a
perusal of Macky's second edition in 1723. Defoe had other informants
and other recent surveys to draw on. But Andrews is certainly right
to detect a sustained assault upon Macky. Even when Defoe departs
from Macky—as when he cites other lines from Charles Cotton's
Wonders of the Peake, not content with the four hundred plus cited
by Macky—he may have been led in that direction by the Scottish
author. Andrews remarks that Defoe's "best authenticated journeys

belong to the period 1704–14." This is a matter that will be explored more fully in chapters 1 and 2; for the moment, it is enough to say that Defoe certainly continued his travels into East Anglia at least as late as 1722 and 1723; and may well have paid recent business trips to the Midlands, possibly in connection with his intended partner John Ward of Nuneaton.[39] All in all, we can say that Defoe assuredly searched through Macky's text for errors, as Andrews observes, and delighted in proclaiming the mistakes he found (e.g., 1: 42, 51; 2: 637). He clearly purloined information from his rival when it suited him.

After the death of Defoe, the passion for travel increased, and with it the demand for information met by successive reissues of the *Tour*. In the seventeenth century most of the travelers had been, if not scholars, at least amateur antiquarians, virtuosi, and collectors. The typical figures were men like Pepys, John Evelyn, or Ralph Thoresby, whose respectability was mixed with a certain independence or non-conformity. As the Georgian period went by, a clear separation grew up between serious archaeological investigation and the new phenomenon that we might call genteel tourism. The round of country houses and gardens became an established part of life for well-bred ladies and gentlemen: one did not need to be a connoisseur to take a general interest in architectural "improvements," to which the Hanoverians were so addicted. There was even something resembling a tourist industry; it was said in the 1750s that "it is well for the county of Norfolk that three or four noblemen have done so much to their places, else very few strangers would visit a country that has so few natural beauties to attract them." But the visitors were not exactly trippers in a modern sense; they were consciously cultivating the art of travel, *ars peregrinandi,* as part of the civilized life.

It is in this context that the many literary travelers of the eighteenth century need to be seen. Disregarding John Wesley, whose ceaseless journeys up and down the country had a very different basis, it was the provincials who had come up to London, and thenceforth adopted metropolitan standards, who devised the most effective literary vehicle for their travels. Smollett in *Humphry Clinker,* Sterne in the *Sentimental Journey,* and Johnson in his *Journey to the Western Islands* proved able to use physical travel as an emblem of mental and moral discovery. By contrast Pope—a great devotee of jaunts—and in turn Horace Walpole, an obsessive visitor of others people's residences, and Thomas Gray, one of the first to enthuse over the Lake District, failed to make direct literary use of their interest. Much the same applies to William Cowper, who traveled rarely but with keen delight. The point is that all these men were in one way or another committed to an anti-metropolitan standpoint. Yet their rusticity had an air of playacting (think of Strawberry Hill, Pope's grotto or his tower at Stanton Harcourt), and something of calculation about it. They were never able to forge an idiom through which to express their undoubted interest in traveling the English countryside.

When we reach the middle of the century, travel has become quicker and more comfortable. In 1700 the roads had been scarcely less dirty, dangerous, and unreliable than they were in the Middle Ages. The gradual spread of the turnpike trusts was accompanied by a new approach to road making, with first John Metcalf and later Telford and Macadam revolutionizing the methods in use. This in turn stimulated innovations in the design of conveyances; by 1784 the first royal mail coach covered the journey from London to Bath in the unprecedented time of sixteen hours. Fifty years earlier, Dover was still a two-days' journey from the capital, with an overnight stop at Canterbury. Exeter took six days to reach, Edinburgh twice that (with a slight speeding up in the summer months). Until well on in the century, there was no direct service to Birmingham; passengers left the Chester road at Castle Bromwich, seven miles away. The defi- ciency was not as serious as it might appear, in that the town basically consisted of a single street, with no street lighting, no assembly room, and for a long time no bookseller's shop. In the same period, Glasgow was still, in G. M. Trevelyan's phrase, a pretty little country town,[40] unimaginably remote from southern England. As this situation slowly changed, and travel grew a less-venturesome business, the literature of topography naturally modified its character also. The formal guidebook came into being, till no less a writer than Wordsworth is found con- tributing to a genre now regarded as somewhat anonymous. His *Topo- graphical Description* of the Lakes first appeared in 1810, appended to a volume of "selected views."

In this heyday of tourism two particular trends make themselves felt. There is first of all the picturesque tour, undertaken as a kind of aesthetic adventure by persons of sensibility. Of this phase of taste Martin Price has written, "The picturesque in general recommends the rough or rugged, the crumbling form, the complex or difficult harmony. It seeks a tension between the disorderly and irrelevant and the perfected form." Moreover, says Price, "its favorite scenes are those in which form . . . is at the point of dissolution. It turns to the sketch, which precedes formal perfection, and the ruin which succeeds it."[41] What is notable is that so many of the picturesque theorists should also have been inveterate tourists—a certain restlessness of temperament contributing to both predilections alike. The most fa- mous of these travelers is of course Rev. William Gilpin. He has usually been treated as a figure of fun, not altogether without justice.

The unguarded remark made at Tintern Abbey, "A mallet judiciously used (but who durst use it?) might be of service in fracturing some of [the gable-ends, which] hurt the eye with their regularity,"[42] seems less eccentric in the context of Gilpin's whole body of thought. It might also be recalled that so serious an antiquary as William Stukeley, who had early made himself an expert on the archeology of Roman Britain and whose *Itineranium Curiosum* (1724) was heavily quarried by succeeding editors of the *Tour,* did not scruple to take away pottery and pieces of mosaic from the sites he described so enthusiastically.[43]

Secondly, there are the "farmer's tours" made by Arthur Young in the 1760s and 1770s.[44] Young's chief interest was ostensibly agrarian improvement, and he affects a blunt no-nonsense manner, as though the sophistications of authorship were worthy only of contempt. In fact Young was an accomplished writer, who used his battery of honorific terms (*improvement, enclosure, fertile, cultivated,* and so on) with an economy both deft and sure. He responded with warm immediacy to any pleasing landscape, and though Cobbett would have found suspect his passion for what was new (fresh plantations, hedges, ditches), Young describes the agricultural revolution of his times with intelligence as well as a great deal of *brio.* Occasionally we detect the glazed eye of the fanatic, but Young has too much common sense ever to be shrill.

One can hardly say as much of William Cobbett's *Rural Rides.* Cobbett undertook his travels as a kind of fact-finding mission; he had already booked space in his own newspaper, the *Political Register,* and at times the journey itself comes to seem like a by-product of this campaign. Like a Royal Commission, Cobbett gave himself terms of reference which made the nature of his findings a foregone conclusion. Bluff, opinionated, iterative, he seldom sticks to the visible scene for long. Cobbett's England, John Derry rightly points out, is a subjective entity. He describes the countryside and the weather, but his real interests are ideas and beliefs. He sets before us a *paysage moralisé,* with a villainous "system" of exploitation eating up English rural life. In this manichean world, notions of pristine rude health are constantly opposed to those of effete and corrupt modernity. Cobbett sprays italics and capitals across the page to lend this dialectic an even more urgent emphasis. He reveals along with ordinary nostalgia for a pre-industrial era what might be termed a displaced yearning—a nostalgia of situation rather than time. Somehow the things Cobbett valued were never quite before him. As a result, there is in *Rural Rides,* for all the wealth of detailed description and close observation, a quality

of impatient polemicism: the vigor derives from what Cobbett doesn't
see, rather than what he does.

In order to show how thoroughly *new* Defoe's method is, in its
functionalism and dry secular tone, it may be helpful to cite some
of his most-important predecessors, as well as his most noteworthy
successor. The full range of English topographic writing over three
centuries—its diverse aims, effects, and methods—can hardly be illustrated in this short space. But some of the main trends between 1530
and 1830 should emerge from a rapid collation of some passages, chosen at random from major contributors to the genre. Leland, for
instance, when he comes to Northampton, potters about
conscientiously:

> The toune . . . stondith on the north side of Avon ryver, on the brow
> of a meane hill, and risith stille [continuously] from the south to the north.
> Al the old building of the toune was of stone, the new is of tymbre.
>
> There be yn the waully of Northampton 4. gates namid by este, west,
> north and south. The Este gate is the fairest of them all.
>
> There is a faire suburb withoute the South gate: and another, but lesse,
> withoute the Weste gate, yn wich is a very pratie house ex lapide polite
> quadrato, it longith to Mr———. . . .[45]

This dogged accumulation of fact mirrors the experience of a foot
traveler, with time to see everything and no particular criteria of
selection. Camden's *Britannia,* on the other hand, has much of the
pomp, the Latinate sense of consequence and the slow-wheeling amplitude of an Elizabethan royal "progress." When Camden makes his
visitation of Northampton, you feel it would be as hard to stop him
in his tracks as a line of state coaches on some grand ceremonial
occasion. He sends forward etymological outriders:

> Beneath these places, the [Aufona, or] Nen, glides forward with a gentle
> small stream, and is soon after encreas'd by the influx of a little river;
> where, at their very meeting, the City, call'd of them after the river,
> *Northafandon* . . . is so seated, that on the west side it is water'd with
> this river, and on the south with the other. Which I was of late too easily
> induced to believe the ancient *Bannaventa:* but I err'd in my conjecture,
> and let my confession atone for it. As for the name, it may seem to have
> had it from the situation upon the north side of the *Aufona.* . . . On the
> wast it hath an old Castle, beautify'd even by its antiquity, built by Simon
> de Sancto Licio, commonly call'd *Senliz,* the first of that name Earl of
> Northampton; who joyned likewise to it a beautiful Church dedicated to
> St Andrew, for his own sepulture; and, as 'tis reported, re-edify'd the
> town. . . .[46]

By contrast, Celia Fiennes is much more interested in getting from place to place, and also much closer to the physicalities of traveling:

> From Warwick we went towards Daventry all along part of the Vale of the Red Horse which was very heavy way and could not reach thither being 14 mile; about 11 mile we came to a place called Nether Shugar a sad village, we could have no entertainment; just by it on the top of a steep hill is Shuggbery Hall a seate of Sir Charles Shuggberys, who seeing our distress, being just night and the horses weary with the heavy way, he very curteously tooke compassion on us and treated us very handsomly that night, a good supper serv'd in plaite and very good wine, and good beds; my Lady Shuggbery was the Lord Leigh's Daughter and that day dineing there her coach drove by us when in distress enquireing for her lodging, which caused Sir Charles to come out and meete us, shewed a generous hospitable spirit to strangers, and with a great deale of good humour my Lady entertained us; the house stands within a good parke. . . .[47]

And so on for another fourteen lines. This straggling style, with its elliptical syntax and chatty miscellany of information, is precisely fitted to Celia Fiennes's mode of tourism. She is the traveler following her own nose, with no ambition to cover any particular region, and wholly unembarrassed about leaving her planned route in the cause of comfort.

Cobbett is not really a topographical writer, and barely a travel writer even when he embarks on his *Rural Rides* (collected in volume form, 1830). His subject is the national mentality, the temperament of the age, the culture of the people in the English countryside, rather than the quiddity of particular places. No single passage can reflect all of his moods, from vehemence to cutting irony and pensive melancholia. But a fairly representative passage would be one like this, which follows a description of the decline at Weyhill sheep fair— Cobbett having visited the fair as a boy almost fifty years earlier:

> From this dismal scene, a scene formerly so joyous, we set off back to Uphusband pretty early, were overtaken by the rain, and got a pretty good soaking. The land along here is very good. This whole country has a chalk bottom; but, in the valley on the right of the hill over which you go from Andover to Weyhill, the chalk lies far from the top, and the soil has few flints in it. It is very much like the land about Malden and Maidstone. Met with a farmer who said he must be ruined, unless another "*good war*" should come! This is no uncommon notion. They saw high prices *with* war, and they thought the war was the *cause*.[48]

Here is much of Cobbett in little. The language is clear and direct; the style moves readily to exclamation and emphatic contrast. Cobbett has a good fund of comparative knowledge, at any rate as regards southern England. He is aware of geology but basically his concerns are human; his anecdotes are recounted not to illumine life's little ironies but to forward a running argument. There is just enough literal circumstance ("a pretty good soaking," "on the right of the hill") to convince us that Cobbett really has been in Hampshire. That much established, the narrative can shift to its real locale of social criticism ("this dismal scene," and so on).

All these varied approaches have their own merit. Yet it was surely Defoe who achieved the most satisfactory mode of literary tourism. That is, he hit on the best blend of objective fact and personal commentary; the neatest amalgam of gazetteer and traveler's tale; the densest mixture of history and prophecy, myth and reportage, observation and impression, formal coverage and informal anecdote. Defoe had perhaps traveled the country over a longer period than any of the writers just considered. With the exception of Camden, he had easily the best-stocked mind. His background as businessman, soldier, economic writer, and spy was as wide as Cobbett's own. He was as responsive to "improvement" as Arthur Young, yet as conscious of an English heritage as ever William Harrison was. He had the shrewd practicality of Celia Fiennes and the same capacity to muse over the ruins of time as Leland. Above all, he had the most deeply creative spirit among this group. He was the only one to evolve a literary vehicle (the "tour" or "circuit") that could straddle the literal and the imaginative. His idiom combines the expressive resources of epic or the novel with the factual fidelity of journalism; his *Tour* shows us the real England but also (in Celia Fiennes's words) "an Idea of England."

IV

In the simplest sense, it is evident that the "design" of the *Tour* depends on its formal structure. This is not primarily a matter of the putative "letters" in which Defoe communicates his information, for this is the thinnest of literary pretenses. Rather, the author is intensely self-conscious about the shape of his journey around the nation. His prose is strewn with remarks that draw attention to the methodical character of his work, no doubt as an implied contrast to that of his rivals. Thus, he writes in Letter XII, "I am now come to the Bank of *Clyde*: My Method here as in *England,* forbids me wandring North, till I have given you a full View of the South" (2: 742). The habitual manner is that of the practiced tourist guide, leaving out nothing essential that a visitor should see:

> I was now at the extent of my intended Journey *West,* and thought of looking no farther this way for the present, so I came away *North East,* leaving *Winchester* a little on the Left. . . . Here I remember'd that I had yet left the Inland Towns of the Two Counties of *Kent* and *Sussex,* and almost all the County of *Surrey* out of my Account; and that having as it were taken a Circuit round the Coast only, I had a great many places worth Viewing to give an account of; I therefore left *Windsor,* which was within my View, on one side of the River, and *Hampton Court* on the other, as being the Subject of another Letter; and resolv'd to finish my present View, in the Order I had begun it; *That is to say,* to give an Account of the whole Country as I come on; that I may make no incongruous Transitions from one remote Part of *England* to another, *at least as few as may be.* (1: 142–44)

Notice how the Thames runs through the narrative as a marker, dividing the text as it divides historical counties and regions.

The prefatory matter in each volume serves an important function in directing the course of the journey, and insists on a shapeliness which might not otherwise be apparent to most readers:

> I have now finished my account of the several Circuits which I took the last Year, compleating the Southern Parts of the Isle of *Britain;* my last brought me to the Banks of the River *Trent* and from thence back to *London,* where I first set out. (2: 539)

The aim of such passages is rhetorical rather than geographical, in that no more ground is covered in the physical sense—the information is simply presented in a more lucid and connected manner.

As we have just seen, the immediate and effective model for the book is often supposed to be John Macky's *Journey though England.*[49] The most cursory glance at this work will reveal how defective is its organization. Macky writes a series of short letters, many of which have no organic base as regards subject matter. A chapter finishes when Macky has used up enough pages, rather than when geographic necessity prescribes. London sprawls over from Letter IX in the first volume to Letter XIV, and turns up again in the second volume. Macky has to make a special "excursion" to Bedfordshire: otherwise, as he remarks, it would have been left out. He digresses quite shamelessly on the state of the English language, improved by Sir Roger L'Estrange among others—the hack of Swift's *Tale* could do no more. Beleaguered in the Isle of Man, he calmly observes that he has omitted certain "excrescences" and proceeds to fill the gaps. Cornwall might perhaps qualify for this description, stretching a point, but the Lin-colnshire fens cannot be said to lie very far from the heart of the country. At this point, too, Macky introduces an account of the orders of society, more appropriate perhaps to the *Almanach de Gotha*.[50] Much more serious is the fact that Macky confines himself to largish towns and to seats of gentry. There is virtually nothing about the intervening countryside or about the route taken. In short, "Journey" is a misnomer. What Macky gives us is a guidebook—a series of places of interest. It would scarcely matter if the putative topographical framework were demolished, and the work presented as an alphabeti-cal sequence—Blackheath, Blandford, Blenheim, Bodmin, Boston, and so on.

With Defoe everything is different. Not only does he maintain a clear itinerary, with the progress from one county to another carefully charted, but he also employs a number of shifts to give the reader a sense of movement. Prospects unfold as we pass through the country; landscapes emerge before our gaze and fall away; contrasting scenes follow one another in smooth succession. This is partly a matter of Defoe's greater visual acuity as compared with Macky's, but it also has to do with fundamentals of his literary method. The "letters" or "circuits" are the signifiers; the physical journeys are the signified. Moreover, the strong sense of an individual observer prompts readers to think of Defoe as a traveler on a real highway on a real trip. This is why it would be a betrayal of the rhetoric to disembody the autho-rial voice, and to speak of him constantly as "the narrator," rather than of "Defoe."

From the outset of the first journey, it is evident that Defoe has a marked awareness of formal design:

> I began my Travels, where I Purpose to End them, *viz.* At the City of London, and therefore my Account of the City itself will come last, that is to say, at the latter End of my Southern Progress; and as in the Course of this Journey I shall have many Occasions to call it a Circuit, if not a Circle. . . . (1: 5)

Again, at the start of Letter V: "As I am now near the Center of this Work, so I am to describe the great Center of *England*, the City of London, and Parts adjacent" (1: 316). When Defoe added his third volume, partly in response to Macky's *Journey through Scotland* (1723), this second observation ceased to be literally true. But this does not effect the major issue: London is repeatedly described as the nexus of trade, society, fashion, wealth, and its fulcral position in the

economic life of the nation stressed. It is therefore appropriate that
Defoe should construct his first two volumes around a series of trips
to and from London, now in one direction, now in another. The layout
of the tour enacts the processes of human geography.

As the book develops, Defoe employs one crucial strategy to forward this "enactment" function. What he does is to choose expressions that apply both to the progress of his (in effect, fictional) tour
and to the description that he is offering to the reader. Often this is
simple enough—a matter of a single word ("But to return to my Passage up the River," 1: 41).[51] It may be explicit in a passage of explana-
tory comment: "I had still the County of *Cambridge* to visit, to
compleat this Tour of the Eastern Part of *England,* and of that I come
now to speak" (1: 77). On other occasions, there is a more complex
and effective intermingling of the progress of the journey and the
progress of the narrative:

> I now draw near to *Cambridge,* to which I fansy I look as if I was afraid
> to come, having made so many Circumlocutions beforehand; but I must
> yet make another Digression before I enter the Town; (for in my way, and
> as I came in from *New Market,* about the beginning of *September;*) I cannot
> omit, that I came necessarily through *Sturbridge* Fair . . . (1: 80)

Here the term "Digression" has much the force of pun. It is through
such linking devices that Defoe establishes the "reality" of his tour,
while at the same time advancing the course of his own narrative.

So vital is this bonding technique, and so important is simple repetition in Defoe's rhetoric, that further illustration is needed. At times,
the author spells out the connection between his artistic plan and the
actual route he is covering: "From *Cambridge,* my Design obliging me,
and the direct Road, in part concurring, I came back thro' the West
part of the County of *Essex*" (1: 88). Sometimes Defoe appears to
admit that the union of effects is a mere whimsical fancy, to be in-
dulged but not believed: "About four Miles, over those delicious
Downs, brings us to *Epsome,* and if you will suppose me to come there
in the Month of *July,* or thereabouts, you may think me to come the
middle of the Season" (1: 159). In places, the punning intent comes
to the surface with conscious wordplay: "My last Letter ended the
Account of my Travels, where Nature ended her Account, when she
meeted out the Island, and where she fix'd the utmost *Western
Bounds of Britain*" (1: 254). The word "digress" is exploited more
than once, because of its ability to straddle journey and narrative:
"And, having mentioned *Andover,* though out of the Road that I was
in, I must digress to tell you, that the Town of *Andover* lies . . ." (1:

289). A similar use is made of "excursion," as at the start of Letter VI: "I have spent so much Time, and taken up so much room in my Description of *London,* and the adjacent Parts, that I must be the more cautious, *at least,* as to needless Excursions in the Country near it" (1: 381).[52]

In this connection the motif of the "tour" or "circuit," mentioned in the very first paragraph I quoted (p. 46), is of special value to Defoe. The word "circuit" figures about thirty times throughout the book. More than half of these occurrences are found near the start or the end of a journey, where the narrator is most conscious of his aims and means. A representative passage comes in Letter VIII:

> The only Towns of any Note that are to be found on the North Bank of *Trent,* are *Nottingham,* and the other *Burton,* of which I shall speak in their Order; at present, as I took a different Circuit in my Riding, I must do so in my Account of it also, or else if my Pen does not follow my Foot, I shall wander rather than travel, at least in my Paper, whatever I did on my Horse. (2: 546)

A major part of the *Tour's* rhetorical energy is expanded in the ambi- tion to make Defoe's pen follow his foot. Often this desire is reflected in a direct appeal to the reader: "I cannot but . . . desire you, my Friend, to travel with me through this houling Wilderness in your Imagination, and you shall soon find all that is wonderful about it" (2: 566). Even where apostrophe as such is not in question, Defoe employs a sort of indirect address: "It would require a long Treatise of Commerce to enter into that [question]: But that I may not bring you into the Labyrinth, and not show you the way out, I shall, in three short Heads, describe . . ." (2: 613).

A crucial development of the idea of the tour occurs in Letter VIII also. It occurs in this passage:

> Having thus passed the Rubicon (*Trent*) and set my Face Northward, I scarce knew which Way to set forward, in a Country too so full of Won- ders, and on so great a Journey, and yet to leave nothing behind me to call on as I came back, at least not to lead me out of my Way in my Return. But then considering that I call this Work, a *Tour,* and the Parts of it, *Letters;* I think, that tho' I shall go a great Length forward, and shall endeavour to take Things with me as I go; yet I may take a Review of some Parts as I came back, and so may be allowed to pick up any Fragments I may have left behind in my going out. (2: 552)

The most striking element in this paragraph is the constant interaction between what might be called topographic placing and narrative placing (note especially *passed, set my Face, set forward, leave behind, came back, out of my Way, in my Return, go a great Length forward, as I go, take a Review, and going out*). It is clear that Defoe effects the interplay chiefly through verbs and adverbial phrases. Throughout the work, indeed, he makes verbs do most to leap this aperture: "But I must land, lest this Part of the Account seems to smell of the Tarr, and I should tire the Gentlemen with leading them out of their Knowl-edge" (1: 351). Or "But though I am backward to dip into Antiquity, yet no *English* Man . . . can go to *Carlisle*, and not step aside to see the Monument of King *Edward* I." (2: 687). Again, "If I may straggle a little into Antiquity" (2: 508). More strikingly: "I am now at the utmost Extent of *England* West, and here I must mount the Alps, traverse the Mountains of *Wales*, (and indeed, they are well compar'd to the Alps in the inmost Provinces)" (2: 451). A common adverbial formula is "in my Course" (1: 299), which has the same capacity to look both ways.

By this means Defoe gives point and direction to his tour, so that it acquires a trajectory—something Macky's seriatim technique forbids. Even where he is forced into what could be an awkward explanation, he manages things far more adroitly and naturally than Macky, who seems clumsy and naive by contrast. A good example can be found in the passage on leaving Windsor, in his second letter, which has already been quoted (p. 45 above). The impression conveyed here that Defoe is taking the reader into his confidence comes to Defoe's aid more than once. As for example, "Before I go forward I should mention *Burrow Bridge*, which is but three Miles below *Rippon* . . . and which I must take in my Way, that I may not be obliged to go farther out of the Way, on the next Journey" (2: 627). Similarly in the Scottish portion: "He that will view the Country of *Fife* must, as I said before, go round the Coast; and yet there are four or five Places of Note in the Middle of the Country which . . . must not be omitted; I'll take them as I go, though I did not travel to them in a direct Line" (2: 775). Once Defoe achieves an almost Shandean self-consciousness, when he comes to Chatsworth ("perhaps it shall be as many Years describing as it was in building, and the Description be no more finished than the Building", 2: 581–82). Usually he stops well short of this, seeming content to dovetail the "progress" of his journey and its literary analogue.

On one occasion, Defoe makes use of literal orientation—the points of the real compass—to explain his mode of progression. This is at the start of Letter III:

I intended once to have gone due West this Journey; but then I should have been obliged to croud my Observations so close, (to bring *Hampton-*

Court, Windsor, Blenheim, Oxford, the Bath and Bristol, all into one Letter; all those remarkable Places lying in a Line, as it were, in one Point of
the Compass) as to have made my Letter too long, or my Observations
too light and superficial, as others have done before me. (1: 172)

Instead, the circuit will be divided, so that Defoe can take Hampton
Court on his outward journey, and Windsor on his return, to "make
my Progress the more regular." In the previous paragraph, Defoe had
found "so many Things to say in every Part of *England*" that his
journey could not "be barren of Intelligence, which way soever I
turn." Whichever way the traveler points his horse; whichever direction the narrative takes.

A number of refinements on this basic technique can be detected.
For example, various motifs are combined—in the third paragraph of
Letter I, Defoe refers both to "what I think, I may very honestly call
a Circuit in the very Letter of it" and to "some Little Excursions,
which I made by themselves" (1: 5–6). Or he dramatizes his double
progression in a sudden vivid phrase: "I am now at the Gates of
Edinburgh; but . . . give me leave to take it in Perspective" (2: 707),
or when he gets to Land's End, "I am now at my Journey's End . . .
I must now return *Sur mes pas*" (1: 243).[53] But these are sophisticated
applications of a method that is in essence notably simple in proportion
to its rhetorical utility.

Without disturbing the primacy of this particular constructional
aid, Defoe introduced a number of other devices as the work pro-
gressed, again with the idea of promoting drive and impetus. In the
second and third volumes especially, he made regular mention of the
small "compass" of his book as contrasted with the bulk of the material
he had to cover. This served a number of rhetorical ends. It constituted a kind of apologia in the face of any observable defects of gaps
in coverage. It stressed the plenitude of England, the sheer weight of
phenomena to be encountered throughout the nation. This was a
leading purpose of his tour, as I shall show in a moment. Third, the
recurrent use of this notion—infinite riches in a little room—serves
to reaffirm Defoe's ambition to create a literary vehicle appropriate
to the material described. In this case, of course, Defoe is saying it
can't be done. The confines of the book are too narrow to allow him
to render the whole teeming multiplicity of British life. But in deplor-
ing the particular failure, Defoe is restating the general or ideal aim
of his work. The literary survey will be as faithful a copy as can be
achieved of the face of England: its failings result (the implication
goes) from a lack of space and from that alone.[54]

Some examples will make the point clearer. The word "compass" occurs some fifteen times; scarcely any of these appear in the first third of the book. Not surprisingly, Defoe's sense of being hemmed in grows steadily more apparent as the book proceeds. The first significant use comes at the start of the fifth letter, when the author comes to speak of London:

> This great Work is infinitely difficult in its Particulars, though not in itself; not that the City is so difficult to be described, but to do it in the narrow Compass of a Letter, which we see so fully takes up Two large Volumes in Folio, and which, yet, if I may venture to give an Opinion of it, is done but by Halves neither. (1: 316)

Again we have the transference from narrational issues ("narrow Compass of a Letter") to those of topography. For within a few lines, Defoe is writing that "*London* . . . might, indeed, be viewed in a small Compass" and then speaking of the Roman walls as "Fifty Miles in Compass." Sometimes he uses the word as a simple spatial term: "That Part of the River *Thames* which is properly the Harbour . . . begins at the turning of the River out of *Lime-House* Reach, and extends to the *Custom-house-Keys:* In this Compass I have had the Curiosity to count the Ships" (1: 350). More commonly, Defoe aligns the word with a term such as "description," referring to his own constructional procedures. For example, speaking of the Pool of London, "In what Manner can any Writer go about it, to bring it into any reasonable Compass? The Thing is a kind of Infinite, and the Parts to be separated from one another in such a Description, are so many, that it is hard to know where to begin" (1: 349). (See also chapter 6, on the "compass" of the journey.)

However, it is only in the second half of the book that this emphasis grows really insistent. Defoe became so conscious of the idea that he extended it to time when writing the preface to his final volume:

> If all these Additions are to be found in the small Interval between the publishing the second Volume and this of the third, and that in so narrow a Compass, what may not every subsequent Year produce? and what Encouragement is here for new and more accurate Surveys of the country? which, whoever travels over it, will always furnish new Materials, and a Variety both profitable and delightful. (2: 536)

On another occasion, Defoe turns a deft compliment on Burley in the Hill (rather nobly, as it was the house of his antagonist, the Earl of Nottingham) by utilizing this ploy (2: 503). A similar passage occurs in the description of Alloway House, near Stirling (2: 800).

That last reference serves as a reminder that the Scottish sections are particularly rich under the aspect I have been considering: "Our Account of *Scotland* being confined to so narrow a Compass, must necessarily want many Things . . ." (2: 536). This may arise partly from Defoe's awareness that he was skimming over very large tracts of ground in a short space. He wrote at the head of his last volume, "The Tour is now finish'd; and you have the Account contracted into as narrow a Compass, as, considering the Extent of Ground pass'd over, with the Number of Cities, populous Towns, and a Country infinitely Rich, Populous and Prosperous, to be described, could reasonably be expected" (2: 535). But this excuse hardly served for the vast spaces of Scotland with which he had to deal in Volume III. Even though contemporaries were ignorant of the Highlands, and even though there was relatively little to detain the curious traveler of pre-Romantic tastes (in any case, Wade's roads were only half-built), there is a definite sense in the last part of the *Tour* that Defoe is anxious to get things completed. He may even have been under some pressure from the bookseller Strahan to cut down on space. Witness a remark in the Introduction to the Scottish section:

> *Scotland* is here describ'd with Brevity, but with Justice; and the present State of Things there, plac'd in as clear a Light as the Sheets, I am confin'd to, will admit; if this pleases, more particulars may be adventured on hereafter. . . . (2: 690)

A number of other hints can be found to support this line of argument, as for example the following:

> From hence there is nothing remarkable till we come to *Aberdeen,* a Place so eminent, that it commands some Stay upon it; yet I shall contract its Description as much as possible, the Compass of my Work being so great, and the Room I have for it so small. (2: 808)

It seems to follow that Defoe's consciousness of restriction was greatest for opposite reasons, in the dense metropolitan area and in the scattered, lightly populated, outback regions. Judging purely by acreage, Defoe is about two hundred times more generous in space allotted to London and Westminster than to Scotland. But of course this reflects not just his own intent, but also the demographic facts of the time (London accounting for something like an eighth of the British population, higher than a century later)[55] and the taste of the age, when readers were no more interested in hearing about the natural splendors of the Highlands than Defoe was in gratifying such an interest.

It is possible that Defoe did feel himself genuinely cramped towards the end, but it is certain that he was capable of making abundant rhetorical capital from the feeling.[56] Nor does this sense of compression impair the structural identity of the book—its cleanliness of outline and purposeful trajectory. Macky, as remarked, makes a series of ill-charted trips in any direction that takes his fancy. He supplies no route: one moment he is in Ipswich, the next in Bury St Edmunds, and in principle there is no reason why his magic carpet should not loft him a moment later to Glasgow. Defoe, on the other hand, plans his itinerary so as to bring in the maximum amount of information as he goes—he likes the phrase *en passant* (e.g., 1: 350)—and so as to give the reader a definite impression of covering all the ground. Where Macky floats high over the landscape, Defoe hedgehops.

Finally, Defoe's tour is much more intelligently conceived that Macky's journey. Initially, Defoe keeps to the idea of a "circuit," with London as the start-and-finish line. Letters I and II are complete in themselves. Letter V is a perambulation of the capital (the fifth of ten English sections). Other trips occupy two letters: thus, III and IV describe a "progress" to Land's End, out and return—similarly VI and VII, with Anglesey the hinge of the journey. When Defoe reached his final volume, he obviously could not retain this scheme—a tour of Northern Scotland could hardly have its base camp in London (a good two weeks' traveling distance even as late as the time of the battle of Culloden). What he did was to effect something of a compromise, but a sensible compromise. Letters VIII, IX, and X all describe a route taken northwards from the Midlands, starting from the far-thest point reached in earlier journeys—either the Trent or the Mersey. Scotland is simply parceled up into three convenient units: XI, the border to the Forth, including Edinburgh; XII, the border to the Clyde, with Glasgow; and XIII, the circuit of the rest of Scotland, going counter-clockwise on the map. As a result of these shifts in the third volume, the *Tour* loses a little in the way of symmetry of design. Yet it retains a shapeliness in its organization that is far beyond Celia Fiennes, Stukeley, or Cobbett—not to mention John Macky.

The following spatial diagram, crude as it must be, gives some approximation of the structural layout, viewed chiefly from a London base.

out	I	return
out	II	return
out	III	
	IV	return
London	V	Westminster

out	VI	
	VII	return
Trent—	VIII	Tees
Trent—	IX	Border
Mersey—	X	Border
Border—	XI	Forth/Clyde valley (E)
Border	XII	Forth/Clyde valley (W)
Forth/Clyde valley (E)	XIII	Forth/Clyde valley (W)

The carpentering work extends a little further than this table reveals. Letter VI ends at Chester, and Letter VII begins there. Both Letters VIII and IX open effectively at Nottingham. Letter X ends at Carlisle, and Letter XII starts there. Similarly, Letter IX ends at Berwick, and Letter XI begins there. Both Letters XI and XII take us to Edinburgh, while the capital is the starting point of Letter XIII—it thus serves as a hub in Scotland almost in the same way as London in the opening seven sections. The book finally comes to a conclusion on the Clyde, near Glasgow, thus meeting up with the earlier progress of Letter XII. The "hinges" in the northern sections (Chester/Liverpool; Nottingham) were important regional centers out of which radiated a variety of social activity. Such twinings reflect an attempt on Defoe's part to assert an unified nation, each part bound to others by a set of strong affiliations, economic and political. This complex interlocking pattern is beautifully adapted to Defoe's aim of comprehensive, yet intelligible, coverage. He has ordered his material so that the formal contours of the book mirror geographic, social, and economic reality. Literary expression and human ecology are wedded in the *Tour's* grand design.

One obvious way of perceiving the shape of a country (at least an island) is to navigate around it by sea. This was indeed the means Defoe had contemplated, as he tells us at the start of Letter IV:

I had once, indeed, resolved to have coasted the whole Circuit of *Britain* by Sea, as 'tis said *Agricola* the *Roman* General did, and in this Voyage I would have gone about every Promontory, and into the Bottom of every Bay, and had provided myself a good Yacht, and able Commander for that Purpose; but I found it would be too hazardous an Undertaking for any Man to justify himself in the doing it upon the meer Foundation of Curiosity, having no other Business at all, I gave it over ... as a hopeless, and too dangerous Adventure, and satisfied myself, to make the Circuit very near as perfect by Land, which I have done with much less Hazard, though with much more Pains and Expence; the Fruit of which you have, in Part, communicated in these Letters. (1: 254–55)

We may recall at this point that Defoe had himself been associated with the coasting trade in his younger days. However, it is intriguing to observe that a later traveler, Paul Theroux, also decided that a coastal voyage, albeit an inland one, would give him a sense of the British nation:

> It answered every need. There was only one coast, it was one undeviating route, and this way I would see the whole of Britain. In many respects, Britain *was* its coast—nowhere in Britain was more than sixty-five miles from the sea. Nearly the whole of the coast was unknown to me. And so as soon as I decided on this coastal route for my intinerary, I had my justification for the trip—the journey had the right shape; it had logic; it had a beginning and an end; and what better way was there to see an island than circumambulating its coast?[57]

Theroux, as an expatriate American, formed the "logic" of his trip around a series of selective stopping-off points around a Britain he knew (outside London) scarcely at all. Defoe, an elderly Englishman, found that his "journey had the right shape" when he devised his sequence of "circuits."

A paradox in this area has been identified by Jonathan Raban, who contends that "England is hardly big enough to make a proper journey around it at all." Yet Raban had just sailed round the British mainland (as opposed to hugging the terrestial shore, as Theroux did), a trip recounted in his book *Coasting* (1987). And he is forced to concede that "The English journey is by nature an epical affair. The terrain to be surveyed is conceived of as vast. The route is arduous."[58] To document the point, he cites Defoe's opening description of "the most flourishing and opulent Country in the World":

> In travelling thro' *England,* a Luxuriance of Objects presents it self to our View: Where-ever we come, and which way so ever we look, we see something New, something Significant, some well worth the Travellers Stay, and the Writer's Care; nor is any Check to our Design, or Obstruction to its Acceptance in the World, to say the like has been done already, or to Panegyrick upon the Labours and Value of those Authors who have gone before, in this Work: A compleat Account of *Great Britain* will be the Work of many Years, I might say Ages, and may employ many Hands: Whoever has travell'd *Great Britain* before us, and whatever they have written, tho' they may have had a Harvest, yet they have always, either

by Necessity, Ignorance or Negligence pass'd over so much, that others
may come and Glean after them by large handfuls. (1: 1–2)

Raban is right to detect the stress here on authorial labor. Beyond
that, we can see an effort to show the writerly enterprise as fulfilling
a "Design," with the task envisaged as an act of Georgic husbandry
(see chapter 5).

However, the question may still be asked: on the global scale by
which we now operate, is Britain a large enough subject to be worth
so much detailed attention? To answer this, in the light of our earlier
discussion, it may be useful to invoke Paul Fussell's categories. In
Abroad (1980), Fussell makes a broad distinction on historical lines:
"Exploration belongs to the Renaissance, travel to the bourgeois age,
tourism to our proletarian moment."[59] Defoe's book surely predates
tourism in the modern sense, and might seem most naturally to belong
to the bourgeois moment. But there is just a hint of exploration in it,
too. Admittedly, by this time, only the most remote corners of the
nation—especially in Scotland and Wales—were altogether lacking
in basic provision such as negotiable roads. But the entire *Tour* shows
that much of the country still remained a sort of frontier territory,
ripe for development and open to economic invaders. Hence Defoe's
enthusiasm for the new system of turnpikes, setting up a *system* of
highways—the very mark of human control and civilization which
Defoe wishes to enact in his own literary map of Britain. Again, it is
true that Britain is not and was not "abroad" in Fussell's sense. For
a time, travel—or more accurately travel writing—became identified
with a certain sort of upper-class globe-trotting. Some of the literature
of abroad has to do also with cultural exile, that is with the home
thoughts of those in flight from domesticity. The point about the *Tour*
is that Defoe could describe a nation largely unknown to most of his
readers: any sense of "abroad" was confined to a very few individuals,
predominantly male, in the upper echelons of society. The further
reaches of Britain were exotic enough for most citizens. Leaving aside
Scotland, which had only recently been politically incorporated, there
can hardly have been ten people alive who were closely familiar with
both Cornwall and Northumberland.

The tour seems a natural way of navigating the country, and it is
a surprise to discover that nobody had ever quite hit on this exact
form before. The very first paragraph of the opening letter defines the
undertaking in terms of separate "circuits," which blend utility and
elegance in a remarkable way. The British mainland is by no means a
symmetrical stretch of land—rather, an irregular series of bumps and
excrescences. Defoe manages to make his journeys not just intelligible,

but even sequential and to some degree cumulative. Like a later German traveler, he could have claimed, "*Veni, vidi, scripsi.*"

A great deal of Defoe's own experience went into the *Tour*. Yet it is far from a direct transcript. Although there is so much shrewd observation of contemporary Britain in its pages, the inner momentum of the book derives from an astonishingly clear sense of history. Defoe reordered his personal memories, interlarding his own tours (made over half a lifetime) with borrowing from published sources. What he gives us is not a tour, straight, but the experiential equivalent of a tour. He imbued the work, too, with a crotchety, sometimes literal-minded poetry of his own. For this task he needed all his literary art, acquired not just as a great reporter, but as a great imaginative creator, too. So Defoe achieved the true English epic. (Significantly it is a non-martial epic, perhaps closer to Virgil than Homer.)[60] His chosen vehicle was not that of the vainglorious *Brutiad*'s that writers of the age so often projected, but the homely guidebook form, within which he dramatized his sense of the British nation, in its fullness and all its contrasting moods.

Defoe comes early in the story of tourism, as an organized form of spending leisure time—indeed, the phenomenon does not properly begin until the second half of the eighteenth century.[61] More significantly, he is at the very start of the literary *tour*: it is not generally appreciated that Defoe's book is the first work of literature in English that has any lasting currency to employ this word in its title.[62] In this introduction, I have attempted to show that this primacy derives from Defoe's unique vision of Britain and from his mastery of formal and rhetorical devices. The rest of the book will seek to illustrate these matters in more detailed ways.

Part I
Pre-Text

The Preparations for this Work have been suitable to the Author's earnest Concern for its Usefulness; seventeen very large Circuits, or Journeys have been taken thro' divers Parts separately, and three general Tours over almost the whole *English* Part of the Island; in all which the Author has not been wanting to Treasure up just Remarks upon particular Places and Things, so that he is very little in Debt to other Mens Labours, and gives but very few Accounts of Things, but what he has been an Eye-witness of himself. (1: 3)

1

The Making of Volume I

We begin with the issue of composition. The primary question is one of dating—when, as precisely as we can tell, did the author commit the *Tour* to paper? In other words—what did Defoe know, and when? But we shall also be investigating related issues: what kind of research had he embarked on, and at what period of his life? How comprehensive, accurate, and up-to-date is his information? What sources can be identified, and what use did he make of earlier writers of topography? What revisions can be identified, and at what stage? It is laborious of course to follow Defoe minutely through every line of the text; but this is the only way to catch him in the act of writing— to pursue him to his very desk, as we can do so much more easily with modern masters such as Joyce or Eliot.

I

Defoe remains disconcertingly remote. We have grown so accustomed to the testimonies of authors that his anonymity comes to seem almost sinister. He wrote a remarkable fictive *Journal*, but left no private diary. Defoe compiled more than one set of diverting *Memoirs*—but they were not his own. As we now recognize, he built on the puritan tradition of spiritual autobiography: yet his direct contributions to the genre scarcely go beyond casual exercises in apologia. The authorship of some two hundred fifty books "by" Defoe, included in the standard *Checklist* of his writings, have now been called into question. Of his extant letters (once more, just over two hundred fifty), all but a dozen were written in seventeen years around the middle of his career; we have none whatsoever till Defoe is into his forties, none from that productive phase 1721–27. And it is not merely the externals of biography that are missing. There is a comparable gap with respect to artistic matters. Defoe, for example, never mentions his output as a novelist in his surviving correspondence.[1]

Hence, Defoe's major books are almost wholly bereft of clues as to his working methods or his techniques of composition. Even to set a date on the writing of his novels is a task beyond our present scholarly capacities. A priori there is nothing to show that *Robinson Crusoe* had not lain seven years in a drawer before April 1719. We tend to assume that the book was written quickly, because Defoe was a fast worker: in 1719, apart from the two parts of *Crusoe*, J. R. Moore lists fourteen separate books, some quite extensive.[2] Yet this evidence is purely inferential. We simply do not know in what fashion Defoe put together his masterpieces. Only one composition, in fact, allows us to study the writer at work: the *Tour*.

This book follows on an unprecedented lull in Defoe's output. From 1701 to 1730 he averaged over sixteen publications a year (disregarding periodicals); the annual total never falls below five (1708 and 1709, with Defoe in Scotland; 1730, when he was dying, and in hiding).[3] In the second decade of the century the tally never drops below twelve: from 1710 to 1719 the average is twenty-six. Then in 1721 the score is only six, including a collected edition of earlier works. The nine entries for the following year include two sets of miscellaneous letters from Mist's *Journal*. In 1723 only *two* items are listed by Moore, neither of these very long, one of them a conjectural attribution. Plainly, Defoe was up to something, for the graph soon begins to rise again. He might have been ill, but we have no proof. He may have been busy with Applebee's *Journal*: but hectic activity of this sort had never been a check on creative energy up till then. He was, of course, writing fewer political pamphlets, and more full-dress novels. The *History of the Pyrates* (1724, 1728) would have been an obvious drain on his time, yet this is basically a compilation (if indeed it is by Defoe at all). One is forced to the conclusion that the sudden fall in productivity has something to do with the *Tour*.

Now, this circumstance has not gone wholly unobserved. William Lee offered one tentative account of this phase: "From the fact that Defoe published very few works during 1723, I think the Tours, to which he alludes in [*The Great Law of Subordination Consider'd*, 1724], must have been made in that year."[4] The suggestion has not found general favor. Those of Defoe's biographers who take account of the *Tour*—some ignore it altogether—incline towards a different emphasis. For example, Thomas Wright:

Most of the material for "A Tour Through the Whole Island of Great Britain" was obtained, not, as Mr. Lee supposed, in 1723, but some forty years previous—during the five years that succeeded Monmouth's rebellion, 1684–1688..... With "Camden's Britannia" as his guide, and "an ancient gentleman" of his acquaintance as his companion, [Defoe] travelled "in three or four several tours, over the whole island," critically observing, and carefully informing himself of everything worth observing in all the towns and counties through which he passed. . . . But though the notes taken during these tours, which covered a period of "near four years," formed the principal material upon which Defoe founded the present work, still he had frequently travelled over the island since, and every journey would necessarily increase his store of knowledge. In England he had made as many as seventeen large circuits, or separate journeys, and three general tours through the whole country; and as regards Scotland, not only had he travelled critically over a great part of it, but he had lived there. The north part of England, and the south part of Scotland, he had viewed "five several times over. . . ."[5]

This looks more authoritative than it is. Wright appears to stick close to what Defoe says, in paraphrasing both the *Tour* and the *Law of Subordination* (see p. 21). However, Wright extrapolates from the facts and comes to a conclusion far in excess of that warranted. James Sutherland is more cautious, but his main contention is similar. In the *Tour,* Sutherland argues,

Defoe was only working up material which he had collected in almost forty years of travelling to and fro in England and Scotland; but the mere task of transforming his notes into a readable narrative was a formidable one.

This is to move beyond Sutherland's earlier, fully measured statement:

His *Tour* . . . appeared when he was over sixty; but many of the observations in it were first made when he was still a young man, riding about from one little market town to another to another on his business and his pleasure.[6]

That much is unarguable. But it is another matter to go on and speculate, as G. D. H. Cole did, that Defoe could have written the *Tour* without ever stirring out of his lodgings in London. In fact, as Cole added, we know that Defoe did travel a good deal; and so the book becomes "a compilation of memories." But the damage was done when Cole referred to Defoe as "one of the world's great liars, with a peculiar art for making fictitious narrative sound like truth."[7] Many readers must have taken away the impression that Defoe simply wrote up information long gathered, relying either on total recall or on careful notes—depending on the authority consulted—and making little effort to produce an up-to-date survey of the nation.

A careful review of the evidence suggests that the truth lies the other way: and that Lee's supposition was in many respects justified. It is certain that Defoe did use his earlier observations. But a careful study of the text shows that the *Tour* is chock-full of recent information. This means not just incidental facts (a house burnt down, say), but whole blocks of the work—the running theme provided by the South Sea Bubble and its after effects, for instance, or the continuing rebuilding of London. This evidence relates to a third major point of distinction, that is, the clues in the *Tour* concerning the actual process of writing. These hints are spread unevenly through the text, indicating a differential in the extent to which Defoe's facts were up-to-date in various parts of the country. However, there is abundant proof throughout to show that Defoe was dealing with things as they were, not as they had been. G. M. Trevelyan's assertion that "the tours on which [Defoe] based his observations were largely taken in the early and middle years of Anne" rests on a flimsy support.[8] It can be shown that the author did use his experience as Harley's spy in a number of places—whereas with Wright's conjecture there is virtually no direct evidence, only circumstantial—but this of course does not mean that later journeys were not also undertaken. To be more positive, I shall attempt to demonstrate that the *Tour* is more of a new concoction, less of a warmed-up ragout, than has been imagined. In this chapter I confine myself to the first volume, reserving the later installments for the next chapter.

II

The *Tour* appeared serially as follows: Volume I, 21 May 1724; Volume II, 8 June 1725; and Volume III, 9 August 1726 (though dated 1727). These afford a definite terminus ad quem. The issue is how long Defoe had spent in preparing and writing the book. To put the last two verbs in apposition is perhaps to invite a misapprehension. Defoe sometimes presents himself as composing "on the spot" (e.g., 1: 242; 2: 468, 707), and always seeks to identify the progress of his physical tour with the progress of his narrative "tour." We ought not, then, to make a sharp disjunction between the gathering of material and the composition of the text. Defoe might have been collecting information for Volume II while writing Volume I: or, for that matter, while already writing Volume II. It begs the whole question to speak of Defoe "writing up" his earlier notes. Apart from anything else, even where we know that the *Tour* is based on earlier observations, we have no proof that Defoe used notes at all.

First let us consider Defoe's own statement of the position, this time in his own words rather than Wright's paraphrase. The opening lines have already been used as an epigraph to Part I.

> The Preparations for this Work have been suitable to the Author's earnest Concern for its Usefulness; seventeen very large Circuits, or Journeys have been taken thro' divers Parts separately, and three general Tours over almost the whole *English* Part of the Island. . . .
>   Besides these several Journeys in *England,* he has also lived some time in *Scotland,* and has Travell'd critically over great Part of it; he has viewed the North Part of *England,* and the South Part of *Scotland* five several Times over; all which is hinted here, to let the Readers know what Reason they will have to be satisfy'd with the Authority of the Relation, and that the Accounts here given are not the Produce of a cursory View, or rais'd upon the borrow'd Lights of other Observers. (1: 3)

A confirmatory touch is inserted at the start of Letter X:

> Having thus finished my Account of the East Side of the North Division of *England,* I put a stop here [the Tweed], that I may observe the exact Course of my Travels; for as I do not write you these Letters from the Observations of one single Journey, so I describe Things as my Journies lead me, having no less than five times travelled through the North of *England,* and almost every time by a different Rout; purposely that I might see every thing that was to be seen, and if possible, know every thing that is to be known, though not (at least till the last general Journey) knowing or resolving upon writing these Accounts to you. (2: 664)

This is quite unequivocal; and there are other places where Defoe clearly indicates that he had undertaken a special journey for the purpose of the book, although this is the only mention of "the last general Journey." It is demonstrably true that Defoe had lived in Scotland, and had traveled all over Britain in earlier years. He need not have mentioned the fact, however: and if he was bent on fabricating a spuriously "authentic" background to the *Tour,* he could just as easily have exaggerated the *recency* of his fact-finding missions. In other words, there is little obvious advantage to be detected in telling the truth in one case and not in the other. Defoe's rhetorical purposes were such that he wished to stress above all the firsthand quality of his observation. With this in mind, he makes a calculated admission that the earlier journeys were undertaken before he had thought of writing his *Tour.* If he can get away with that concession, it hardly seems needful to invent a totally fictitious "general Journey." Quite how comprehensive this journey really was, is another matter.

  We are left, then, with the fact that Defoe supplies at the outset a specific departure date:

> I set out, the 3d of *April*, 1722, going first Eastward, and took what I
> think, I may very honestly call a Circuit in the very Letter of it. . . . (1: 5)

Of course, this could be as deceptive a precision as Crusoe's own. The
timing would accord neatly enough with the publishing lull mentioned
before. Seven of Moore's nine entries in his *Checklist* for 1722 were
published by March (these include *Moll Flanders* and the *Journal of
the Plague Year*); one of the remainder was a compilation based on
earlier material, while the title page of *Colonel Jacque* (published on 20
December) contains a giveaway to show that the work was originally
planned by the summer of that year at the latest.[9] These facts supply
a negative kind of evidence: nothing in Defoe's career, as it can be
established, forbids a journey at this date. Are there more positive
clues?

It should be noted first that an election was under way at this
particular juncture. Defoe generally took pains to inform himself on
the political temperature in the constituencies, when such a moment
came, either on his own behalf or another's. Moreover, Applebee's
Journal contains certain articles, reprinted by Lee, that have Defoe
written all over them, notably the issues for 14 and 21 April.[10] We
can be reasonably sure that Defoe would be more occupied by the
face of England in April 1722 than by lunar landscapes, Madagascan
coastlines, or the diverse exotica that sometimes claimed his attention.

Second, there is an aspect of Defoe's business affairs that bears on
the point. In the *Tour*, his progress through East Anglia is represented
as fairly leisurely and, as we shall see, it is possible to infer that he
did not complete his journey before well into autumn. Colchester is
reached by a somewhat circuitous route, and there Defoe makes a
passing reference to the high steward of the town "(this Year, 1722)."
In the same paragraph, he mentions Lord Cowper as recorder, which
firmly places the writing before 10 October 1723, when the former
Lord Chancellor died.[11] However, there are grounds for supposing
that Defoe would indeed have been in Colchester a year or more prior
to that event. On 6 August 1722 he was granted a lease of farm
property owned by the corporation of Colchester. The transaction,
made in favor of his daughter Hannah, was a typically complex one,
involving further legal agreements dated 1 September 1722 and 29
September 1723. To help him, Defoe had an agent on the spot, an
Evangelical clergyman in the borough.[12] But he was not the sort of
man to do business by proxy where he could carry it through himself.
All in all, it seems humanly certain that Defoe would have visited
Colchester in the summer of 1722, the very time when the ongoing
narrative of the *Tour* would require his presence there. Whether he

reached the town by way of the elaborate coastal trip described in his book, or rode by the direct route through Chelmsford, is a more speculative issue.

There is a third factor that prompts the conclusion that Defoe did actually take a journey into East Anglia around this period (or journeys, for there is nothing that precludes a series of visits, punctuated by occasional sojourn at Stoke Newington). This occurs when we reach Suffolk. "Being come to *Newmarket* in the Month of *October*," Defoe writes, "I had the opportunity to see the Horse-Races" (1: 75). Now of course this might be proof of the usual theory, Defoe recollecting in shameless tranquillity his earlier days, perhaps the time when he was associated with Godolphin.[13] The mention of the trainer Tregonwell Frampton, whose great days were around the end of Anne's reign, might support that view.[14] However, a couple of pages later Defoe alludes to a visit to nearby Rushbrook, which house he found in mourning:

> The Family being in Tears, and the House shut up; Sir *Robert Davers*, the Head thereof, and Knight of the Shire for the County of *Suffolk*, and who had married the eldest Daughter of the late Lord *Dover*, being just dead, and the Corpse lying there in its Funeral Form of Ceremony, not yet Buried; yet all look'd lovely in their Sorrow, and a numerous Issue promising and grown up, intimated that the Family of *Davers* would still Flourish. . . . (1: 77)

Curiously, both the second and third baronets of this name died within the relevant period, respectively in October 1722 and June 1723. However, the reference to Davers's marriage and his children make it clear that the father is meant. It is true that Defoe had mentioned this man as far back as 1704, in a newsletter to Robert Harley from Bury St Edmunds.[15] It is therefore conceivable that he learned in London of Sir Robert's death, and cunningly slipped in a reference that tallied with the October visit to Newmarket. This seems devious even for a notoriously resourceful inventor. Moreover, Defoe seems to be ignorant of the death of Lady Davers, which occurred a few days later and was reported in the London press. The passage is also remarkably tasteless if we suppose it to be written in the knowledge of the second family bereavement. A more natural explanation would be that Defoe visited Rushbrook in October 1722, and transcribed his impressions shortly afterwards—before the following June, at all events.[16]

Concerning Cambridge, which comes within a few pages, the position is more complicated; but it is still perfectly possible to correlate what Defoe says with the supposed journey. He names Andrew Snape

as Vice-Chancellor of the University; at that time the office was held
from the start of November, rather than from the new calendar year
(as later) or the academic year (as today). Snape's tenure thus ran
from November 1722 to November 1724, when he was succeeded by
William Savage. This is the sort of fact that Defoe could have obtained
from a handbook, but again the facts are easy to reconcile with the
schedule. A more difficult problem is posed by Defoe's allusion to the
celebrated quarrel between Richard Bentley and the University. He
writes that

> the *Dr. flying to the Royal Protection,* the University is under a Writ of
> *Mandamus,* to shew Cause why they do not restore the Doctor again [to
> his degrees], to which it seems they demur, and that Demur has not, that
> we hear, been argued, at least when these Sheets were sent to the Press;
> what will be the Issue Time must shew. (1: 87)

Plainly, Defoe was cheated here of a desire to include stop-press news,
something he does manage in several places. The sequence of events
is a little hard to piece together, but it was broadly this. First, Bentley
was deprived in 1718; during the Hilary and Easter terms of 1722,
consultations with counsel were held regarding Bentley's suit in the
King's Bench against the Vice-Chancellor's court. Then, in April
1722, the Master of the Temple was consulted, and by Easter 1723,
the University were obliged to make their return to a writ of mandamus. Finally, on 7 February 1724, Lord Chief Justice Pratt issued a
peremptory mandamus enjoining the University to restore Bentley;
and on 26 May, the University complied—just too late for Defoe's
last-minute additions.[17]

   In the remainder of the first letter, there are several incidental clues
that enable us to date the composition, if not the fieldwork. Defoe
alludes to the Earl of Oxford and his son Lord Harley at one point
(1: 88), thus indicating that the text was written prior to Oxford's
death in May 1724. Earlier, the narrator had spoken of "the Duke of
Grafton, now Lord Lieutenant of *Ireland*" (1: 51). Grafton was recalled in April 1724, though he was not officially supplanted by Cart-
eret until the summer. A reference to the Dukes of Manchester (1:
37, 89) shows that Defoe was writing in the knowledge of the late
Duke's death in January 1722. The Members of Parliament listed (e.g.,
at Ipswich, 1: 36) are those elected at the 1722 election. A number
of allusions to the South Sea Company (e.g., 1: 44) and its officers (1:
37) reveal that Defoe has in mind the new schemes devised in an
attempt to restore the Company's tarnished reputation, that is, from
1721 onwards. Defoe writes of struggles "lately" concerning the

choice of burgesses at Ipswich (1: 47): these were doubtless protracted, but one identifiable flare-up took place in 1721.[18]

In Norfolk, the *Tour* is less up-to-date. Only in the appendix to this letter does Defoe report a significant event:

> Since these Sheets were in the Press, a noble Palace of Mr. *Walpole's*, at present First Commissioner of the *Treasury* ... is, as it were, risen out of the Ruins of the ancient Seat of the Family of *Walpole*.... (1: 92)

The foundation stone of Houghton Hall was laid on 30 May 1722; by the end of that year, the first stone-course was in position. It looks very much as if Defoe had not been on the spot since that time. There is also a slightly discrepant reference when Defoe reaches Norwich. After mentioning the acts against importing calico in 1720 and 1721—the most important measure was 7 Geo. I, c.7 (1721)—he says he "pass'd this part of the Country in the Year 1723" (1: 62). Now if the narrative accurately reflected a real tour, Defoe should have reached Norwich in the autumn of 1722: this of course is to judge by the itinerary already charted. But the discrepancy is not alarming, though it may be awkward. It suggests that Defoe had shaped his tour to East Anglia out of one or more journeys that actually followed a different route from that described. Looking at the matter in another way, we have further indications that Defoe was busy in 1722/3 collecting material for his new book.

Only one area of the text shows any marked lack of acquaintance with present circumstances. Most surprisingly, this is at the start, where Defoe is treating of the suburbs of London on the Essex side—townships scarcely three or four miles from his own home in Stoke Newington. For example, he refers briefly to "Sir *Tho. Hickes's* House at *Ruckolls*" (1: 7)—that is, Ruckholt, near Leyton. He must have meant Sir Henry Hickes, the third baronet, for there was no Thomas in this line. But Hickes had sold the estate about 1720 to the trustees of Robert Knight, one of the principal villains of the South Sea Bubble episode. Similarly, the following page brings mention of "Sir *Tho. Fanshaw,* of an Antient Roman Catholick Family, [who] has a very good Estate in this Parish [Barking]" (1: 8). There had not been any-one so styled since 1705, and though an Irish peerage survived in the family, the last Lord Fanshaw died in 1716. There had been a con-tested will but the estate had passed to William Humphreys in the second decade of the century, probably around 1717. Now these are strange errors for anyone as observant as Defoe to make, stranger still for a resident of northeast London with strong Essex attachments. It must be remembered that they would still have been errors if the information had been gleaned many years before.

Defoe's vagueness here may arise from the fact that these two estates lay too near London to be likely stopping places. If he did undertake a journey through Essex, Defoe may well have thought he knew outer London well enough for them not to require fresh research. As soon as he leaves the metropolitan fringe, his accuracy returns.[19] The account of Viscount Barrington (1: 14–15), whose seat lay near Chelmsford, is full and reliable. It is also remarkably discreet; as the entry concludes, "His Lordship is a Dissenter, and seems to love Retirement. He was a Member of Parliament for the Town of *Berwick* upon *Tweed*." True enough: but, as we have seen (p. 31), Defoe suppresses the unfortunate mode of Lord Barrington's retirement from the House—he was expelled on 15 February 1723 for alleged complicity in a fraudulent lottery scheme. Defoe no doubt remained loyal to him as a Whig and a dissenter: but later on it was rumored that Barrington had himself sold the dissenters down the river.[20] Defoe is similarly confident on City figures such as Sir John Lethieullier (1: 91) and Lord Castlemain (1: 89–90). Wanstead House, described as "built," dates from 1715–20. But the higher echelons of society were covered adequately, too. Whatever his general social ethos, Defoe all his life displayed a keen interest in matters of family succession and genealogy. It is therefore no occasion for surprise that he should incorporate a little court-register material:

> At *Lees*, or *Lee's* Priory, as some call it, is to be seen an antient House, in the middle of a beautiful Park, formerly the Seat of the late Duke of *Manchester*, but since the Death of the Duke, it is sold to the Dutchess Dowager of *Buckinghamshire*; the present Duke of *Manchester*, retiring to his antient Family Seat at *Kimbolton* in *Huntingdonshire*, it being a much finer Residence. His Grace is lately married to a Daughter of the Duke of *Montagu* by a Branch of the House of *Marlborough*. (1: 37)

The facts behind this passage are that the first Duke of Manchester died on 20 January 1722, while the third Duke married Isabella, granddaughter of John and Sarah Churchill, on 16 April 1723.

One final clue in respect of the first letter. In the entry for Bury St Edmunds, Defoe allows himself a lengthy paragraph on the subject of an attempted murder perpetrated in the town, involving a barrister and his brother-in-law. He writes, almost with relish, of the exemplary punishment meted out to the barrister and his hired assassin when their brutal intent was averted. On 21 April 1722 a paper appeared in Applebee's *Journal* which Lee, with abundant justification, printed as the work of Defoe. Its principal subject is the Coventry election, a topic he had made very much his own. Halfway through the article, attention is shifted to the Bury St Edmunds murder. The crime is treated in directly parallel terms to those employed in the *Tour* (1: 50–51). Again it looks as if Defoe may well have had East Anglia in his mind at the critical period; he may just have been there or may have been on point of taking a journey into the eastern counties.[21]

Thus far I have considered a single tour, which forms no more than two-fifths of the opening volume. The evidence assembled prompts a tentative interim summary. Defoe almost certainly did visit Essex and Suffolk at least once between April and November 1722. According to his own statement he was in Norfolk in 1723, and there is no good reason to challenge this assertion. The writing of this opening letter can be allocated with some confidence to a date between November 1722 and June 1723:[22] certain information that came to hand after that period was incorporated into the text, and final additions were made in the Appendix to this letter. All these conjectures, as it happens, will find support when Volume I is reviewed as a whole. But even if we take the first letter in isolation, there is a striking measure of congruence among the facts. This portion of the text gives no warrant for the habitual skepticism that critics have affected. There is much to support Defoe's claim of recent firsthand knowledge, virtually nothing to upset it.[23]

III

Having established this approximate schedule for the tour of the Eastern counties, we can deal in a more summary fashion with the remainder of Volume I. The major clues as to the making of the tour of the South-East will be set out in a less discursive form.

(i) The composition cannot be allotted to a time earlier than 1722, to judge from the passage on Ham House. Defoe says that in Petersham there

> stood a most delicious House, built by the late Earl of *Rochester,* Lord High Treasurer in King *James II*'s. Reign, as also in part of Queen *Ann*'s Reign ... I am oblig'd to say only, that this House *stood* here; for even while this is writing the Place seems to be but Smoaking with the Ruins of a most unhappy Disaster, the whole House being a few Months ago burnt down to the Ground with a Fire, so sudden, and so furious, that the Family who were all at home, had scarce time to save their Lives. (1: 163–64)

This fire, in which much of Lord Clarendon's library was destroyed, took place on 1 October 1721. Defoe is habitually a trifle vague in fixing such intervals of time, but one would suppose that the margin implied by his phrasing would be of the order "three months to a year ago."

(ii) A slightly later period is indicated by another section. In this case we have explicit testimony that additions were made at the proof stage. But, quite apart from that, it looks as if the text of the Sussex portions was written at the end of 1722. At Petworth, Defoe mentions a fire to the house, the damage now "fully repair'd":

> but another Disaster to the Family can never be repaired, which has happen'd to it, even while these Sheets were writing; Namely, the Death of the *Dutchess* [of Somerset], who dy'd in November 1722, and lies buried in the Burying Place of the Family of *Seymor* . . . in the Cathedral Church of *Salisbury*. (1: 132–33)

Defoe's phrasing in the paragraph immediately preceding this one seems to imply that the Duchess was still alive when he wrote.

A moment later, Defoe passes on to the nearby estate of Goodwood. There ensues a parenthesis highly relevant to this enquiry:

> (This Family also is in Tears, at the writing these Sheets, for the Death of her Grace the Dutchess [of Richmond], who dyed the beginning of the Month of *December*, and is bury'd in *Westminster Abbey*; and here the Year closing, I think 'tis very remarkable, that this Year 1722, no less than Five Dukes and Two Dutchesses are Dead (*viz.*) The Dukes of *Bucks*, *Bolton*, *Rutland*, *Manchester*, and *Marlborough*, and the Dutchesses of *Somerset* and *Richmond*; besides Earls, (*viz.*) the Earl of *Sunderland*, of *Stamford*, *Exeter*, and others; and since the above was written, and sent to the Press, the Duke of *Richmond* himself is also dead.) (1: 133–34)

The facts relayed by Defoe are not quite precise. In reality, the necrology should run: On 31 January 1720, Earl of Stamford d. (his widow d. 9 November 1722—could this have been confused by Defoe ?). On 2 February 1721, Duke of Rutland d. On 24 February 1721, Duke of Buckinghamshire d. On 6 December 1721, sixth Earl of Exeter d. On 21 January 1722, Duke of Bolton d. On 20 January 1722, Duke of Manchester d. On 9 April 1722, seventh Earl of Exeter d. On 19 April 1722, Earl of Sunderland d. On 16 June 1722, Duke of Marlborough d. On 23 November 1722, Duchess of Somerset d. On 9 December 1722, Duchess of Richmond d. On 27 May 1723, Duke of Richmond d. It is possible that Defoe was confused by Old Style dates when inserting the names of Rutland and Buckinghamshire. Nevertheless, despite the fuzziness engendered, it is easy to discern the broad pattern: with the original draft written around November/December 1722, revised subsequent to May 1723.

(iii) In this second letter, Defoe makes just as many direct references to his fact-finding journey. Unfortunately, few of these contain any element that would enable us to date the visit or, for that matter, to demonstrate that it really took place. On the score of dating—though not of authenticity—there is an exception at 1, 165: "Mr. *Temple* created Baron *Temple,* of the Kingdom of *Ireland,* even since this Circuit was perform'd. . . ." This event took place on 12 March 1723. Defoe wrongly names the new baron as son of the famous Sir William, which warns us against putting too much confidence in what he says. Again, however, this is a misapprehension that the writer could have fallen into fifty years before or five days earlier.

(iv) For the rest, it is clear that Defoe's observations were often of recent date. Lady Morden's death took place in 1721 (see 1: 96); since Defoe had known her husband, this may suggest personal information rather than a special trip to Blackheath. Vanbrugh's building operations around Greenwich (1: 95) date from the end of the previous decade—he actually purchased the property in 1717. Rather more vague is the following:

> In the Gardens of this Episcopal Palace, the Lady Dowager *Onslow,* Mother of the present Lord of that Name . . . was very unhappily drown'd about Two Year since, in one of the Fish-Ponds; whether she did it herself, or whether by Accident, or how, 'tis not the business of such a Work as this to enquire . . . (1: 157–58)

In fact, Lady Onslow drowned herself—as is generally agreed—as early as 25 November 1718. But it would plainly be unwise to build too much on the phrase "about Two Year since."

Beyond this there are the customary references to the Bubble and its aftermath (e.g., 1: 159–60) and to prominent City men. The reference to Humphrey Parsons as Sheriff of London fixes composition between November 1722 and the same month in the following year (1: 155–56).[24] While it would be rash to be too positive on the basis of such evidence, the impression is strengthened that the *Tour* took shape relatively late in Defoe's mind and that its central inspiration is the desire for a national stocktaking after the Bubble. Apart from anything else, the face of the landscape in the Home Counties must have been changed by the expropriation of South Sea directors' estates. Both of the first two letters move at their close to a plangent elegy on the "fine Parks and new-built Palaces [that] are fallen under

Forfeitures and Alienations by the Misfortunes of the Times, and by
the Ruins of their Masters Fortunes in that *South-Sea* Deluge" (1:
91: see 1: 169). Defoe cannot even leave the subject aside when he
comes to a pleasure resort such as Epsom:

> for abating one unhappy *Stock Jobbing* Year, when *England* took leave to
> act the Frantick, for a little while; and when every Body's Heads were
> turn'd with Projects and Stocks, *I say,* except this Year, we see nothing of
> Business in the whole Conversation of *Epsome.* (1: 160)

So pervasive a theme can hardly have been introduced as an
afterthought.[25]

I turn now to the third letter, which concludes Volume I of the
Tour. It describes a journey to Land's End; the return is kept for
Volume II. This is remarkably bare of concrete evidence from the
point of view of dating; *prima facie,* a sign that it may be based on
more distant recollections. However, the composition at least must be
fairly recent. Allusion to "the late Sir *Christopher Wren*" (1: 189) fixes
the writing as subsequent to 25 February 1723, when that eminent
nonagenarian passed away. On the next page there is a further reference to the death of the Duchess of Somerset, adding here the joint
burial of her daughter "who dy'd for Grief at the loss of the Dutchess
her Mother,"[26] and the removal of her son's remains to the same tomb.
These events are described as "lately" taking place (1: 190). Defoe's
comments on the memorial proposed may, but do not certainly, indicate his own presence in Salisbury at this juncture.

This letter, like the others, must have been written (or revised) no
earlier than 1722. Defoe's entry for Falmouth, which is full and informed, includes this comment on the Lisbon trade:

> These Packets bring over such vast Quantities of Gold in Specie, either
> in *Moidore* . . . or in Bars of Gold, that I am very Credible [*sic*] inform'd
> the Carryer from *Falmouth,* brought by Land from thence to *London,* at
> one Time, in the Month of *January,* 1722, or near it, Eighty Thousand
> Moidores in Gold. . . (1: 239)

He writes, too, of the "late setting up of the English Packets"—a
service attendant on the commerce with Portugal that followed on
the Methuen Treaty of 27 December 1703. This is important because
it shows that Defoe was aware of developments in the locality that
took place after his visit on behalf of Harley in 1705. But there is no
clear proof in this section that Defoe had actually traveled down to
the West Country in recent years. Throughout the third letter, only
one passage seems to hint as much, and this occurs at Portland:

To prevent [the] Danger [caused by Portland Race], and guide the Mariner in these Distresses, they have, within these few Months, set up two Light-Houses on the two Points of [the] Island; and they had not been many Months set up, with the Directions given to the Publick for their Bearings, but we found three outward-bound *East-India* Ships which were in Distress in the Night, in a hard extream Gale of Wind, were so directed by those Lights, that they avoided going on Shore by it, which, if the Lights had not been there, would inevitably happen'd [*sic*]to their Destruction. (1: 213)

The Trinity House patent for these lighthouses was granted in May 1716, but I do not know when they were ready for service. Defoe had certainly been to Weymouth as Harley's agent,[27] and in the *Tour* he recounts an experience "while I was here once" (1: 212). All the same, his account of the new lighthouses appears to derive from recent contact.

As suggested, however, this is not the case with the letter in its entirety. The third circuit is distinguished from its predecessors by the extent to which it is palpably based on earlier knowledge. In the tour of East Anglia, we have only references to Defoe's childhood visit to Ipswich in 1668 (1: 40), as well as a later passage from Harwich to Ipswich (*c*.1688?: 1: 42) and an anecdote concerning the Mayor of Cambridge (1: 86), which Defoe had picked up on his travels in October 1705.[28] In the second letter there is a recollection of having been entertained by Sir Robert Fagg in 1697 (1: 131). In short, the two initial journeys rely only to a small extent on Defoe's adult memories—though the second, like the first, incorporates some sharp impressions of his youth (1: 149–52). For the most part, the facts are recent and the observation fresh.

The circuit of the southwestern counties is a different matter. Defoe makes widespread and open use of his former experiences. Thus, he describes a sudden furious wind blowing up at Plymouth, mounting in a tempest that caused severe damage to ships riding at anchor. Defoe places this "the next Year after [the] great Storm, and but a little sooner in the Year, being in *August*" (1: 229). Actually the gap was almost two years. The Great Storm, as Defoe has pointed out on the previous page, occurred on 27 November 1703. The second disaster took place in August 1705, as a dispatch from Defoe to Harley makes clear.[29] It might be argued that such dramatic events naturally stuck in Defoe's memory, and that they would not have been ousted by any degree of recent traveling. And certainly Defoe recounts another story of the Great Storm at Helford (1: 240–42), besides describing an equally stirring event—a sea battle off the Lizard, which Defoe had witnessed during the French war (1: 246).

Yet more mundane recollections also figure. The account of the peaceable town of Dorchester (1: 210) plainly derives from the observations which Defoe had made for Harley in 1705.[30] Again, the narrator alludes briefly to the state of Whitehall "before the burning" (1: 195), that is, the fires of 1691 and 1698. This observation is made at Wilton, where Defoe had clearly been more than once: "On the left of the Court was formerly a large Grotto . . . but the last time I had the Curiosity to see this House, I mist that Part; so that I suppos'd they were remov'd" (1: 194). Finally, Defoe quotes at length from his own proposal to settle the Palatinate refugees in a kind of New Forest new-town (1: 200–6). The plan confessedly dates from Godolphin's time as Lord Treasurer, and can be placed around 1709.[31] Defoe was proud of his initiative in such matters, and it is readily explicable that he should have reverted to the subject in his tour of Hampshire. Nevertheless, the inclusion of this material strengthens the impression that this letter is fabricated from a comparative dearth of fresh information.[32]

All we can say with confidence is that the third letter was composed or revised no earlier than February 1723 (I include here the so-called "Appendix to Letter III," which is formally rather than temporally distinct). Much more definite evidence is furnished by the "Addenda" at the close of Volume I. "Since the Closing this Volume," Defoe writes, "there are several Great and Magnificent Buildings begun to be Erected, within the Circuit of these Letters, which however, not being finish'd, cannot now be fully described . . ." (1: 250). There follows a list of five current building operations. It must be acknowledged that here Defoe was right up with events, if not ahead of them. One entry reads, "The Lord *Onslow's* Seat, re-edifying near *Guildford.*" It is generally thought that Leoni's alterations to Clandon Park belong to the period 1731–35. On the other hand, Sir Gregory Page's house, Wricklemarsh, near Blackheath, sets a different problem. It was built by John James reputedly within a year. Page bought the site from the executors of Lady Morden (widow of Defoe's erstwhile acquaintance) after her death in 1721. Most authorities imply that the house was built directly afterwards. Defoe's phrasing clearly suggests that building was still in progress: see also 2: 535. Lastly, there is the following entry: "The famous Addition, or Square begun at *King's* College Chapel in *Cambridge,* of which the Foundation is but even now lay'd." The first stone for James Gibbs's Fellows Building was in fact laid on 25 March 1724, one day before Bentley's restoration (a deliberate piece of timing by the University). Defoe conspicuously makes no reference to the Senate House, whose foundation stone went into place on 24 June 1722. The conclusion must be that Defoe's addenda derive from the news sheets or secondhand information: and this is, after all, only what we should expect.

We can now review the evidence as regards the making of Volume I, working backwards from publication. The book was issued on 21 May 1724. The "Addenda" were probably compiled about the end of March or the beginning of April 1724. It was possibly at this time that the Preface, which refers to the additions, was written (1: 4). The Appendix to the first letter was inserted at proof stage, along with certain other corrections to the text of the whole. This stage was reached after May 1723, perhaps around the autumn of that year. The main composition of the first two letters was undertaken a few months earlier: Letter I, perhaps around November 1722; Letter II, if Defoe's own testimony is to be credited, around December. With Letter III, it is impossible to be equally specific, but there are no grounds for supposing that the timetable was radically disturbed.

As to the more speculative issue concerning the date of Defoe's visits, a similar disjunction can be made. Letter I is assuredly based on recent experience (unless there has been gross fudging and some strange coincidences). Letter II probably takes account of recent ex' perience, particularly in the sections nearer London that felt some visible impress from the Bubble. Letter III might incorporate material specially gathered but probably does not. It is safe to say that here Defoe relied much more on his earlier travels. Yet Defoe's England throughout this volume (as indeed through the entire text) is essen' tially the Hanoverian world, no matter how remote his own literal "tour"—the facts with regard to commerce, population and navigation are as nearly as he can make them the contemporary data. His anxiety to appear up'to'date is indicated by the weight of additions and appen' dices he tacked on to each volume.

I have intimated that the *Tour* may have had its origin in Defoe's unquenchable interest in elections, along with certain business trips required in 1722. Moreover, there are clear signs that his developing theme was England in the wake of the Bubble. The effective cause of the work has usually been put down as Macky's *Journey.* But the early references are all to the first volume of Macky's work, which had appeared as far back as 1714. Moreover, if Defoe did begin in 1722, he cannot possibly have taken account of Macky's Scottish journey, which did not come out till the following year. (And of course Defoe's intention to cover Scotland is explicit from the outset, in the title as well as the Preface to Volume I.) Two other books were at least as effective in turning Defoe's mind to this undertaking. *Magna Britan' nia* had been coming out in serial form since 1720. Even more im' portant, Edmund Gibson's edition of the great original by William

Camden was reissued in 1722. In fact it was the 1695 edition that
Defoe used: but the reappearance of *Britannia* must have brought it
back to his attention. His references to this source are far more numerous than any others; and as the book evolved, it was Camden/Gibson
that lay behind Defoe's venture. Despite the manifest differences in
style, coverage, and overall intention, it was *Britannia* that inspired
Defoe to emulation, that encouraged his innovations, and that set the
standard by which he expected to be judged.[33]

IV

What conclusions can be drawn regarding the making of the *Tour?*
It is possible to discern two in particular. First, we can observe Defoe's
layered, agglomerative technique. *Prima facie*, this may not seem revelatory: one expects a guidebook to be a compilation. But Defoe used
personal recollections, secondhand anecdotes, borrowed information,
in his "creative" works, too—consider the *Journal of the Plague Year,
Memoirs of a Cavalier, Captain Singleton*. We know enough of Defoe's
use of narrative sources in his fiction to realize that the *Tour* is not
different in kind simply because it draws together in a single harmoni-
ous vision widely discrete materials. It is true that the *Tour* yokes
personal and vicarious experience, that it modulates between historic
fact and imaginative re-creation, and that it blurs remote and recent
observations. But all these things are true, in greater or lesser measure,
of *Crusoe*, of *Moll Flanders*, and of *Colonel Jacque*.

Second, we can study the processes by which Defoe gave form and
direction to his developing "tour." The work has a trajectory, something equivalent to the narrative urgency that is found in a novel. One
principal recourse is the claim of novelty—"Since our last Volume, we
have to add . . ." Again, Defoe constantly stresses the dynamic state
of contemporary Britain—"This is still an encreasing flourishing
Town, and if they go on in Trade, as they have done for some time,
'tis probable it will in a little time be as big as the City of *Dublin*. . . ."
Or "it has certainly been a good Town, and much bigger than it is
now: At present like an old Beauty, it shews the Ruins of a good Face;
but is also apparently, not only decay'd and declin'd, but decaying and
declining every Day, and from being the fifth Town in *Scotland* . . .
is now like a Place forsaken." (See below, p. 124). This rhetoric of
growth and decay needs to be backed by a sense of contemporaneity,
as an antiquarian survey does not.[34] Hence the importance Defoe
places on catching a locality at a particular moment in time. He seeks
to convey the impression of a here and now, even where his real

journey (as distinct from the literary *Tour*) was demonstrably some time in the past. Indeed, Defoe has spread a patina of contemporaneity so skillfully over the text that he has deceived generations of readers. Many sources place all the observations as "1724–26"; Wright, as we have seen, allots "most" of them—quite without warrant—to the 1680s; while Trevelyan, on not much more substantial grounds, implies that Defoe made his observations "largely . . . in the middle years of Anne." The truth, as a detailed analysis shows, is both more complex and more interesting. To watch Defoe piecing together his cento of facts and impressions, weaving in a memory here and grafting on a stop-press addition there, is to catch high literary craftsmanship in the very act.

2

The Making of Volumes II and III

It is always difficult to follow a major success, something Defoe had found out with *Robinson Crusoe*, a few years earlier. As we have just seen, the first volume of the *Tour* was published on 21 May 1724, having been composed mostly in 1722 and the first half of 1723.[1] The first edition of the work was completed by the appearance of Volume II on 8 June 1725 (containing Letters IV to VII) and of Volume III on 9 August 1726 (containing Letters VIII to XIII). The former installment covers parts of the West Country, the Midlands, Wales and London; whereas the last volume is devoted to the Northern counties and Scotland. In fact the letters are not numbered continually throughout the whole set, but begin a fresh series with each volume; thus Volume II comprises Letters I to V.[2] So in fact does Volume III, because the style "Letter III" is erroneously used both for the conclud-ing portion of the North of England and for the opening section of Scotland. These are clearly different letters, in the convention used throughout the *Tour;* they are divided by a special introduction to the Scottish portion. The three letters in Volume I had been separately paginated: here the pagination (ignoring preliminaries, index, and the like) is divided into two series for Volume II, corresponding to two letters each. In Volume III the pagination begins afresh with the Scottish portion.[3]

Clearly the work was designed as a comprehensive guide from the very outset. The very title, and the "Author's Preface" set at the head of Volume I, make that certain. There is a natural link between the first and second installments, since on the former occasion his third letter had carried Defoe out to the extremity of England, that is, the Cornish peninsula and Land's End. The last words of the main text of Volume I had promised a continuation, rather more adroitly than, five years earlier, Robinson Crusoe had promised a sequel to *his* strange surprising adventures:

> I might take up many Sheets in describing the valuable Curiosities of this little *Cherosonese,* or Neck Land call'd the *Land's End,* in which there

lyes an immense Treasure, and many Things worth Notice, I mean besides those to be found upon the Surface: But I am too near the End of this Letter. If I have Opportunity, I shall take Notice of some Part of what I omit here, in my Return by the Northern Shore of the County. (1: 249)

As routine a gesture of cliff-hanger journalism as this may seem, it does indicate that Defoe had already mapped out a return journey to London. When he wrote the preface to his second volume, he mentioned the response of the public to its predecessor: "The Reception which the first Part of this Work has met, has not been so mean as to discourage the Performance of the Second Volume, nor to slacken the Diligence in our Endeavours to perform it well" (1: 251). Clearly Defoe was keeping a watchful eye on public taste, and was prepared to make adjustments as he went along in order to supply what he judged was most likely to succeed with his audience. Nevertheless, he was already committed to the first itinerary in his new volume. (I shall call this "Letter IV," following the practice of modern editions.)

The facts I have outlined do not establish anything beyond the certainty that Defoe intended to continue his *Tour* in 1724, and that he had closed certain options to himself in the way that the continuation should proceed. As a result, there is little doubt that nearly all the basic "research" for the later volumes was already completed. To anticipate my conclusions a little, it will emerge that there is *less* recent material in the subsequent installments than there had been in the opening volume. Of course, Defoe makes valiant efforts to disguise the weakness, and makes conspicuous play with a selection of topical snippets of information. In the London section, especially, he is able to show a convincing grasp of up-to-date developments, hardly surprising for one who had been observing the varying fortunes of the capital for sixty years.

Elsewhere Defoe's information is patently less fresh, and this is the more true the further from London the *Tour* proceeds. Hence the slightly defensive note of the preface to Volume II:

As we observ'd in the first Volume, and frequently in this, there will always be something new, for those that come after; and if an Account of *Great Britain* was to be written every Year, there would be something found out, which was overlook'd before, or something to describe, which had its Birth since the former Accounts: New Foundations are always laying, new Buildings always raising, Highways repairing, Churches and publick Buildings erecting, Fires and other Calamities happening, Fortunes of Families taking different Turns, new Trades are every Day erected, new Projects enterpriz'd, new Designs laid; so that as long as *England* is a trading, improving Nation, no perfect Description either of the Place, the People, or the Conditions and State of Things can be given. (1: 252)

The technique here draws on what Defoe's admirers like to call his skilled rhetoric, while his detractors would see it as journalistic chicanery. He is attempting to turn the rapid obsolescence of his information to his own advantage; firstly, because it confirms the picture of a thriving, improving, developing society that he is concerned to paint throughout the book; and secondly because Defoe manages to suggest that other new accounts are equally vulnerable to this rapid process of dating. The paragraph is a prelude to a list of up-to-the-minute revisions, including the mention of a bill actually passing through parliament at that very time.

Nothing very relevant had happened to Defoe personally in the interval between the publication of Volumes II and III. Some of his rivals (and concealed sources) had made an advance of their own: further parts of Thomas Cox's *Magna Britannia* had been issued, while John Macky had added *A Journey through Scotland* to the guidebook that had most directly anticipated Defoe's methods in the *Tour*. Defoe makes transparent reference to Macky in his introduction to the Scottish portion of Volume III (2: 689), and the signs are that he had already absorbed Macky while writing the text for Scotland. More interesting in some ways is William Stukeley's *Itinerarium Curiosum* (1724). This was exactly the kind of antiquarian lumber Defoe affected to despise, but it is written with a certain combination of qualities (literalism in mensuration, speculative zeal, and an awkward poetry) that he might have recognized as uncomfortably close to his authorial style. Stukeley had preceded Defoe not merely in visiting archaeological sites, cathedrals, and stately homes, but also in commenting upon such things as lead mining in the Peak district and the Lombe silk mill at Derby.

So much by way of preliminary. I now turn to the detailed evidence that can tell us something of Defoe's working method as he proceeded with the *Tour*.

I

The second volume, as mentioned, followed its predecessor after an interval of barely more than a year, on 8 June 1725. There are some changes in the list of booksellers named on the title page (which is completely reset, although the substance remains the same).[4] A major selling point was the map by Herman Moll, duly emphasized on the title page. At the outset of this volume, Defoe supplies a preface, which clearly was written last and can be deferred for the present.

The text proper begins with the return leg of the journey to the southwestern counties. Again, there are definite signs that Defoe was placing heavy reliance on his earlier observations. This comes out most obviously in the choice of itinerary. In Letter III, Defoe had joined his 1705 route around Dorchester, and thereafter his tour fol-lowed almost the identical course as far as Liskeard. The extreme tip of the Cornish peninsula is described in the *Tour*, although Defoe seems not to have visited it in 1705. Then, in Letter IV, the route is once more taken up at Bodmin. This degree of coincidence looks suspicious, but a glance at Herman Moll's map (published in 1724) will show that this was the obvious course to follow. It not only took in all the most important towns, but in addition it was the most direct road of any magnitude along the south coast route.[5]

Turning to the fourth letter, we find that the situation is not exactly parallel. Here Defoe conducts his progress from Bodmin via Launces-ton to Bideford and Barnstaple. He then turns inland across Exmoor (assenting to Camden's description, "a filthy, barren Ground," 1: 263–64) and describes Tiverton before moving on to Taunton via Welling-ton. It is only at this point that he incorporates a detour to bring in Porlock, Minehead, and Watchet—places that he does not mention in his reports of 1705, and that could well have been reached via Dulverton. From Taunton the tour shifts to Bridgwater, just as Defoe had done when investigating the county for Harley. After this comes a break:

> From *Bridgewater*, there is a Road to *Bristol*, which they call the *Lower Way*. . . . But I must first go back again a little while into *Somersetshire:* The *Northern* Part of the County, I did not visit in this Journey, which, as I hinted before, is only a Return from my long Travel to the Land's End. In omitting this Part, I, of course, leave the Two Cities of *Bristol* and *Bath*, and that high Part of the County called *Mendip Hill*, to my next *Western* Journey, which will include all the counties due *West* from *London;* for these now spoken of, though ordinarily called the *West* Coun-try, are rather *N. W.* [*sic*] than *West*. (1: 270–72)

The 1705 route had proceeded in this very direction, Bristol, Bath, and then Chippenham. Defoe's explanations sometimes have a self-conscious air, as if he were trying to steer around difficulties caused by a divergence from his "real" journey in the past. At all events, he soon goes back on his word. Bath and Bristol are indeed postponed to Letter VI, discussed later in this volume. But the Mendip region follows within a few pages of the declaration just quoted (1: 278–79):

despite a further promise, this is all the coverage that district gets, and it must be concluded that Defoe had not written Letter VI, or even planned it very carefully, at this stage.

Immediately after, Defoe joins his 1705 itinerary once more. True, Chippenham is—rather surprisingly—left out, whereas Harley had received a notably full report on this borough. But Devizes, Trow-bridge, Bradford, and Westbury are covered (1: 281–82), as they had been on the former occasion. At this point, the 1705 journey is trans-posed into Letter VI (2: 438–47), with a trip up the Severn valley described. In Letter IV, Defoe has recourse to a simple expedient. He makes his return to London via Newbury and Reading, that is to say, he reverses his *outward* progress in 1705, which had followed this route westwards.[6]

It is of course possible that these correspondences are a matter of chance. It would not require any great sweep of coincidence to sup-pose that Defoe may have traveled from Newbury to London in 1723 (say), as he had journeyed from London to Henley in 1705. This is true even though Defoe was less a creature of routine than many of us—less likely to take a particular route simply because that was the way he had been before. However, there are a number of circum-stances that indicate that this letter may be built principally around the visit made for Harley.

Often Defoe seems little concerned to disguise the antiquity of his information. "There was, and, I suppose, is still," he calmly observes at Taunton, "a Private College, or Academy, for the Dissenters in this Town; the Tutor, who then managed it, was named *Warren,* who told me, that there were Threescore and Twelve Ministers then preaching . . . who had been his Scholars. . . . The Academy, since his Death, is continued, but not kept up to the Degree it was, in the Days of the said Mr. *Warren*" (1: 267). Matthew Warren (c.1643–1706) was an ejected minister who figures in Calamy; he served at Paul's Meeting in Taunton after his expulsion. A couple of pages later, on a very similar topic, Defoe again falls into the past tense:

> Here, also [in Bridgwater], is a College, or Private Academy, for the Dis-senters to breed up their preaching Youth; the Tutor was one Mr. *Moor,* a Man who, it is own'd, was a Master of good Literature; what Talent he had at Erudition, I can give no Account of, for it is not every Master of Learning, that makes a good Instructor of others. (1: 270)

As a product of a dissenting academy himself, one would expect Defoe to show a closer grasp on the affairs of such institutions. John Moore (c.1642–1717) was educated at Oxford, became a dissenter in 1667, and served as minister to Christchurch Chapel in Bridgwater from 1676. His academy in the town dates from rather later, but was in being by 1691. After his death his son, also John Moore (d. 1747?) conducted the seminary. Defoe is almost certainly referring to the father, who gained renown as master of the academy. His phrasing suggests that he knew that Moore senior was dead, but had no up-to-date information with regard to the academy.

A third dissenting cleric had been named in a characteristic paragraph on Bideford. Defoe alludes to "the Person who officiates at the Meeting-House in this Town," adding that he "happened to have some Conversation" with this man. The minister proved to be learned and agreeable, as well as "very well received in the Place, even by those he differ'd from in Matters of Religion." Defoe concludes: "His Name, as I remember, was *Bartlet*. But this is a Digression: I wish I could say the like of all the rest of his Brethren" (1: 260–61). There are three conceivable candidates, representing three generations, any of whom Defoe could have met. William Bartlet (d. 1682) was another to have suffered ejectment in 1662; his son John predeceased him in 1679; while his grandson William lived from 1678 to 1720. All served in Bideford. Even if we suppose Defoe's contact to be the youngest of the three, this does not argue any very recent acquaintance with the town. Since Defoe spent two days in Bideford in August 1705, conferring with a leading citizen of the town named John Darracott, and since he was traveling with a Professor of Sacred Theology at this time, it seems highly probable that the "conversation" with Bartlet occurred on that visit.[7] He was currently trying to dodge creditors in London, as well as the Devon constables who had instructions to arrest him for seditious activity and "embroiling the people." Consequently, it was a phase of his journey for Harley he was likely to remember. He also had his own account in the *Review* for 25 August to assist his recollections.[8]

It is notable that, in all these cases, the *Tour* alludes to men prominent in the region some time before. Defoe knew of Matthew Warren's successor at Taunton, Stephen James, because James was listed as the distribution agent for that town when Defoe organized the circulation of various pamphlets around 1706. But he describes the academy basically as it was before Warren's death. Again, he makes no reference in the entry for Exeter to the celebrated local dissenters, Joseph Peirce and Joseph Hallett. Peirce was still at Newbury in 1706, and Defoe lists him as distribution agent for the town.[9] In 1713 he moved to Exeter, and in 1718 and 1719 he was involved in the famous Salters Hall controversy—the most factious episode in dissenting history for a generation or more. Defoe is silent on the matter, and it does appear that each place carries for him the set of associations it had twenty years before. He brings facts up to date where he can, but his firsthand touches are those supplied by the 1705 journey.

Here we come on a curious gap. For one ready enough to draw on his youthful memories, Defoe is notably reticent on the Monmouth rising. He simply describes Monmouth's retreat to Bridgwater, and supplies some fairly detailed (but not especially new or graphic) facts regarding the battle of Sedgmoor. The account ends up with a fierce abridgment: "The rest I need not mention" (1: 269). No hint here, though it would have been safe and honorable to acknowledge it forty years on, that Defoe himself was in Monmouth's cavalry, and was forced to flee: indeed he actually fell a prisoner to the King's forces and was pardoned only by exercise of royal grace.[10]

In another part of the fourth letter, Defoe is prepared to use his own memories of the 1680s and the turbulent events the nation witnessed in that decade. The passage in question concerns the Irish dragoons recruited by James II (1: 295–99). Defoe naturally describes the behavior of these troops as mutinous and unruly. He related how he had ridden to Reading, and how in each town on the way he heard more alarming reports of alleged massacres. This is a lively section, with a good deal of firsthand observation and an equal measure of personal investment. No one can regret the use Defoe makes here of his youthful adventures. It might be held, nonetheless, that this letter depends too much and too often on such material, without a compensating weight of recent information.

There are other signs that Defoe was drawing on his capital. There is a strange remark at Bideford: "*Bidiford* was antiently the Inheritance of the Family of *Granville* . . . and the Earl of *Bath,* who is the Heir and Chief of the Family, is now Baron of *Bidiford,* Viscount *Lansdown,* and Earl of *Bath*" (1: 261). This would fit the situation up to the death of the third Earl of Bath in 1711. But in 1724 the Earldom was in abeyance, as it was to remain until William Pulteney's elevation twenty years later. The well-known poet and Tory politician George Granville, "the polite," created Baron Lansdown of Bideford in 1712, had become Duke of Albemarle in the Jacobite peerage in 1721. But Defoe's formulation remains an odd one. Again, his reference to the "late unhappy Lord *Mohun*" (1: 268) and his speculation regarding the disposition of the Dunster estate both suggest an early dating: Lord Mohun had been killed as far back as 1712 in the celebrated duel that features in Thackeray's *Henry Esmond.*

As with Volume I, however, it can be shown that the text of this letter was not completed before well into the 1720s. One indicative passage is this:

The Title of Earl of *Torrington,* was first given to the late General Monk, Duke of *Albemarle* . . . and the Line being extinct in his Son, it was given by King *William* III. to Admiral *Herbert* . . . and since that to Sir *George Bing,* one of our present Admirals, and one who asserted the Authority and Power of the *British* Navy against the *Spaniards,* at the late Sea Fight near *Cape Passaro* in *Sicily:* So that the Town of *Torrington,* seems to be appropriated to the Honour of the Defenders of the *British* Sovereignty at Sea. (1: 262–63)

Byng was made Viscount Torrington on 9 September 1721. His victory off Cape Passaro, when twenty-one Spanish ships had been destroyed, took place on 31 July 1718, some four months after he had been appointed Admiral of the Fleet. A more recent date still is confirmed when Defoe gives the roster of living Knights of the Garter. This is concluded by the names of the Earl of Scarborough and Lord Townshend. They had been admitted to the order on 9 July 1724— the last knights to be installed until Robert Walpole and others in May 1726. Similarly, two pages later (1: 314), Defoe appends the names of the Provost and Fellows of Eton College. His list omits Stephen Weston, a Fellow until 1724 (he was consecrated Bishop of Exeter on 28 December); while it also excludes William Malcher, who became a Fellow at the very end of that year. Obviously these are facts that could be derived from secondary sources. Their only interest is in showing that Defoe was at work on the text after the publication of Volume I. But even where a particular reference shows comparatively up-to-date knowledge ("The River *Kennet,* lately made Navigable by Act of Parliament," 1: 286—there was an act in the first year of George I's reign, but the one Defoe has in mind is 7 Geo. I, c.8, of 1721), we never gain the impression that Defoe has lately been on the spot.

Letter V is the most famous section of the *Tour,* describing as it does London at a critical stage of its development. Obviously, different canons of judgment must be applied. Defoe was a Londoner, not only by birth and upbringing, but also by elective affinity. The City embodied many of the positives that inform his work—property, commerce, thrift, and singleness of purpose. Widely as he traveled, he never stayed away from the capital for very long at a time. Other towns he came to as a visitor, as a political agent, as a journalist or as a businessman. London he knew as an insider.

As we should expect, this letter is the best-informed part of the *Tour* as far as topicalities go. Abundant evidence can be drawn together to show that Defoe was writing a report that was up-to-the-minute in every respect. If the *Tour* had been conceived some time before and begun in 1722, Letter V clearly dates from a later period—1724 at the earliest. Where there are disparities, Defoe is as likely to be trust-worthy as any other source available to us. Thus, Defoe refers three times to the damage caused to the Custom House by "an accidental Fire" (1: 333). Elsewhere this becomes "the late Fire" (1: 344). Twice he says that the restoration of the building is not finished (1: 334, 379). Thomas Ripley began work on the renovation shortly after the fire in 1718, and from the edition of Stow's *Survey of London* by John Strype (1720) it would appear that the work was already completed. But Defoe lists the Custom House explicitly when describing the new buildings going up as he wrote. The other items he includes can be verified from external evidence, and they certainly cover a period well after 1720. It does not seem rash to speculate that Defoe may be faithful to the current state of things in this case too.

The list just mentioned purports to enumerate "new Edifices and publick Buildings, erected or erecting in and about *London*" since the main account in this letter was written (1: 378–80). St Martin's in the Fields is "finished with the utmost Expedition': it depends how one interprets "finished," but Defoe seems to be ahead of the facts here—Gibbs was still at work into 1726.[11] Second on the list is the new Admiralty office, "not yet finished." Ripley's undistinguished work is generally dated 1723–26: but it seems to have been completed by December 1725, when the French visitor Saussure mentions it.[12] Third is Guy's hospital, which will be discussed in a moment. The next is a meeting house in Spitalfields, not precisely datable. Two wings added to Bedlam follow, "this also not finished." The bequest for this purpose by Sir William Withers is mentioned; since Withers died on 31 January 1721, this would leave a comfortable margin of time—however the new wings do not seem to have been built straight away and indeed were not finished for some years after the appearance of the *Tour*.[13]

Sixthly, Defoe names "The *South-Sea* House in *Threadneedle-street*, the old House being intirely pulled down, and several other Houses adjoyning being purchased, the whole Building will be new from the Foundation; this not finished." Again, this partially conflicts with the impression left by contemporary maps; the old house seems to have survived for longer than Defoe suggests. However, the South Sea Company had certainly acquired the adjacent property in 1720, while the building was under way by December 1725.

Other new buildings that Defoe specified as already complete in-clude "A new Street or Range of Houses taken out of the *South* Side of the *Artillery Ground* near *Morefields*, also an Enlargement to the new Burying Ground as it was formerly called, on the *North* Side of the same Ground." In fact the Artillery Company had been granted permission to erect houses on the south side of the ground, near Chiswell Street, as far back as 1698. However it was only about 1722 that the development was completed.[14] Defoe, then, is justified in naming this among buildings recently finished. Slightly less convincing is a reference to Figg's Theatre, the famous boxing booth off the Tyburn Road. John Byrom visited Figg's establishment in April 1725 and it was clearly a novelty for many at this time.[15] However, newspaper advertisements indicate that Figg was in business as early as March 1720. It is possible that alterations had been made on the site: otherwise, Defoe's statement that "*this publick Edifice is fully finished, and in Use*" has the air of stale news.

This leaves a number of new operations in ecclesiastical architecture. The proposed fifty new churches naturally dominate Defoe's commentary here, although he makes separate mention of St. Botolph without Bishopgate—a restoration not connected with Queen Anne's project. The foundation stone of the new building for St. Botolph's was not laid until April 1725, which makes Defoe's phrase "Rebuilding" highly topical. As to the churches that are among the fifty, Defoe names Christ Church, Spitalfields (various starting dates given: the Parish Clerks in 1732 allocate the building to 1723–29); St. George in the East (the consensus of sources would prompt a dating of 1715–23); St. Luke's, Old Street (not consecrated until October 1733, though planned in 1711); St. Anne's, Limehouse (1712–24, according to the Parish Clerks); and St. George, Bloomsbury (not a separate parish until the act of 3 George II, c.19 of 1731: probably completed in the previous year). These splendid churches, for which Nicholas Hawksmoor was chiefly responsible, must have profoundly changed the London landscape with their graceful spires and boldly etched tower lanterns. It would not have stretched the powers of any reasonably observant person, let alone a Defoe, to maintain full awareness of their growth and completion. But it is important to stress that again we are dealing with the world of the mid-1720s: the end of George I's reign, rather than Queen Anne's England.[16]

On the basis of this list, particularly the entries for St. Martin's, St. Botolph, and the South Sea House, Defoe's additions can be tentatively placed around the spring of 1725—not long before publication. What of the main text of this letter? Certainly a number of references suggest that the writing was carried out relatively late. Sir Christopher Wren must have died before composition (1: 335); this event took place on 25 February 1723. A clear reference to Atterbury's disgrace (1: 367) cannot have been inserted before June 1723 when the bishop's deprivation was carried out. From allusions to some of the buildings then proposed (the new Custom House, South Sea House, East India House—the last erected in 1726–30), it looks as though a likely date would be mid-1724.

The matter is complicated by a revision at proof stage. Defoe's extensive coverage of Guy's Hospital is introduced thus:

> This will, I suppose, be called *Guy's* Hospital, being to be Built and Endowed at the sole Charge of one Mr. *Thomas Guy,* formerly a Bookseller in *Lombard street,* who lived to see the said Hospital not only design'd, the Ground purchased and cleared, but the Building begun, and a considerable progress made in it, and died while these Sheets were in the Press. (1: 374)

The account goes on to mention Guy's will, and the surprise caused by its precise terms when they became known after his death. Defoe supplies full details of the will, listing the governors and the managers of Guy's charity. Guy died on 27 December 1724, his will was proved on 4 January, and the first sixty patients admitted to the hospital on 24 January 1725. This sounds like a remarkably rapid succession of events, but it should be noted that Guy lived to see the roof go up on the building. When Defoe came to write the account of "new edifices" already considered, he noted simply that the hospital was "not yet quite finished." This may mean that Defoe's interpolation with regard to Guy was made slightly earlier than the list of new buildings. But clearly both date from the early months of 1725—not before February and not later than June, when the list of Admiralty Commissioners (1: 369) was altered. If we took April, that would allow Defoe time to incorporate the new restoration at St. Botolph's, and would permit the final presswork to be carried through in time for publication on 8 June, given some concentrated work by the printer.[17]

II

Letter VI describes the outward leg of a journey to North Wales. Again, the main part of the composition can be allotted with some confidence to 1724. That is the year Defoe himself announces, if we make a forward calculation at one point (and suppose, as we must, that Defoe overlooked the misprint "1477" for "1447").

> The Body of *Humphry* Duke of *Gloucester* . . . by the most indisputable Authority, must have lain Buried there 277 Years. *Viz.* It being in the 26th of *Hen.* VI. 1477. (1: 389)

Less inferential evidence is provided by a reference to "the late Mr. *Lowndes*" (1: 395), that is the Treasury official William Lowndes, who died on 20 January 1724. Marlborough is spoken of as deceased (1: 394), as are (among the comparatively recent dead) the Duke of Buckingham (1: 395) and the Earl of Oxford (2: 447, 449). Oxford was referred to as alive in Volume I, which clearly fixes the composition of the first two volumes as spaced around May 1724. Rather less recent, but no distant history, is furnished by mention of "the late" Sir William Ashurst (1: 382: d. 12 January 1720). General John Pepper (1: 383) died too late to supply a test case: that is, on 22 December 1725. However, no weight can be placed on a passage mentioning notable seats (1: 392); the owners include Sir Stephen Fox, who had died as far back as 1717—something Defoe well knew, for he mentions Fox's generous bequests in the previous letter (1: 378). In the same list occurs the name of Sir Godfrey Kneller, who had died on 19 October 1723, as well as "the late Earl of *Marr*," who was living in exile and whose property had been forfeited. It is evident that Defoe is identifying residences according to their best-known occupier, rather than naming the current resident.

As regards the supposed "tour" itself, we have only one clear-cut dating: and that, unfortunately, occurs in a suburban London (as it is today) entry. The passage concerns that shortlived piece of princely show, Cannons:

> I left *Cannons* with regret, the Family all Gay, and in Raptures on the Marriage of the Marquis of *Caernarvon,* the Dukes eldest Son, just then Celebrated with the Lady *Katharine Talmash* Daughter of the Earl of *Dysert* which Marriage adds to the Honour and Estate also, of the Family of *Chandos.* (1: 388)

The wedding took place on 1 September 1724—not, as one might suppose, at Edgware, but at Ham. Sadly, the joys of this marriage were to be as fleeting as the splendors of Cannons, for the Marquis died three years later at the age of twenty-seven. That Defoe composed the section on Chandos and his properties not long before Volume II appeared is shown by another passage:

> So far is the Duke from having exhausted himself by this Prodigy of a Building [Cannons]; that we see him since that laying out a Scheme, and Storing up Materials for building another House for his City Convenience, on the North Side of the New Square, call'd *Oxford* or *Cavendish Square,* near *Maribone:* and if that is discontinued, it seems to be so, only because the Duke found an Opportunity to purchase another much more to his

advantage; Namely, the Duke of *Ormond's* House in St *James's* Square. (1: 386)

The sequence of events behind this paragraph can be plotted as follows. Ormond's house was sold on 29 April 1719. Chandos was outbid, but managed to acquire the property by private dealing. He was installed by August 1720. Meanwhile Edward Shepherd was at work for Chandos in Cavendish Square. This development had been planned around 1719 or 1720, but did not get under way until the spring of 1724. By the end of that year, two houses were half-built, though it was not until 1727 that the easternmost house was ready for occupation. It appears likely, then, that Defoe wrote before he knew of Shepherd's renewed activity in Cavendish Square. Again the middle part of 1724 is suggested as the period of composition. Defoe's reference to the Caernarvon marriage may be a last minute addition or it may even have been inserted at proof stage.[18]

As might be anticipated, the metropolitan parts of this tour display more signs of recent knowledge. For example, Defoe allots one paragraph to a new pleasure house set up in Hampstead, "being taken lately by a certain *Projector* to get a Penny" (1: 384). John Macky had made vaguely approving noises with regard to this venture in 1722,[19] but Defoe is far less indulgent:

> This brought a wonderful Concourse of People to the Place, for they were all so effectually gratified in all sorts of Diversion, that the Wicked part at length broke in, till it alarm'd the Magistrates, and I am told it has been now in a manner suppress'd by the hand of Justice. . . . It could not be, no British Government could be supposed to bear long with the Liberties taken on such Publick Occasions: So as I have said, they are reduc'd, at least restrain'd from Liberties which they could not preserve by their Prudence. (1: 384–85)

The background is briefly this: the projector, named Howell, had taken Belsize House in 1720, and it was fitted out for its new purpose by that Easter. As Defoe says, the place soon became a fashionable resort, and the Prince and Princess of Wales were there in the summer of 1721. However, what he calls "the hand of Justice" was soon moved to action. In May 1722 the Middlesex justices at Hickes Hall ordered the High Constable of Holborn to direct his officers to put down unlawful gaming, rioting, and other abuses that had been rife at Hampstead. It does not take very deep reading in muncipal history to know that eighteenth-century local government was not particularly expeditious, and law enforcement notably weak in the fast-growing municipalities on the edge of London. If the abuses were "restrained," it is unlikely to have happened quickly.[20] Certainly, Defoe is dealing with a situation quite different from the one Macky had complacently described in 1722.

As soon as the "circuit" moves away from the orbit of the capital, there is the expected drop in firsthand observation of contemporary facts. One strange oversight looks *prima facie* most suspicious. When Defoe reaches St David's, he gives some account of the diocese:

> They reckon up 112 Bishops of the See, since it begun, to the Year 1712. The last Bishop but two, was Dr. *Thomas Watson,* of whom the World has heard so much, being depriv'd after a long Debate, on a Charge of *Simony;* whether justly, or not, I shall not enquire, but he bestow'd great Sums on Charitable Designs, and is still (living) enclined as I am told, to do much more. (2: 457)

Disregarding the 1712 reference, these points are relevant. (1) Watson had indeed been deprived in 1699, after a great deal of wrangling. Nor was the matter then over, since Watson took the case as far as the House of Lords and it ran on for some years. (2) There was a vacancy at this time until the celebrated George Bull was instituted in 1705. He was succeeded by Philip Bisse, and Bisse in turn by Adam Otley. Otley died in October 1723; his successor, Richard Smallbroke, was appointed on 26 October and consecrated on 2 February 1724. Defoe's phrase "the last Bishop but two" was accurate during Otley's tenure, which began in 1713, but not thereafter. (3) More seriously, Defoe errs with respect to Watson himself. The deprived bishop had indeed lived for some years after the *cause célèbre* in which he figured. But his death at the age of eighty, on 3 June 1717, was not exactly fresh news. All these facts prompt the view that Defoe was recalling the state of opinion within the diocese as it had been some years before, perhaps around 1713. It is true that Watson had left Wales and spent his latter days in Cambridgeshire. But if the people of St David's had entirely lost touch with him, it is hard to see how they could outline to Defoe his charitable intentions.

This is the only clear instance of anachronistic detail in the letter. In general there are fewer signs of Defoe using identifiable travels of his own made in earlier years. A portion of this tour, covering Glouces-ter, Tewkesbury, Pershore, Evesham, Worcester, and Leominster, re-enacts part of Defoe's journey for Harley in the autumn of 1705.[21] In addition, Bath and Bristol are considered in Letter VI, and they too were on the itinerary in 1705. However, we know that Defoe must have visited these towns on other occasions. More than that, he actu-ally mentions in the *Tour* what was in all likelihood his earliest visit

to the region, around 1670: "I have my self drank the Waters of the
Bath above fifty Years ago" (2: 434). Whether Defoe went on into
Wales in his boyhood, we do not know. But since he constantly compares the Welsh landscape to the Alpine prospects he evidently knew
already, it seems that he visited Wales only *after* his Continental
journeys of the 1680s and 1690s. (At one point he states candidly,
"From *Worcester* I took a Tour into *Wales,* which tho' . . . it was not
at the same time with the rest of my Journey; my Account I hope
will be as effectual," 2: 446: but this does not help with dating.) We
know that Defoe must have been at Aylesbury for the races both in
the time of Charles II and again in Queen Anne's reign (1: 394).[22]
Once more, it is impossible to judge whether Defoe traveled further
west on these occasions. In 1710 he advertised in the *Review* for a
walking companion "to travel into several parts of the West," adding—perhaps more disarmingly than truly—"for his diversion only."[23]
If Defoe did make a trip into the West at this time, it was into a
region he already knew well (I exclude Wales, where the evidence is
scanty). Consequently, it would probably not have been necessary for
him to revisit the area in 1723—let us say—in order that the *Tour*
should emerge as it stands. Nor is there clear proof in Letter VI of
such a visit. But if nothing establishes it, nothing precludes it.

There remains the special case of Bristol. Defoe seems to have been
more fully *au fait* with this city than with many others. His account
is quite without the vagueness that attends certain entries. He relates
how the port's trading with Ireland "is prodigiously encreas'd in these
last Thirty Years, since the Revolution" (2: 435) and he describes the
new building in one part of the city. Some of his information proved
to be not quite accurate, and had to be revised in the appendix to
Volume II. It is also true that much of the entry could be based on
secondhand testimony supplied by a local correspondent—Defoe must
have known many Bristol merchants. In 1706 he was in contact with
the important Quaker and businessman Benjamin Coole, as well as a
member of the influential mercantile family of the Wraxalls.[24] Nonetheless, it is likely that Defoe did have close personal relations with
Bristol. We can disregard the story that he fled from his creditors to
the city in the early years of the century, a legend that may somehow
have grown out of Richard Savage's career. But it is possible that he
was in Bristol during November 1714, deriving local intelligence from
a local clergyman (a dissenting minister, no doubt) and writing a
pamphlet on the government's behalf. Some of this intelligence may
have found its way into the *Tour.*[25]

For the rest, we have to rely on fugitive references and dubious
signs in our attempts to date the letter. If Defoe saw a statue of Queen

Anne at Worcester, as he says, this must have been after 1714 (2: 443). The promising-looking phrase used of the River Lugg, "This River is lately made Navigable by act of Parliament" (2: 447), turns out to mean an act of 1696, 7 & 8 Wm. III, c.14, s.2. If we are to take literally the statement that the Earl of Colerain "is now on his Travels" (1: 382), this may indicate the year 1723, when Colerain was on the Continent under no less a mentor than Conyers Middleton. What can be asserted with absolute conviction is that the letter must have been written or revised well into 1724; that the sections concerned with the London hinterland (and perhaps Bristol) display more recent knowledge; and that Defoe was not dependent on a single fact-finding mission, as he might well have been with the extreme South West of England in Letters III and IV.

The return journey from Chester, by a highly circuitous route, occupies Letter VII. A large part of the Midlands is covered in this division of the *Tour,* and Defoe writes in such an assured, bland style that it is hard to believe he was not writing from immediate experience of the districts surveyed. If we try to substitute for impressionism of this kind firmer evidence, a limited number of positive clues can be discovered.

The attention Defoe bestows on Coventry merits especially careful scrutiny: we have already touched on the passage in the Introduction (pp. 29–30 above), but further commentary is needed here, since the dating issues are complex.

> It was a very unhappy Time when I first came to this City; for their Heats and Animosities for Election of Members to serve in Parliament, were carry'd to such a Hight, that . . . the Inhabitants (in short) enraged at one another, met, and fought a pitch'd Battle in the middle of the Street. . . . Nor were these the Scum and Rabble of the Town, but in short the Burghers and chief Inhabitants, nay even Magistrates, Aldermen, and the like. Nor was this one Skirmish a Decision of the Quarrel, but it held for several Weeks, and they had many such Fights; nor is the Matter much better among them to this Day, only that the Occasion does not happen so often. (2: 482)

The occasion was less frequent, because of the Septennial Act: there had been three elections in 1701–2, and seven between 1700 and 1713. But after 1715 the voters had to wait until 1722 to exercise their right, be it freeborn, acquired by the purchase of burgages, or attendant on membership of the corporation. Throughout Anne's reign Coventry had been notoriously volatile, indicating that a large proportion of its fifteen hundred freeholders were floating voters, ready to swim with the national tide. However, it was the 1705 election that saw a particularly contentious struggle for power, and it was then that the affrays described by Defoe took place. According to some reports, the Tories assembled some five hundred hoodlums to discourage intending Whig voters.[26]

Defoe is unlikely to have witnessed this affair, because it took place in May 1705, five months before he arrived in the town on his travels for Harley. He did write two papers in the *Review* on the subject, one as late as August 1706, the other contemporaneously. He also promised Harley "the history at large in print"—a promise apparently unfulfilled. But his informant can be readily identified as Edward Owen, Alderman and formerly Mayor of the borough, with whom he corresponded following his visit in 1705, and who was named as the local distribution agent the following year. This makes it hard to reconcile with the known facts a paper in Applebee's *Weekly Journal* for 21 April 1722, already cited (p. 30 above), that William Lee attributes to Defoe. The assignment seems wholly plausible; in the previous chapter, I quoted its account of the attempted murder in Bury St. Edmunds, and the promise of "a diverting History of *Coventry* Elections for some Time past" could surely only have come from one writer on Applebee's staff at this juncture. We are forced to conclude that the opprobrious references to Alderman O——n and the other "*Coventry* Whigs," for countenancing in 1722 what they had complained of in 1705, must proceed from a change in Defoe's sympathies.[27] It is beyond dispute that he took a close interest in the parliamentary contests in this borough for a number of years; he still kept an eye on events in 1722, but the *Tour* offers no clear proof that he visited Coventry again on that occasion.

When he reaches Coleshill, Defoe is predictably incensed at the overwhelmingly Tory cast of the corporation and indeed the town as a whole. This he attributes to the influence of Lord Digby, so that there is "but one Family of *Whiggs* . . . in the whole Town, and they hoped to drive them out of the Place too very quickly." He proceeds:

> The late Incumbent of this Parish quitted his Living, which is very considerable, because he would not take the Oaths, and his Successor was the famous ——— who, when I was there, was newly proscrib'd by Proclamation, and the Reward of 1000£. order'd to whoever should apprehend him; so their Instructors being such, 'tis no Wonder the People have follow'd their Leader. (2: 481–82)

As we have already seen (p. 29), the first minister is obviously John Kettlewell, the celebrated nonjuror, though he had been deprived of the living as long ago as 1690 and had died five years later. The second can be identified as Thomas Carte, later well known as a historian. Defoe is in error when he states that Carte held the living at Coleshill; he took refuge with the minister there (one Badger) following the 1715 rebellion. Carte was suspected of complicity in the Atterbury plot and was made the subject of a proclamation on 15 August 1722. Applebee's *Journal* on 11 August was one of several newspapers to mention a "diligent" search for "Mr. Cart, the Nonjuring Parson." If Defoe is telling the truth, he must have been in Coleshill at this time or just afterwards. This is not implausible, in that Defoe was on the point of drawing up an elaborate business deal with John Ward of this town.[28]

If we turn from the research for Letter VII to its composition, we can be more explicit. Defoe takes account of the death of the Earl of Sunderland (2: 486), as also that of Robert Heysham, a businessman with interests both in London and in Lancashire, who died on 26 February 1723 (1: 467). Heysham is mentioned in the course of a brief consideration of Liverpool; Defoe returns to the town in Letter X, and I defer any observations for the present. But one important reference in this letter demands notice. When Defoe reaches Bedfordshire, at the end of this current circuit, he gives a list of market towns in the county, ending up with Woburn.

> The last of these was almost demolish'd by a terrible Fire, which happen'd here just before my writing this Account; but as this Town has the good luck to belong to a noble Family [the Russells] . . . there is no doubt but that the Trustees, tho' his Grace the present Duke is in his Minority, will preserve that good Character to the Family, and reedify the Town, which is almost their own. (2: 513)

The house of Bedford did in time rebuild the town. Defoe's allusion fixes the period of composition around the late summer of 1724, since the fire took place in June. He speaks of the Duke as an "Infant"; in fact the Duke was sixteen, and before Volume II appeared in print he had been married.

There follows an Appendix of great interest. The need for such an addendum, Defoe says, is occasioned by the fact that "no Man can take so strict a View of *England,* but something will occur, which the nicest Observer could not possibly see, or the most busy Enquirer be inform'd of at one Journey" (2: 515). He adds, with more conviction perhaps, "some Things will be undertaken and begun in the smallest Intervals of Time, which were not heard of before." The phrasing seems to allow for secondhand information; and the "more exact Enquiry into the particular State of the City of *Bristol*" that follows looks to rely on contributed material. Defoe mentions "an Act of Parliament actually pass'd, Ann. 1723" to permit the construction of a new exchange. He refers also to a change in the proposed site of the building. The *Journals* of the Commons record one bill on this subject introduced in December 1721, but subsequently withdrawn; where-upon another bill was introduced in early 1722. Defoe's comment, "The Citizens do not seem so hasty to Build, as they were to get the Act of Parliament pass'd to give them Power to do it," is quite justified. In the event, the new exchange did not go up until 1740.

After the section on Bristol, there comes one of the most famous parts of the entire *Tour* —a review of the state of roads in England at this time, with a particular emphasis on the effect of the new Turnpike Acts. I say "new," although Defoe covers, inter alia, some of the earliest measures of this kind, including the Ingatestone stretch of the London to Colchester road, 7 & 8 Wm. III, c.9 (1696), and the Dunstable—Hockley stretch, improved as a result of 9 Anne, c.14 (1709). However, there was a burst of activity in turnpike legislation in the early 1720s. Many of Defoe's comments are exceedingly topical. He remarks, "We see also a Turnpike set up at a Village very justly called *Foul Mire* near *Cambridge* . . . but those Works are not yet brought to any Perfection" (2: 523). This bill seems to have been introduced only in January 1725. Similarly, when Defoe says that the "terrible Road" called Baldock Lane, noted for its impassable state, "is now under Cure" (2: 523), he seems to be thinking of equally recent events. A petition referring to the impassable road near Buckden was read by the Commons also in January 1725. Other acts were of slightly longer date, but it is plain that Defoe took a keen interest in these developments, and that he noted the acceleration in turnpike legisla-tion *after* the composition of the letters that make up Volume II.

This leaves the preface at the head of this volume. In it Defoe refers to the reception accorded to the first part of his *Tour*. He repeats his apologia with regard to errors and omissions:

> To describe a Country by other Mens Accounts of it, would soon expose the Writer to a Discovery of the Fraud; and to describe it by Survey, requires a Preparation too great for any Thing but a publick Purse, and Persons appointed by Authority. . . . But to describe a Country by Way of Journey, in a private Capacity, as has been the Case here, though it requires a particular Application, to what may be learn'd from due En-quiry and from Conversation, yet it admits not the Observer to dwell upon every Nicety, to measure the Distances, and determine exactly the Scite, the Dimensions, or the Extent of Places, or read the Histories of them. But it is giving an Account by way of Essay, or, as the Moderns

call it, by Memoirs of the present State of Things, in a familiar Manner. (1: 251)

Defoe's uneasiness here must have sprung from the realization that Volume II, apart from the London sections, was less detailed and less up-to-date than its predecessor had been. At all events, he goes on to mention recent developments, such as the entry of the South Sea Company into the Greenland trade—an unsuccessful venture, whose inception it is hard to date with precision.[29] More revelatory is this sentence:

> Another Article has happened, even between the Writing the APPENDIX to this Work, and this PREFACE; namely, That an Act of Parliament is passing, and will soon, we suppose, be pass'd for making the River *Nyne* navigable from *Peterborough* to *Northampton,* a Work which will be of infinite Advantage to the Country. . . . 'Tis true, this may be long in doing, it being above fifty Miles in Length by the River; and they had once before an Act granted for the same Thing; yet, 'tis said, they intend now to go about it in good earnest, and that they will be content with performing it piece-meal. (1: 252)

The earlier act was that of 13 Anne, c.19 (1713); the present measure, 12 Geo. I, c.19. It was brought in during January 1725 and passed the Commons on 12 March. Defoe presumably implies that the bill was awaiting the royal assent, but in any event the spring of 1725 is indicated.

This makes it possible to draw up the following rough schedule, working backwards from publication. Volume II issued on 8 June 1725. "Preface" written c. March/April 1725. The "Appendix" probably dates from about this period, though completed before the "Preface." The list of new buildings in London appended to the text of Letter V c.February 1725. The additions to the main text of that letter, concerning Guy's Hospital chiefly, date from January or February in all probability. The four letters written, or at least put into shape for the press, June-September 1724. Unless there was substantial revision, none of these letters could have been finished before June 1724. Defoe may have been working from rough drafts made earlier; indeed, all the signs are that much of Volume II was heavily dependent on former observations, with Letter IV making extensive use of the 1705 journey. But if his own running remarks are to be trusted, the actual writing was performed in the summer and autumn of 1724.

III

The third volume, as stated, came out on 9 August 1726, fourteen months after Volume II. The work is clearly divided into two sections. Following the "Preface" and the "Introduction," Defoe's tour of the Northern Counties occupies Letters VIII–X. Then comes the peregrination of Scotland, headed by its own "Introduction," and comprising Letters XI–XIII. These two sections are separately paged and can be regarded as the effective units of composition in Volume III. Accordingly, I shall take these sections, rather than individual letters, as the basis of discussion. In following this course, I do not mean to prejudge the question as to whether some areas may not have been visited, and some parts of the text compiled, at different times.

The tour of the northern counties begins with an "Introduction." Here Defoe contrasts two, presumably imaginary, gentlemen "who travelled over the greatest Part of *England* in several Journies together" (2: 540). One took brief notes only, respecting the most notable things he observed, and then "he wrote a very good and useful Account of his whole Journey after his Return." This account Defoe claims to have seen, and by its aid to have corrected and enlarged his own observations. The second traveler made a detailed journal of every matter that came to his attention, whether trivial or significant. Defoe does not say directly that the second traveler was wasting his time, or that the first exemplifies his own working method. He does not need to; the application is clear enough.[30]

In the tour proper, the first substantial town described is Nottingham. This is one of those places, like Bristol, where Defoe appears in full control of his material. He writes with aplomb even where he is least informative: "I might enter into a long Description of all the modern Buildings erected lately in *Nottingham,* which are considerable, and of some just now going forward. But I have a large Building in the whole to overlook; and I must not dwell too long upon the Threshold" (2: 551). Defoe had obviously been in the district more than once—"the last time I was there," he says, the Trent overflowed. He was evidently at the races in Nottingham on a former occasion (2: 553): his pretense that his current "tour" involved another visit to the course may be false, but it is impossible to be sure. From what he says, Defoe knew Nottingham during the sojourn there of the exiled French general, Marshal Tallard, who had led the defeated army at Blenheim.[31] He remarks of the garden Tallard had constructed in the French fashion, "It does not gain by *English* keeping" (2: 549).

In the following paragraph, Defoe abruptly changes the subject:

There was once a handsome Town-House here for the Sessions or Assises, and other publick Business; but it was very old, and was either so weak, or so ill looked after, that, being overcrowded upon Occasion of the Assises last Year, it cracked, and frightened the People, and that not without Cause. As it happened, no Body was hurt, nor did the Building fall directly down. But it must be said, (I think) that Providence had more Care of the Judges, and their needful Attendants, than the Townsmen had, whose Business it was to have been well assured of the Place. . . . We are told now that they are collecting Money, not for the Repair of the old House, but for erecting a new one, which will add to the Beauty of the Town. (2: 549–50)

The borough records appear to be silent on the accident itself. But they do mention a resolution of 1722/3 that a new town hall be erected with all convenient speed, as well as a minute of 22 April 1724, deputing the Mayor and two aldermen to attend a meeting at Rufford with JP's and gentlemen of the country, on the subject of a new hall. It is not clear whether the first resolution followed on the accident, or was prompted by alarm at the ruinous state of the building as Defoe describes it. But certainly the information was not in any way ancient history—the events were in the very recent past.[32]

From Nottingham, Defoe was "called aside" to Southwell Abbey, and once again the entry gives proof of modernity. Defoe inserts "An Account of the Town and Church of Southwell" (2: 554–61). This, he says, came from "a Reverend and very good Friend, and one of the present Prebendaries of the Place." Such contributed material might have been obtained by personal application on the spot, or Defoe may simply have written for it. His phrase "report of Inhabitants" is ambiguous. All that can be asserted with confidence is that Defoe was in communication with his Southwell friend shortly before publi- cation of the Tour. Checking the list of prebendaries supplied against John Le Neve's Fasti, we find that several appointments dating from 1720 (three cases) and 1721 (also three) are recorded, along with others from 1718 and 1719. The list indeed incorporated Edward Parker, whose tenure began as late as 24 September 1724: and it is up-to-date except that the prebend of South Muskham is allotted to John Lloyd. According to Le Neve, Lloyd was succeeded by Robert Dannye on 4 January 1724. Perhaps Le Neve's date should really be 1724/5, or it may be that Defoe's informant had a lapse of memory. In any case, two references in the account to Sir William Dawes as the "late" Archbishop of York firmly place the writing after 30 April 1724.

As soon as the tour leaves these towns, and begins to proceed through the county into Derbyshire, the sense of recent contact be-

comes less marked. There is a distinct impression that Defoe knew
Welbeck in the days of the former Duke of Newcastle, rather than
those of the celebrated statesman, Horace Walpole's "burlesque
Duke," who had succeeded to the title in 1715; the Welbeck estate
did not pass to him but (after protracted litigation, involving the
notorious Peter Walter among others) went to Lady Harley, later
Countess of Oxford, widow of Pope's friend. In the same sentence (2:
562) Defoe speaks of the Duke of Kingston, that is doubtless the first
Duke (father of Lady Mary Wortley Montagu), who had died in
March 1726, before Volume III appeared: and the Marquis of Halifax,
a title extinct for many years. Other references (2: 551, 553) make it
clear that the text here is concerned with identifying residences, rather
than naming the present occupant.

A still-more-betraying reference follows. Defoe comes to the "antient Seat, large, but not very gay, of Sir *Nathaniel Curson*, a noted
and (for Wealth) over great Family, for many Ages Inhabitants of this
County" (2: 564). The county is Derbyshire and the seat Kedleston,
though Defoe does not care to name it. Now Nathaniel has been a
favorite name in the Curzon family for centuries, and remains so. The
second baronet, who died in 1718, bore it; as did the fourth, who
succeeded in 1727. Unfortunately, at the time Defoe was allegedly
visiting the county, the baronetcy had devolved upon Sir John Curzon.
It looks very much as if Defoe had been caught out by his distance
from the county; at that time the family consisted of local magnates
rather than national figures.

A measure of negative evidence can be gleaned from Defoe's omissions in the Northern tour. For one so keen to mention river navigation, it is interesting that he does not mention the Idle, which was
opened up in 1725. He does refer to the Act of Parliament "some
Years ago" to make the Aire and Calder navigable, but this dates from
1699 (10 Wm. III, c.25). The comment that Castle Howard "is not
finished, and may not, perhaps, [*sic*] in our Time" (2: 642) is vague
enough to be discreet. But at York, Defoe seems to know nothing of
the new Mansion House, which the Earl of Oxford saw going up
during his tour in the summer of 1725. (Burlington's Assembly Rooms
did not materialize until the early 1730s.) As for the visit to the site
of the battle at Marston Moor, we can only assume that, like some of
the southern battlefields visited, it was made in good time for *Memoirs
of a Cavalier* (published c.May 1720). Similarly with the well-known
description of a hazardous journey over the Pennines (2: 596–600),
which corresponds to the passage over Blackstone Edge in the *Memoirs*. When Defoe recounts a conversation with a clergyman in Halifax
"some Years ago" (2: 605), it must be assumed that Defoe means Rev.

Nathaniel Priestley, with whom he had been in contact as far back as 1706. (It is true that Wright and others date this acquaintance to 1712, when Defoe was—according to their account—living in Halifax. But today this story is discounted.)[33] In the celebrated description of the West Riding wool trade, in short, there are no signs of a special visit just made for the purposes of the *Tour*. Defoe mentions "three Journeys" into the West Riding: probably none was very recent.

Three areas of the text may be singled out for special attention. Defoe's visit to Buxton, when he sampled the waters (2: 574), was almost certainly made in 1712, when he was ordered by his physicians to take the Derbyshire waters. The same applies to Matlock (2: 567), where the phrasing implies that the visit was made some time past.[34] More explicit is the entry for Liverpool—that is, the second entry, which comes at the start of Letter X. Defoe tells of his first visit in 1680, of a second in 1690 (these look suspiciously like round numbers), and of a third, undated, undertaken as part of the present tour. His mention of the "new Church" (2: 667) plainly relates to St Peter's, which was built at the turn of the century in response to petitions that Liverpool should be separated from the parish of Walton. The church was consecrated in 1705. Defoe names as a principal benefactor "the late Mr. *Heysham*," who died in 1723, as previously observed. He gives, too, an enthusiastic account of the new "wet Dock," which had been mentioned in Letter VII (2: 468). The proposal for such a venture had been made in 1708, the enabling act had been passed in the following year (8 Anne, c.25), while the work was completed around 1715. Defoe writes as though the scheme were fully under way. He could have obtained the information at a distance, but it is not certain that he did so. Certainly Defoe shows a real apprehension of the growth of the town; for once, his speculations of geometric "increase" are supported by economic and demographic figures. Significantly, too, he alludes to Edmund Gibson's edition of Camden (1695) as being written "about two and thirty years ago" (2: 668).

On another occasion, Defoe explicitly refers to 1726 as the year in which he himself is writing (2: 644). This is in the entry for Beverley. Here, Defoe seems to be unaware of the restoration operations on the Minster carried out in 1725/6. He mentions a story concerning two Danish soldiers involved in a duel at the town at the time of William III's Irish campaigns. Defoe speaks of a memorial tablet, quotes the first line, and then adds: "There are other lines mentioning the Story . . . but I do not remember them, it being some Years since I made this Observation" (2: 647). In this case, it may be that Defoe made a brief note at the time, which he was later unable to supplement from his memory. The relevant considerations are: (1) The tablet still exists, at St Mary's church (a place Defoe fails to mention). It shows that the duel took place in December 1689. (2) On his journey northwards in 1712, Defoe had to get from Lincoln and Gainsborough to Newcas-tle. The likely route would involve that rough passage over the Humber that Defoe had characterized in sharp terms in Letter VII (2: 493) and that would bring him to Beverley. Finally, Defoe mentions almshouses built by the executors of Michael Warton. This does not refer, as one might suppose, to the contemporary MP, Sir Michael Warton, who died on 25 March 1725, and made generous charitable bequests, but to his father (d. 1688). In fact, the information has obviously been filched from Gibson's edition of Camden, like much of the entry for Beverley.[35]

Throughout the northern tour, Defoe makes more insistent and obvious use of his printed sources than hitherto. Camden and his editor, Bishop Gibson, are drawn on with particular frequency. More-over, Defoe gives fewer indications of sustained familiarity with a given region. He does mention two visits to Tadcaster, no doubt in the course of a journey to or from Newcastle and Scotland. Now we know that Defoe was in Newcastle at least three times, in 1706, 1710 and 1712. He had close relations with a local printer, Joseph Button, who actually issued some of his pamphleteering work, and also with John Bell, the postmaster for Newcastle and an agent of Harley. Fi-nally, Defoe maintained a keen interest in the keelmen's hospital that had been set up in the town in 1701. He wrote a number of papers in the *Review* on the subject in 1712, and it is predictable that the *Tour* should contain a somewhat barbed paragraph on the topic (2: 659–60).[36] The fullness of Defoe's entry for Newcastle confirms the suspicion left by the thin and derivative character of other sections. The Northern tour is most impressive in covering those localities that Defoe had known from the 1680s onwards—Nottingham, Derbyshire, Liverpool, and the West Riding, as well as Newcastle. This suggests that he had little recent information to go on, except in towns where he already had good contacts and reliable correspondents—as, most obviously, with Nottingham and Southwell. The text must have been written or revised no earlier than September 1724; if incidental refer-ences are to be trusted, its composition ran into the year of publication, 1726, but there are fewer concrete pointers than in Volumes I and II.

IV

We come finally to the Scottish sections. The "Introduction" refers to previous accounts of the nation, written by "Natives of that Country, and that with such an Air of the most scandalous Partiality" (2: 689). Defoe probably has Macky in mind, as well as writers like Lockhart and Ridpath, who had produced tendentious accounts of recent Scottish history. In this sense there is ample evidence that the tour constitutes a direct reply to Macky's *Journey through Scotland*,[37] published in 1723; Defoe adopts a tone of studied impartiality, and places deliberate emphasis on the balanced judgment he seeks to achieve: "as I shall not make a Paradise of *Scotland,* so I assure you I shall not make a Wilderness of it" (2: 691). There is no sign that the "Introduction" dates from a later phase of composition than the letters that follow.

Defoe tells us at the outset of the work that he has "lived some time in *Scotland,* and has Travell'd critically over great part of it; he has viewed the North Part of *England,* and the South Part of *Scotland* five several Times over," so that readers should be satisfied with "the Authority of the Relation" (1: 3). (See further discussion, pp. 189–90.) This seemingly open admission on the subject of his earlier period of residence in Scotland might prompt the belief that the last three letters are based on the state of the nation fifteen years before.[38] It is certainly the case that Defoe makes little attempt to disguise just how antique some of his observations had become. For example, a long entry devoted to Drumlanrig Castle, seat of the Dukes of Queensberry, has at its center a warm tribute to the second Duke. Clearly Defoe's most vivid memories of the place (to put it in the most open terms) derive from the lifetime of this nobleman, who had died in 1711.[39] Witness an anecdote at the close of this section:

> While I was at *Drumlanrig,* being desir'd by the late Duke to make some Observations on his Grace's Estate there, which is very great, in Order to some *English* Improvement (*sic*), I, in particular, view'd some of the Hills to the North of the Castle, and having a *Darbyshire* Gentleman with us, who was thoroughly acquainted with those Things, we discover'd in several Places evident Tokens of Lead-Mines . . . and to confirm our Opinions in it, we took several small Pieces of Oar in the Gulls and Holes. . . . But the Duke's Death put an End to these Enquiries, as also to several other Improvements then in View. (2: 729–30)

It would be apparent to every reader that this was fairly ancient history. Less so with the following paragraph:

> Here we were surpriz'd with a Sight, which is not now so frequent in *Scotland,* as it has been formerly, I mean one of their Field Meetings, where one Mr. *John Hepburn,* an old Cameronian, preach'd to an Auditory

of near 7000 People, all sitting in Rows on the steep Side of a green Hill. (2: 730)

We are in a privileged position here, thanks to the survival of Defoe's letter to Harley of 26 December 1706. In this, Defoe passes on to the minister a report from "Our Itinerant," that is, one Pierce who was accompanying Defoe on his Scottish journey. The account in the *Tour* tallies so closely with that given by Pierce concerning Hepburn's preaching as to leave no doubt of its source.[40] Much the same applies when we come to the lengthy recital of a murder committed by a young nobleman at Inverkeithing. Defoe concludes his narrative with the explanation, "This Tragedy, and its Circumstances, I think, merits to be recorded, and the rather, because most of the Circumstances came within the Verge of my Knowledge, and I was upon the Spot when it was done" (2: 773). Once more we can check this against Defoe's report to Harley at the time, that is, in a letter of 25 April 1707.[41]

But this is to establish what has never been seriously doubted. That Defoe made extensive use of his period of residence in Scotland, no one is likely to challenge. The more difficult question remains—had he revisited the country since 1712, and how up-to-date is the bulk of his information? There are few direct pointers: Defoe's claim that he covered the southwestern counties of Scotland "at another particular Journey from *England*" (2: 724) leaves open the possibility that he had in mind two separate trips during his service for Harley. As to the final "circuit," that of the Highlands, there is little in the way of concrete temporal reference. It should be noted, however, that Defoe makes no mention of Wade's roads, which had been foreshadowed in a report of 1724 and were begun in 1726. Nor does he seem to know anything of the building of Fort William at this time. If Defoe did indeed make a "general journey" for the purposes of his book, it seems most unlikely that the more remote Caledonian fastnesses would figure on the itinerary. Some people have doubted whether Defoe ever went into Northern Scotland at all. There is nothing like conclusive evidence to back this supposition, and there are many signs that Defoe did take a lengthy journey into Ross and Sutherland about 1700.[42] He makes a number of allusions to the Jacobite troubles of 1707 and 1715: more to the point, his statement that the Earl of Mar "had" a noble seat appears to indicate familiarity with the act of sequestration imposed by the Forfeiture Commissioners as late as 1723. On the whole it seems that Defoe was well informed on the fate meted out to various families implicated in the 1715 rising (see, for instance, 2: 798–800), and it seems possible that he had at least some recent contact with

Stirling, Alloa, and Perthshire—more recent than that made in No-vember 1706, at all events.

Among the explicit references we may note one to the improvement in the Perth linen trade, occasioned by "the late Act of Parliament in *England,* for the suppressing the Use and Wearing of printed Cal-licoes" (2: 798). Defoe means the act of 7 Geo. I, c.7 (1721). Another providential dispensation of Hanoverian rule is the gift by the King of £1,000 annually to the General Assembly to support missionary work. A visit to Queensferry appears to be "in the Time of the late Wars," (2: 721), that is, prior to 1713:[43] but the description of Win-ton, if, as it offers to be, based on personal testimony must date from after 1716. On the very first page of the Scottish tour, Defoe refers to the minister of Mordintown, as the well-known author of *The Cyprianick Age:* "His Name is *Lauder*" (2: 692). Defoe seems to be confusing *The Principles of the Cyprianic Age* (1695: reprinted 1717), by John Sage, with Alexander Lauder's *The Ancient Bishops Consid-ered* (1707) and *The Divine Visitation of the Bishops* (1711). This argues a shallow acquaintance with the locality, but not necessarily a distant or nonexistent one.

An area where Defoe seems in more control of his facts is that concerned with legal luminaries, those characteristic Scottish culture heroes. For example, the mention of "the Family of *Dalrymple* en-nobl'd in the Earl of *Stairs* [sic], and honour'd in several Branches of that House, the eldest being now Lord President of their Session, and another lately Lord Advocate, &c." (2: 703–4). Sir Hew Dalrymple was Lord President of the Session from 1698 to his death in 1738: Sir David Dalrymple, Lord Advocate from 1709 to 1720. The first Earl of Stair had himself been Lord Justice Clerk and Lord President of the Session. Later in the same paragraph, Defoe turns his attention to "*Ormistoun,* the Seat of the present Lord Justice *Clerk,* of the anti-ent House of *Cockburn.*" Adam Cockburn, styled Lord Ormistoun, held office from 1705 to 1710, and again from 1714 to 1724. The slight antiquity of Defoe's facts here may suggest that he was behind events in another place. This is where he speaks of "The Family of *Elliot,* of whom one is, at present, one of the Lords of Session in *Scotland,* and is call'd Lord *Minto,* in Virtue of his Office, being otherwise no more than Sir *Gilbert Elliot* of *Minto*" (2: 764). This statement was true from 1705 to 1718, when the first baronet died. His son and successor, who bore the same first name, was not ap-pointed a Lord of Session until 4 June 1726. It seems improbable that Defoe could have received this information in time to incorporate it so smoothly into the text, prior to publication in August. When the

Tour appeared, the information was unimpeachable; we may take leave to doubt whether Defoe really knew why it was so.[44]

There are several other loose dating indications, showing that Defoe at least had his spies out in 1716 and later (see 2: 739, 750).[45] But these are slender threads on which to construct an argument; and it is safe only to say that Defoe writes of a post-1715 world, incorporating a number of events that took place in the early 1720s, but relying for some of his local color and firsthand evidence on the years he had spent in the kingdom on Harley's business. It is more constructive to turn to a portion of the work that can be placed with greater accuracy.

This is the "Preface" to Volume III, in all likelihood the last words of the *Tour* as far as actual composition went. "The Tour is now finished," Defoe writes (2: 535), and in case we have missed the relief in his accents, the Preface concludes, "Without any more Apology, [we] recommend our Work to the Candor of the Reader, and close the Account of a Tedious and very Expensive five Years Travel" (2: 537). This sentence came before the public in August 1726, and appears to conflict with the starting date named at the outset, 3 April 1722. (That is, supposing the order of the printed tours is that of Defoe's real or assumed journeys, and this is the rhetorical pretense at least.) In any event, the "Preface" was certainly written in 1726. Defoe says that Walpole's house at Houghton is "finished, at least the Outside Work and Figure of the Building is" (2: 536). This was the stage reached during 1726, when the house was habitable, although further additions continued to be made for another decade (see also p. 69). Another edifice now completed is the South Sea House, also the work of 1726. Sir Gregory Page's house is generally thought to have been finished rather earlier, but the evidence is scanty. Defoe's statement regarding the progress of Guy's Hospital also suggests a date around May 1726 (see p. 90).

The growth of the new "City" at the west end of Hanover Square is too vaguely described to give a firm indication; development in this area, as Sir John Summerson points out, soon slowed down,[46] and what Defoe says appears to fit the latest possible date consistent with the publishing history. The "terrible fire" at Wapping had occurred in 1715 (2: 536). "To close all," says Defoe, "There is the erecting a new Stone Bridge over the *Thames* at *Putney* and *Fulham,* for which an Act of Parliament was obtained last Sessions, and preparations are now actually making to set about it, which is likely to be a very stately and magnificent Work." Not surprisingly, Defoe was caught out by events here. A bill had been brought in during March 1726, and passed later in the session despite a number of opposing petitions. But the vested interests against the measure were numerous and powerful, and the bridge was not yet to come into existence. In the light of this statement and the others mentioned, it would seem that Defoe wrote the "Preface" after April 1726—perhaps in May or June.

V

On the basis of this chapter and its predecessor, general conclusions may be drawn about the making of the *Tour* as a whole. The composition of the *Tour* can be allotted to the period from November 1722 to May/June 1726. Some parts only of the text are datable, but all these fall within the period named. Moreover, an appraisal of the evidence permits a broad chronology to be drawn up. This shows that Defoe carried out the main task of writing a year or eighteen months prior to the publication of each volume. Between four and eight months prior to publication, sheets were corrected, additions made, and, where necessary, appendices supplied. Shortly before the volume was issued, not more than a month or two at most, the final touches were added, including the preface (always written last). The evidence suggests that Defoe worked in concentrated bursts: the bulk of Volume I being written in the autumn and early winter of 1722, most of Volume II in the summer of 1724. Volume III is harder to fix with assurance, but the likeliest time of writing is the second half of 1725. The earliest possible date is the end of 1724. The separate volumes were basically independent productions, and Defoe takes account as he goes along of the reception accorded to earlier parts. His working method, in brief, was consecutive and synthetic in character.

With regard to the materials that went into the *Tour*, it is evident that Defoe used a wide variety of information. Some of it was cribbed from previous authorities; some drew on his experience as a young man; some depended on his travels for Harley; some was contributed by his contacts up and down the country; some was based on fresh observation of his own. There is a marked differential in this matter between particular circuits. Few signs of recent firsthand knowledge can be detected in Letters VI (Welsh sections) and XIII. Letter IV, especially, appears to draw heavily on the years spent in the service of Robert Harley. On the other hand, the last section of this letter, along with much of the first volume, goes back to Defoe's younger days—to 1688 and earlier. Letters XI and XII, along with Letter IX, make undisguised use of his missions to Scotland in 1706–10. Letter V is based on a lifetime of close attention to London and its doings— the observations ranging from those of the 1680s, or earlier, to the very eve of publication. Letters VI, VII, and VIII are patchy, but the

treatment of certain important towns—Bristol, Nottingham, Coventry, and Liverpool—indicates some recent contact. Letter I and, in a
rather less sustained fashion, Letter II embody up-to-date findings.

The conclusion prompted is that Defoe undertook something of a
"general tour" when planning the book, but probably carried this no
further than the Home Counties and the Midlands. This means that
East Anglia and southeast England were thoroughly covered, and the
sector lying northwest of London, straddling in approximate terms
the Bath Road and the Great North Road, was dealt with more skimp-
ily. But it is probable that he had recently taken the Dunstable road
(as Moll and her highwayman husband had done), perhaps on a business trip to Coleshill. Unless his imagination was even more preter-
naturally vivid than we have believed, Defoe had been on the new
turnpike roads—many dating from the decade preceding the Tour's
publication. It should be stressed that, whenever Defoe made his visit,
he took great pains to bring his material up to date.

If we look back at the composition of all three volumes, it becomes
apparent that the amount of obsolete or secondhand information is
decidedly greater in the latter sections of the Tour. One reason for
this may be weariness on Defoe's part, and possibly haste as he undertook a number of large nonfiction works around 1725. However, there
is no doubt that he had less firsthand acquaintance with the districts
covered in the latter half of his book; in addition, the acquaintance
had less often been renewed by visits in the Hanoverian era. He
perhaps had fewer contacts and informants in regions far from London.

Nevertheless, the broader literary conclusions reached in connection with Volume I do for the most part survive this reservation. We
can still see Defoe tinkering and fiddling, adjusting a fact here and
abridging an anecdote there. The impromptu quality that often mars
the artistic effect of his fictional narratives, as in the ramshackle structure of The Farther Adventures of Robinson Crusoe, is much less of a
disability here. Opportunistic and eclectic though his working methods may have been, Defoe managed to turn a journalist's enterprise
into something like high art. The Tour would no doubt be better as a
report if it had been based on sustained and up-to-date personal knowledge of all the places described. But it would also be from a literary
standpoint less rich and enticing: its perspective would be narrower
and its final effect, paradoxically, less personal. For Defoe is never
more himself than when he is caught in the act of borrowing, tidying
up, or varnishing over the cracks.

3

The Uses of Plagiarism: Camden's *Britannia* in the *Tour*

Eᴀʀʟɪᴇʀ sections of this book should have made it plain that Defoe employed a wide range of sources and manipulated them with considerable skill, not to say deviousness. His policy with regard to John Macky's *Journey* is an example of this (see p. 38). But the most considerable debt is that owed to Camden's *Britannia*, as it had been brought up to date by Edmund Gibson and his collaborators, and this area of his borrowing requires separate attention.

In 1929 Godfrey Davies reviewed briefly "a very attractive reprint of the first edition" of Defoe's *Tour*.[1] He observed that the introduction by G. D. H. Cole did "little more than point out the general importance of the *Tour* to the economic historian" and that it left untouched "the question of Defoe's sources," apart from some vague and misleading comments regarding Defoe's use of existing guidebooks. In particular, Davies was skeptical regarding the alleged influence of John Macky's *Journey through England* (1714–23):

> Usually Defoe mentions Macky only to refute him, and when his descriptions are similar to those of the earlier writer, it is probable that both authors were borrowing from a common source. Defoe frequently mentions his indebtedness to Gibson's edition of Camden, and his debt is even greater than he acknowledges. Before the value of the *Tour* as historical evidence can be determined it is essential that it be compared with earlier descriptions of England. This would reveal the new information incorporated, which in its turn could be partially tested at least by sources not available when Defoe was writing. At present it is impossible for a student of the *Tour* to tell whether a passage is merely a rehash of what had already appeared in print, an accurate description of what Defoe had actually witnessed, or whether a fertile imagination is supplying the place of observation. Unfortunately Cole's introduction will furnish little guidance towards the solution of these difficult problems.

There Davies left the matter. He did not take it up again himself in a later article on the *Tour*, and few attempts have been made to grapple with "these difficult problems."

A fuller review of the evidence than Davies was able to undertake provides abundant justification for his suppositions. Space precludes a full citation of the numerous textual references that have been found to support his case (they are, besides, somewhat repetitive in charac-ter). However, it is possible to summarize the main conclusions reached, as they affect what Davies wrote in the only consideration to date of these important issues.

Macky's second volume was advertised in the *Daily Post* on 4 May 1722, thirty-one days after the nominal starting date of Defoe's own tour. It is possible that its appearance stimulated the writing of a rival "journey"; and it is certain that Defoe often had Macky in mind, though the latter often figures only as "a late Writer" or something similar.[2] It is also true that Defoe took over errors from his predecessor, for instance, his misnomers in the account of Cannons.[3] However, Davies's basic point holds. Macky is most useful to Defoe as a target whenever he wishes to proclaim his own superior accuracy. And the borrowings he makes from the *Journey* are seldom extensive or very literal.

Against this, it can be shown that the *Tour* makes an extremely heavy levy upon *Britannia,* and specifically the edition of 1695 edited by Edmund Gibson.[4] This was not the first full translation of the Latin text, which had originally been issued in 1586: Philemon Holland had produced an English version in 1610. But Gibson had greatly aug-mented the survey. He assembled a team of distinguished scientists and antiquarians to assist him, some of them leading members of the Royal Society such as John Ray. These men were deeply imbued with the need for what might be termed "thick description" of empirical data. Defoe mentions Camden or Gibson by name about eighty times. But he makes silent use of *Britannia* in many more passages. In all I have identified some two hundred places where Defoe draws directly on his predecessor for facts or observations, but this is certain to understate the scale of the debt. The *Tour* contains marginally more references to the sections added by Gibson than to the original text of Camden, but both writers may be drawn on in a given block of the work.

Borrowings from *Britannia* are found in every area of the *Tour,* except Letter V, dealing with London. For this section, specialized works were used, notably John Strype's recent edition of the great Elizabethan *Survey* by Stow, and there is less about antiquity here, anyway. The borrowings tend to be most frequent, in their disguised form, in those parts of the work that concern districts remote from London or regions with which Defoe had little recent contact. How-ever, this applies more to northern and western parts of England, for example, Letters VII through X, than to the southern part of Scotland in Letters XI and XII (borrowings become more numerous in the Highland regions). Naturally, the loan-rate increases in the *Tour*'s coverage of historic towns, cathedral cities, and the like, but the process is not confined to such places.

The contributions supplied by *Britannia* undergo varying treatment when they reach the *Tour*. Defoe uses methods ranging from direct quotation and metaphrase to broad paraphrase. In the latter instance, Defoe tends to amplify rather than compress his source, which lends a measure of support to the view that he was habitually a prolix writer. For example, the account in Gibson (col. 356) of the Dunmow Flitch custom runs to 82 words. In Defoe (1: 37–38) it requires 121 words, about half again as long.[5]

The *Tour* often conceals its indebtedness by a variety of means. Prose is converted into verse (compare Gibson, col. 723, with Defoe, 2: 578); material is reordered (as the same comparison will show); and, especially where inscriptions or epitaphs are quoted, spelling and punctuation are altered.[6] It is virtually certain that Defoe took his versified form of the grant of Hatfield Forest (1: 39–40) from Camden (col. 344); but he seeks to add authenticity (". . . which I find in the antient Records") and in the process alters the text in small particulars. In fact, the alleged charter is completely bogus, and contains anachronisms both in content and in language.

Occasionally the "editing" of *Britannia* amounts to a creative undertaking. Thus, Defoe builds up a list of Devon worthies (1: 223–24) from widely scattered references by Gibson (cols. 38–42).[7] Again, the rebuilding of Bury St Edmunds by Canute is achieved by a sort of imaginative infilling by Defoe (1: 49–50) of Camden's account (col. 368).

In places, however, the pilfering is more direct. This is especially the case in Letters VIII–X, dealing with Northern England. Compare for example Defoe, 2: 654–57, on East Yorkshire, with *Britannia,* cols. 739, 741, 746–50, 772, and 777. The most notable single example occurs at Beverley (2: 644–47), where about nine hundred words are lifted whole from Gibson (cols. 743–44), for the most part *literatim* and with no attempt to disguise the theft. For once Defoe avoids his usual paraphrases and variations, and simply inserts the text of *Britannia* into his own work. But the material must have been transcribed for the press, since it differs in typography and presentation, with a few variants in punctuation. In the most sustained stretch of borrowing, there is only one important verbal difference, but it is highly revelatory: where the text of *Britannia* has "But to come to the condition of the town" (col. 744), the *Tour* reads, "But to come to the present Condition of the Town" (2: 646).

J. H. Andrews was the first to point out this case of plagiarism.[8] He noted that Defoe's "own" writing begins again with a reference to the tradition of sanctuary in Beverley, a passage that seems to belong several paragraphs earlier with the mention of the "frith" or "freed" stool (col. 644 in Camden). From this Andrews deduced that another hand apart from Defoe's was at work: the mistake "can be ascribed more plausibly to an editor or collaborator than to the author." Further, the slip reveals "the carelessness and haste with which Defoe's masterpiece was written." The first conclusion seems ill-founded, and the second seems a little harsh. The small blunder in misplacing the reference to sanctuary is very simply explained, since it occurs at the moment when Defoe resumes his own narrative after the long passage copied from *Britannia*. It is the only place in the entire *Tour* where such a lengthy direct borrowing can be traced, and it is not too surprising that Defoe should have become muddled. There is not a shred of evidence that any collaborator was involved. Actually, Defoe's confusions go slightly further. He introduces the passage by saying, "As to this Privilege of Sanctuary, Mr. *Cambden* gives us the description of a Stone Chair . . ." (2: 644). In fact, the borrowing comes from a section added by Edmund Gibson in 1695, as many internal references make clear. There is also an oddity in that Defoe retains a reference in *Britannia* to "our Author," by which Gibson meant Leland—the effect in the *Tour* is to leave the impression that Camden is meant. All in all, the section shows Defoe at his most feebly dependent, and shows the limitations of his method when such sustained reliance is placed on a secondary source.

A more representative picture will be afforded if we look at a section of the work chosen at random. This is a portion late in the second letter, where Defoe is not far from his home territory. In a matter of twenty pages or so, describing the area around Guildford, the narrator employs Camden in a variety of ways. There are what might be called critical citations, where Defoe accepts information from *Britannia* but adds his own gloss: as, for example, "a good River, call'd *Arun*, which signifies, says Mr. *Cambden*, the swift, tho' the River it self is not such a Rapid Current as merits that Name; at least it did not seem to be so to me" (1: 132: see Camden, col. 169, and Gibson's addition, col. 181). There are semiconcealed debts, as where Defoe writes about Clandon, with a brief aside "as appears in Mr. *Camden*" (1: 147), almost totally eliding his complete reliance on this source (Camden, col. 162). On the other hand, his reference to Camden on the River Wey (1: 143) is sufficient acknowledgement, since Defoe brings his own knowledge of the economic life of the district to this section. He corrects Camden on the usage "the Swallow," concerning the underground streams near Dorking (1: 150); but although Defoe had lived in Dorking when he was young, and supplies a long recollection of events there in his childhood (1: 150–52), he actually splices a good deal of Camden's text into the whole section.

When he reaches the region known as the Weald, he quotes two lines of verse, which "they retain here in Memory" (1: 155). Probably it was Camden who actually retained them (col. 155), but—possibly to conceal his indebtedness—Defoe cites them in an altered form. Even in a matter one would expect to be entirely personal, that is the mention of a fine view across the Weald to the South Downs (1: 154), we find that Camden had also referred to this prospect (col. 164). The only substantial "correction" in this sequence is that made to Camden and Gibson regarding the course of the Wey (1: 148–49: see Camden, cols. 156 and 163). Elsewhere, Defoe is about his usual business siphoning off material here, adapting there (as when he alters Gibson's statement of the age of the orange trees at Beddington from a hundred years to eighty years, 1: 158), and generally making free with his most important source. Once he cites Camden apparently verbatim, but quietly alters the tense: "Portsmouth is populous in time of war" (col. 123) becomes "was populous" (1: 138). At such moments, the discursive practice amounts to weaving Defoe's own weft onto the warp of Britannia.

Although sustained dependence on Camden is rare, in the form found in the entry for Beverley, the reader can never safely assume, especially in the northern sections, that the extent of Defoe's debt is made clear in the text. A favorite device is to appeal to Camden's authority for one fact, and then silently to raid his work for many more.[9] This technique is illustrated in the coverage of Penrith, where Archdeacon William Nicolson had carried out research for Gibson. When Defoe remarks, "At Penrith also we saw several remarkable things, some of which I find mentioned by the Right Reverend Continuator of Mr. Cambden, and which I was glad to see, so confirm'd my Observation" (2: 686), it should be a warning to us that all the essential facts are present in Gibson. Most of them appear, undiluted, in the Tour. "Fame reports" that there were once fifty churches in the lost town of Dunwich (1: 54): actually it was Camden who so reported, quoting the historian Spelman (col. 380). Equally when "the Country People" tell "us" a long story about waterspouts known as "gypsies" (2: 655), we are not surprised to find that it was Gibson in truth who printed a communication by John Ray on the subject (cols. 748–50).

Defoe alludes to a number of earlier topographers, such as John Leland, and authors of county histories such as Robert Plot and Richard Carew. He had certainly read some of William Dugdale's works, but there is no concrete proof that he had any firsthand familiarity with most writers mentioned.[10] He simply lifts their names from *Britannia*.

In general, it may be said that Defoe, without outright lying, consistently manipulates the text so as to play down (or misdescribe) his indebtedness to existing sources.[11] He seems under a compulsion to decorate whatever he has purloined; and for long stretches, *Britannia* forms a base around which Defoe introduces embellishments, personal glosses, and general updating.[12] Yet the presence of Camden and Gibson usually produces no feeling of intrusion. Defoe has made the blood of *Britannia* circulate through his own *Tour,* and amazingly the body displays every sign of rude health, for the borrowings are part of the design.[13]

There is one particular factor that enables Defoe to achieve this effect. His own "design" is quite different from that of his predecessor. Camden/Gibson is organized by counties, and starts from the remote southwestern peninsula of Cornwall. More importantly, these counties are themselves defined by the British tribes who lived in a given area at the time of the Roman occupation. Thus, the work proceeds not as a series of tours, or indeed by any sort of formal itinerary. It follows another traditional form of topographical writing: it is a survey, and that survey is at root antiquarian in nature, as expressed by its reliance on the model of *Roman* Britain. Defoe's text looks so different because it deals ostensibly with the contemporary: the book starts from London and, for the first seven letters, returns there on a regular basis. It takes no particular notice of county boundaries, even though the individual letters refer in their titles to the counties which are traversed. Finally, it simulates an actual journey, and it takes account of features (such as landscape, the agricultural character of a district, or the weather encountered) that Camden's method almost entirely precludes. The result is that Defoe's non-antiquarian form allows him to slip in a mass of antiquarian matter, largely filched from those who had gone before.

Part II

Text

But to describe a Country by Way of Journey, in a private Capacity, as has been the Case here, though it requires a particular Application, to what may be learn'd from due Enquiry and from Conversation, yet it admits not the Observer to dwell upon every Nicety, to measure the Distances, and exactly determine the Scite, the Dimensions, or the Extent of Places, or read the Histories of them. But it is giving an Account by way of Essay, or, as the Moderns call it, by Memoirs of the present State of Things, in a familiar Manner. (1: 251)

4

The Rhetoric of Growth and Decay

W E now move from the way Defoe compiled his book to its rhetorical form and literary components: in particular, to habits of style, to
use of allusion, and to techniques of rendering a narrative progression.

I

In the "Introduction" to the first volume of his *Tour,* as we have
seen, Defoe sets up an elaborate contrast between past and present.
One image he employs to bring out the constant process of national
re-creation is that of a growing child:

> But after all that has been said by others, or can be said here, no Descrip-
> tion of *Great Britain* can be, what we call a finished Account, as no
> Cloaths can be made to fit a growing Child; no Picture carry the Likeness
> of a Living Face; the Size of one, and the Countenance of the other always
> altering with Time, so no Account of a Kingdom thus Daily altering its
> Countenance, can be Perfect. (1: 4)

Defoe understood perfectly well that the changing countenance of
Britain implied removal as well as addition. While his main stress is
on the rising prosperity of the country, there is another aspect of
change that is often neglected. Witness this section from the "Preface"
to Volume III:

> As I mentioned in the last Volume, every New View of *Great Britain*
> would require a New Description; the Improvements that encrease, the
> New Buildings erected, the Old Buildings taken down. . . . These Things
> open new Scenes every Day, and make *England* especially shew a new
> and differing Face in many Places, on every Occasion of Surveying it.
> (2: 535)

It is easy to overlook that phrase about "Old Buildings taken down,"
yet a close inspection of the text shows that Defoe was fully conscious

of the dual face of change. One of his favorite devices is the use of contrast, sometimes couched in terms of growth—"rising" towns or "flourishing" country—against a set of counterimages of exhaustion—"barren" land or "broken" ruins. Together these body forth the plenti-tude of the island, expressed in the rhetorical variety of the text.

This is not the picture given us by most commentators on the *Tour*, who see it as a celebration of the new England. G. D. H. Cole, for example, writes with enviable confidence, "Defoe's *Tour* is to be read, then, to-day above all for the light it throws on the economic and social condition of England half a century or so before the coming of the Industrial Revolution."[1] Cole believed that Defoe was at his best in describing "what seemed to him really living and important," i.e., "the great social transition he saw proceeding around him."[2] More explicit still is this passage:

> The things he looked for on his journeys were by no means those which appealed to the ordinary tourist of his day or our own. For "antiquities" he had something of scorn; he liked towns which excelled not in the "tumbledown picturesque," but in good, clean, well-built modern houses; he liked a countryside full of corn and cattle, rather than views and roman-tic wildness; and, above all, his interest was always in the present rather than the past. Not that he was unable to appreciate a fine old building or a "view" which conformed to his sense of beauty. But these were not the thing he was in search of, and he gave them but a passing mention. What really interested him was the state of the country in a social and eco-nomic sense.[3]

This is a splendid account of the "official" meaning of the book. The deeper implications of the *Tour* run in a different course, however. Defoe, true, has a marvelously acute sense of *process*. And this comes out not only in his joyous welcome to the new commercial ventures of his day. He does write of the emerging order in graphic and warmly appreciative language. But he repeatedly sets against his picture of health and plenty an idiom of devastation. His *Tour* is pervaded by a sense of the fragility of human contrivances, very close to Pope's in that most central Augustan document, the *Epistle to Burlington*.

Take the account of Dunwich in Suffolk:

> This Town is a Testimony of the decay of Publick Things, Things of the most durable Nature. . . . The Ruins of *Carthage*, of the great City of *Jerusalem*, or of antient *Rome*, are not at all Wonderful to me; the Ruins of *Nineveh*, which are so entirely sunk, as that 'tis doubtful where the City stood; The Ruins of *Babylon*, or the Great *Persepolis*, and many Capital Cities, which Time and the Change of Monarchies have Over-

thrown; these, I say, are not at all Wonderful, because being the Capitals of great and flourishing Kingdoms, where those Kingdoms were Over-thrown, the Capital Cities necessarily fell with them; But for a private Town, a Sea-Port, and a Town of Commerce, to Decay, as it were of itself (for we never read of *Dunwich* being Plundered, or Ruin'd, by any Disas-ter, at least not of late Years); this I must confess, seems owing to nothing but the Fate of Things, by which we see that Towns, Kings, Countries, Families, and Persons, have all their Elevation, their Medium, their Decli-nation, and even their Destruction in the Womb of Time, and the Course of Nature. It is true, this Town is manifestly decayed by the invasion of the Waters, and as other Towns seem sufferers by the Sea, or the Tide withdrawing from their Ports, such as *Orford,* just now named; *Winchelsea* in *Kent,* and the like; So this Town is, as it were, eaten up by the Sea, as above; and the still encroaching Ocean seems to threaten it with a fatal Immersion in a few Years more. (1: 54).

This is not an isolated purple passage. Throughout the book we get the same sensitivity to the depredations of time, in the manner almost of an Elizabethan sonneteer. It is this that gives tension and energy to what might otherwise be a perfunctory survey of "the improving temper of the present age" (1: 44).[4]

If we look closely at the passage quoted, it is evident that the leading terms—the words and images that carry the principal emotional charge—have very little to do with anything Cole described. These include *decay, Ruins* (three times), *Time and Change, Overthrown* (twice), *fell, Decay* again, *Plundered or Ruin'd* (note the capitals, very rare here for verbs), *Disaster, Fate, Declination, Destruction, Womb of Time and Course of Nature, decayed* yet again, *invasion, sufferers, eaten up, encroaching, threaten,* and *fatal Immersion.* This is the vo-cabulary of elegy, or of a medieval *ubi sunt* lament (the idea of the wheel of fortune is very close), and not the language of confidential social prophecy.

Since this conclusion departs so widely from what has been the accepted view of the literary substance of the *Tour,*[5] a more detailed and scrupulous analysis of this idiom is plainly required. I shall take, first, the language of growth; second, that of decay; and third, the passages of juxtaposed imagery that lend to the *Tour* its most distinc-tive artistic effects.

The vocabulary of growth, then, corresponds to that celebratory element in the "official" *Tour,* located by Cole and others. It makes heavy use of words such as *plenty* (often with *vast*), *health(y), bounty, growing, prolifick, rise/rising, improve(ment), luxuriant, nourish, thriving* and so on. An important class of words is that of *flourish(ing), fertile,* and *fruitful.* The first of these occurs some thirty times: in about ten of those cases, *flourish* comes in immediate proximity to another key term, *increase.* As for *fertile,* it is found fifteen times, mostly in the first three-quarters of the book—Scotland, understandably enough in Defoe's terms, rarely inspires the word. *Fruitful* is more common, with forty instances spread quite evenly through the *Tour.* This compares with the most common term of general approbation implying a smiling landscape or a prosperous town—*pleasant,* which turns up over ninety times. This count is in some ways misleading—*pleasant* sometimes figures in a rather negative context, as where it is used four times in a description of the disadvantages from which the site of Edinburgh appears to suffer (2: 710).[6]

The most significant individual word, however, is *increase,* either as noun or verb. (Defoe more commonly spells it with an initial *e,* though the variant *i* creeps in steadily towards the close.) This appears at least 140 times in the text, an extraordinarily high figure compared with its frequency in ordinary discourse.[7] In no author-concordance that I have checked with does *increase* figure among the hundred commonest words listed. Even if one included particles such as *and, the,* and *of,* Defoe must use *increase* among his fifty commonest. Moreover, as with *quantity,* this overall dominance goes with exceptional density in specific regions of the text. Sometimes Defoe repeats *increase* with almost reckless unconcern. It occurs five times in ten lines in the description of refugees employed in Canterbury (1: 118). Exactly the same ratio appears in the entry for Bristol (2: 435), where *prodigious, flourishing, magnitude,* and *swell'd* are also in evidence. Four instances at a short interval, allied with *prodigious, quantity, populous,* and *number,* are found here:

> If they were so populous at that time, how much must they be encreased since? and especially since the late Revolution, the Trade having been prodigiously encouraged and encreased by the great Demand for their *Kersies* for clothing the Armies abroad, insomuch that it is the Opinion of some that know the Town, and its Bounds very well, that the Number of People in the Vicaridge of *Hallifax,* is encreased one fourth, at least, within the last forty Years, that is to say, since the late Revolution. Nor is it improbable at all, for besides the Number of Houses which are encreased, they have entered upon a new Manufacture which was never made in those Parts before, at least, not in any Quantities, I mean, the Manufactures of *Shalloons.* . . . (2: 605)

There is something very revelatory about Defoe's adjustment of sense in "which was never made . . . before, at least not in any Quantities, I mean." Literal nouns such as *trade* and *manufacture* call for little gloss, frequent as they are. The point about *increase* is that it is used in a whole gradation of meanings, from literal to the quasi-figurative.

Sometimes it is both subject and predicate, applied to persons and things, indicative and conditional, active and passive all at once:

> The *Manchester* Trade we all know; and all that are concerned in it know that it is, as all our other Manufactures are, very much encreased within these thirty or forty Years especially beyond what it was before; and as the Manufacture is encreased, the People must be encreased of course. It is true, that the encrease of Manufacture may be by its extending it self farther in the Country, and so more Hands may be employed in the County without any encrease in the Town. But I answer, that though this is possible, yet as the Town and Parish of *Manchester* is the Center of the Manufacture, the encrease of that Manufacture would certainly encrease there first, and then the People not being there sufficient, it might spread it self further. But the encrease of Buildings at *Manchester* within these few Years, is a Confirmation of the encrease of People. . . . (2: 670–71)

Some degree of repetition might be put down to journalistic haste or clumsiness. But nine occurrences in so short a space lead one to the conclusion that Defoe is doing something analogous to poetic reshaping—scrutinizing a word as he repeats it, as with "wit" in the *Essay on Criticism*. There is an even greater huddle in the account of Dumfries (2: 725). Here Defoe argues that the growth of trade and the growth of population are interdependent. His main rhetorical bridging device is the bare word *increase*.

This brings us naturally to another leading idea, generally covered by *populous*. The word is endemic in nineteenth-century gazetteers of Britain and America, and Defoe makes less personal capital out of it than he does with *increase* or *quantity*. Nonetheless, a term that is not exactly ubiquitous in everday speech crops up a scarcely credible 120 times. One sign that the expression carries a lower resonance for Defoe, despite its currency, is the fact that it never appears in high concentration—rarely more than twice in a given paragraph. It is habitually found in conjunction with *exceeding(ly)* or with a number of syntactically parallel adjectives—*rich, large, well-built,* and the like. *Populous* might have been considered above, along with *abundance,* but it generally occurs in a "growth" context, whereas *abundance* is a routine trick of speech with Defoe and can turn up anywhere.

Directly opposed to this set of terms we find a whole thesaurus of "decay." The more regular expressions include *destroy/destruction;* as well as *decrepid, sterile,* and *desert.* In the late sections particularly *sink* becomes an important antonym of *rise.*[8] *Remains* is common, while *ruin* and its derivatives can be found forty-odd times. But much the most important single term is *decay* itself, with just over a hundred instances. Many of these form part of an oxymoron, with *growth* the contrary idea. But the word claims attention for its own sake, especially in the Scottish portions. This passage on Ayr does employ the growth—decay paradox, but the sheer iteration of this latter component stands out just as conspicuously.

> *Air* . . . was formerly a large City, had a good Harbour, and a great Trade: I must acknowledge to you, that tho' I believe it never was a City, yet it has certainly been a good Town, and much bigger than it is now: At present like an old Beauty, it shews the Ruins of a good Face; but is also apparently, not only decay'd and declin'd, but decaying and declining every Day, and from being the fifth Town in *Scotland,* as the Townsmen say, is now like a Place forsaken; the Reason of its Decay, is, the Decay of its Trade, so true is it, that Commerce is the Life of Nations, of Cities, of Towns, Harbours, and of the whole Prosperity of a Country; What the Reason of the Decay of Trade here was, or when it first began to decay, is hard to determine. . . . (2: 739)

An equally marked concentration is found in the passage on Dunfermline, where Defoe spells out the "threefold" decay of the town. The word occurs six times, along with *demolish'd, ruins, fallen* (in and down), *monuments, sinking, moulder'd away, injury of time,* and *irrecoverable.* "We may now call it," the text glumly observes, "the Monument of a Court" (2:774).

As already indicated, this notion of decay is frequently associated with a sense of the lapse of time. The most striking single instance is perhaps "Time, the great Devourer of the Works of Men" (2: 447). Among other phrases used are "defac'd by time," "Time has made it look gross and rough," "the very ruins almost eaten up by time," "defaced with age," "sunk into time," "sunk into their own ruins by the mere length of time," "to crumble and suffer by time," and "the meer injury of time." At the end of Letter IX, Defoe allows himself a more sustained meditation on the ruins of time, in a vein quite different from anything Cole's description would suggest:

> I cannot but say, that since I entred upon the View of these Northern Counties, I have many times repented that I so early resolved to decline the delightful View of Antiquity, here being so great and so surprizing a Variety, and every Day more and more discovered; and abundance since the Tour which the learned Mr. *Cambden* made this Way, nay, many since his Learned Continuator; for as the Trophies, the Buildings, the religious, as well as military Remains, as well of the *Britains,* as of the *Romans, Saxons,* and *Normans,* are but, as we may say, like Wounds hastily healed up, the *Calous* spread over them being removed, they appear presently;

and though the Earth, which naturally eats into the strongest Stones, Metals, or whatever Substance, simple or compound, is or can be by Art or Nature prepared to endure it, has defaced the Surface, the Figures and Inscriptions upon most of these things, yet they are beautiful, even in their decay, and the venerable Face of Antiquity has something so pleasing, so surprizing, so satisfactory in it, especially to those who have with any Attention read the Histories of pass'd Ages, that I know nothing renders Travelling more pleasant and more agreeable. (2: 663)

A portion from this piece of prose will be quoted subsequently (p. 144): but the whole passage deserves notice, since it brings together so many of the recurrent topoi I have considered.

Nor is the succeeding paragraph any less revealing: here Defoe adopts a curious self-dramatizing mode, full of the vocabulary of puri-tan discipline.

But I have condemn'd my self (unhappily) to Silence upon this Head, and therefore, resolving however to pay this Homage to the Dust of gallant Men and glorious Nations, I say therefore, I must submit and go on; and as I resolve once more to travel through all these Northern Countries upon this very Errand, and to please, nay, satiate myself with a strict Search into every thing that is curious in Nature and Antiquity. I mortify my self now with the more ease, in hopes of letting the World see, some time or other, that I have not spent those Hours in a vain and Barren Search, or come back without a sufficient Reward to all the labours of a diligent Enquirer; but of this by the way. (2: 663)

With its slightly chastened air of anxious self-inquiry, the tone here is closer to that of Defoe's novels, particularly *Robinson Crusoe*, than anywhere else in the book. Significantly, the extra imaginative potency enters the *Tour* in the shadow of the ruins of time.[9] Not for the only time, Defoe shows himself an antiquarian *manqué*.

Third and lastly, we come to Defoe's strategic contrast between the two elements I have just considered, growth and decay. At its simplest, the device consists of a violent oxymoron set up within these terms. Thus, we find *full perfection of decay* and *very perfection of decay* with similar phrases. (There is an equivalent paradox used to underline the emphasis on *quantity;* several times, Defoe speaks of *an innumerable number!*) However, the opposition is often more elaborate and more interesting. "If contraries illustrate . . .," Defoe once muses (2: 583); and his technique does indeed rely heavily on the interplay of favorite Augustan antinomies—Nature and Art figured in the last quotation, and they appear together on half a dozen further occasions.[10]

Nevertheless, it is the contrast between expansion and contraction that most occupies Defoe. On the one side there is *overplus, enlarge-ment,* the world of *profitable* and *delightful* activity. Set squarely up against this is the world of *neglect,* of *shattered* buildings, and *desert* countryside. One pole connotes life, health, and fecundity; the other suggests *dying of age, sinking into rubbish* (a surprisingly common noun), and *burying beneath time.*[11] Images of *plenty, bounty,* and *wealth,* are directly confronted by *disaster, calamities,* and *delapida-tion.* Filtered through one set of terms, Britain is *populous, growing,* and *prolific:* through the other, it is seen as *stript, sterile,* and *waste.* The nation's treasure is *inexhaustible,* her citadels *so undemolished still* (1: 170, a strange locution). Yet in the same breath Defoe will show us mines *quite exhausted* or towns *all demolished.*[12]

There are some sixty passages in which this contrast is drawn out most explicitly. In my view they are the key sections by which the imaginative contours of the *Tour* are defined. The general character of their contribution to Defoe's purposes can be gauged from a sample survey. Apart from the passage on Dunwich already quoted, there is the carefully etched "View of the Difference between the present and the past Greatness of this mighty City, called *London*" (1: 332); and the detailed comparison of English and Scottish palaces:

> *Greenwich* and *Nonsuch* are demolished,
> *Richmond* quite out of Use, and not able to receive a Court.
> *Winchester,* never inhabited, or half finished.
> *Whitehall* burnt, and lying in Ruins . . .
> *Westminster,* long since abandon'd . . .
> Whereas the Kings of *Scotland* had in King *James* the VIth's Time all in good Repair, and in Use, The several Royal Palaces . . . (2: 776)

Of course, added force is imparted to this contrast by the fact that it runs in the opposite direction from the prevailing antithesis between prosperous England and economically backward Scotland.

There is a highly representative example in a short space when the narrative reaches Stirling. The castle here prompts characteristic musings:

> The Palace and Royal Apartments are very magnificent, but all in Decay, and must be so: Were the Materials of any Use, We thought it would be much better to pull them down than to let such noble Buildings sink into their own Rubbish, by the meer Injury of Time: But it is at present the Fate of all the Royal Houses in *Scotland* . . . (2: 753)

It is the loss of "noble" and "magnificent" buildings that makes their current state so unbearable to contemplate.

Defoe returns obsessively to this way of polarizing the data available
to him. The town of Bideford has *flourished;* its twin, the town of
Barnstaple rather *declined,* because of an involuntary rivalry (1: 260).
Again, "if we calculate Things present, by Things past, the Town of
Minehead is risen out of the Decay of the Towns of *Porlock* and *Watchet*" (1: 268). The town of Ancaster *swelled* up into a city, but is
now *sunk* again out of knowledge (2: 501). York is none the less
beautiful because its ancient fortifications are now demolished, "for
the beauty of Peace is seen in the rubbish" (2: 636). Appleby was
once a *flourishing* city, but is now a *scattering, decayed,* and *half-
demolished town* (2: 681: many other similar examples). Haddington
shows the marks of *decayed beauty:* it is easy to see it is not what it
had been, but an "old half ruin'd, yet remaining Town" (2: 700).
Nothing will save Ayr from death, if trade does not revive; Ludlow
shows in it decay, what it was in its flourishing estate. Defoe often
extracts a wry humor from this contradiction: at Worcester, he says,
"I went to see the Town-House, which afforded nothing worth taking
notice of, unless it be how much it wants to be mended with a new
one" (2: 443). While at Doncaster:

> This Town, Mr. *Cambden* says, was burnt entirely to the Ground, *Anno*
> 759, and is hardly recovered yet; but I must say, it is so well recoverd,
> that I see no Ruins appear, and indeed, being almost a thousand Years ago,
> I know not how there should; and besides, the Town seems as if it wanted
> another Conflagration, for it looks old again, and many of the Houses
> ready to fall. (2: 589)

Abbotsbury, Defoe observes with contempt, is a town "anciently famous for a great Monastery, and now eminent for nothing but its
Ruins" (1: 214). The abbey at Bury St. Edmunds is demolished, and
"its Ruins are all that is to be seen of its Glory" (1: 50).

Two personal elements can be detected in all this. In the first place,
Defoe was obviously keenly interested in the process of restoration
after a disaster. It does not seem rash to attribute this to his own
experience of the Great Fire and the subsequent rebuilding of London.
Possibly, one might see the Restoration of the monarchy, that crucial
event for the people of seventeenth-century England, as going some
way to explain Defoe's perpetual recourse to phrases like "a general
Ruin a little recover'd" (1: 118) or, used of York, "'tis risen again"
out of decay (2: 636). Of course, Defoe does explicitly refer both to
the rebuilding operations and to the King's return; but it may be that
his attitudes were affected on a deeper level too. The Civil War had
riven the nation as no other event in recent English history, and its

consequences still hung around in the nation's awareness. Indeed, there were still many physical traces in the landscape of the great seventeenth-century struggles that a traveler could not miss (see chapter 5, pp. 138–39).

In the second place, as previously noted, there is a notable tendency to harp on the calamitous effects of the South Sea Bubble.[13] As one who had twice known bankruptcy, it is to be expected that Defoe would have this recent trauma in the national expeience strongly imprinted on his mind. All the same, Defoe seems even more obsessed by the topic than one would have anticipated. He just cannot keep off it. And it is not simply that he mentions the Bubble and its effects so regularly: his writing takes on a special plangency at such moments, and the familiar imagery of growth and decay is invested with a poetry rarely found in his "creative" work. For example, after dilating on the glory of the houses on the outskirts of London ("they reflect Beauty, and Magnificence upon the whole Country, and give a kind of Character to the Island of *Great Britain* in general"), Defoe turns to the wealth of the city that makes possible building on such a scale: but there is another side. This has already been quoted in the Introduction to the present book (p. 32), but it needs to appear once more:

> It would also take up a large Chapter in this Book, to but mention the overthrow, and Catastrophe of innumerable Wealthy City Families, who after they have thought their Houses establish'd, and have built their Magnificent Country Seats, as well as others, have sunk under the Misfortunes of Business, and the Disasters of Trade, after the World has thought them pass'd all possibility of Danger. . . . (1: 169)

An even more lyrical passage on the "Misfortunes of Business, and the Disasters of Trade" occurs at the end of the first letter. Defoe describes with enthusiasm Wanstead House, the home of the mercantile Child family, and then sets out a threnody on the "general Possession" of South Sea (quoted on p. 32). This is much more than a diatribe against the villainy of stockjobbing. It outlines a little tragic plot, where pity and grief unite in a studied lament on the mutability of things.

How conscious was Defoe of what, on this showing, he was providing through the rhetoric of his *Tour*? Reasonably so, it would appear. His preface announces at the very start all the leading themes—*the most flourishing and opulent Country in the World*, and *a flowing Variety of Materials*, as well as *Novelty* opposed to *Antiquity*. In the third paragraph, *encrease* turns up three times; other metaphoric terms include *luxuriance, harvest, face of things, glean*, and *fruitful*. And by the second page, it is evident that the growth—decay syndrome is present in the writer's mind:

The Fate of Things gives a New Face to Things, produces Changes in *low* Life, and innumerable Incidents; plants and supplants Families, raises and sinks Towns, removes Manufactures, and Trade; Great Towns decay, and small Towns rise; new Towns, new Palaces, new Seats are built every Day; great Rivers and good Harbours dry up, and grow useless; again, new Ports are open'd, Brooks are made Rivers, small Rivers, navigable Ports and Harbours are made where none was before and the like.

Several Towns, which Antiquity speaks of as considerable, are now lost and swallow'd up by the Sea, as *Dunwich* in *Suffolk* for one; and others, which Antiquity knew nothing of, are now grown considerable: In a Word, New Matter offers to new Observation, and they who write next, may perhaps find as much room for enlarging upon us, as we do upon those that have gone before. (1: 2)

It would be futile to list all the favorite items from Defoe's vocabulary here. Enough to recognize the general effect, which is distinctively Augustan—antithetical, elevated, sententious, *eloquent* to its nerve ends. One can hardly doubt that, in setting these pointed lines at the head of his work, Defoe knew what he was doing. This is the idiom of one habituated to *placing* things; to comparing, contrasting, sorting, and arranging experience. It is a rhetoric of process, which disposes and aligns facts within a historical sequence.

II

It is ironic that the *Tour* has been left aside as prosaic and literal, compared with Defoe's fictional output. The truth is that, if anything, it is Defoe the novelist who sticks within the possible, and rates verisimilitude above what might be summed up by "the marvelous." The *Tour* is a sustained exercise in the marvelous. Skeptical as Defoe may be with regard to folk tales, and to "wonders" of the kind encountered in the Peak (see chapter 7), he is warmly hospitable towards wonders of another kind. He is fascinated by extremes of scale, of volume, of age, of frequency, of wealth, of abundance—in short, any distributable or variable feature of life. His rhetorical forms are driven constantly towards exaggeration.[14] Not, that is, the exaggeration of "stretching," where all figures are doubled and all exceptions quietly forgotten. Rather, Defoe exaggerates by seeking out and citing the extreme case. He does not necessarily falsify matters: he simply fixes his attention on the most striking data he can find. His *Tour* of Britain incorporates the function of a publication such as the *Guinness Book of Records;* he collects all-time highs like an avid cricket or baseball statistician. Arguably, this is the common coin of journalism, but few pass the currency with such spendthrift profusion.

There are three ways in which this concern affects the words on the page: that is, three varieties of hyperbole that sustain this rhetoric.

The first is the direct superlative. Almost every paragraph in the three volumes contains a real or implicit superlative; I will take a single example, chosen pretty much at random (other passages would certainly show a higher density of cases):

> The best Ornament of the City [Chester], is, that the Streets are very broad and fair, and run through the whole City in strait Lines, crossing in the Middle of the City, as at *Chichester:* The Walls, as I have said, are in very good repair, and it is a very pleasant Walk around the City, upon the Walls, and within the Battlements, from whence you may see the Country round; and particularly on the side of the *Roodee,* which I mentioned before, which is a fine large low Green, on the Bank of the *Dee.* In the Winter this Green is often under Water by the Inundations of the River, and a little before I came there, they had such a terrible Land Flood, which flow'd 8 Foot higher than usual so that it not only overflowed the said Green, call'd the *Roodee,* but destroy'd a fine new Wharf and Landing-Place for Goods, a little below the Town, bore down all the Warehouses, and other Buildings, which the Merchants had erected for securing their Goods, and carried all away Goods and Buildings together, to the irreparable Loss of the Persons concern'd: Also beyond the *Roodee,* one sees from the Walls of *Chester* the County of *Flint,* and the Mountains of *Wales, a Prospect best indeed, at a Distance.* (2: 469)

In this paragraph of 219 words, Defoe employs (i) grammatical superlatives, as *the best Ornament,* and *a Prospect best indeed;* (ii) grammatical comparatives, as *8 Foot higher than usual;* (iii) what might be termed implicit superlatives, as *very broad and fair, very good Repair,* and *very pleasant Walk;* (iv) words connoting totality or absolute state, as *the whole City, the Country round, all the Warehouses,* and *carried all away;* (v) terms of "ultimate" state—this constitutes another hyperbole, and is exemplified by *irreparable;* (vi) words whose semantic basis includes a superlative or comparative notion, as *fine large low Green, often under Water,* and *such a terrible Land Flood;* and (vii) other phrases with an additive effect, as *not only . . . but . . . also.*

Some of these categories call for no special comment. As regards the method of the entire book, it should be noted that a common locution, *the most* ———, may qualify for either (i) or (iii).[15] The most important class, however, in its bearing on the *Tour* at large, is item (vi). This is like (ii), except that there is no modifier such as *most, very, exceeding(ly)*. All the superlative force comes from within the lexical unit itself. Good examples are *prodigious*, which occurs over seventy times in the text along with *prodigy*, a rarer variant. The word commonly comes up in juxtaposition to nouns such as *sum, number, trade, increase, expence*, and *quantity*. (*Vast* is often attached to the same nouns, as of 1: 82.) Each of these is a significant term in the idiom of the *Tour*, and several will be mentioned again. Another instance is the word *immense*, with its adverbial form. This comes about twenty times, generally with application to a noun like *estate, wealth*, and *sum*, or the adjective *rich*. A third case is furnished by *infinite(ly)*. Here there are forty occurrences, often in relation to *populous, full*, and *number*. Finally, there is *exceeding(ly)/excess(ive)*; I have noted thirty usages, with *populous, rich*, and *fine* common adjuncts. A number of other expressions turn up with slightly less regularity, but they serve a similar purpose. Among these are *eminent(ly), extraordinary* (with *more than ordinary*, etc.), *monstrous(ly)*, and *extreme* with its derivatives, all of which appear eight or more times. "Monsters for Magnitude" (1: 347) is a noun-based variant.

For the rest, the true superlatives include two curious forms, *beautifullest* (twice) and *frightfullest*. In category (iii) certain adverbial phrases are of common resort, for instance, *without exception, beyond (without) comparison, to the last extremity*, and *heightened to such a degree*.[16] *A pretty many* is one unusual expression.

The second mode of hyperbole could be described as the use of "terms of ultimate state." The simplest form this takes is the verbal shape IN(UN)——IBLE(ABLE). Frequent examples are *incredible, innumerable, impossible, inexhaustible*, and *invaluable*. Others that occur more sporadically are *insupportable, indelible, unaccountable, irresistible, unpassable, indefatigable, intollerable, inexpressible, inestimable, invulnerable, inaccessible, impregnable, indissolvable* (of the Union with Scotland), and *irreparable*. There are closely allied forms like *unprecedented*. However, Defoe can achieve the same effect with a phrase, for example, *all the magnificence . . . imaginable, in the fewest words imaginable* (a pure superlative, looked at in another way), *never to be exhausted, not to be matched, hardly to be valued*, and *not to be described*. This last belongs to a group of negative formulae that Defoe uses freely: *so beautiful no pen can describe* is another variant. There is a strange concentration of these negatives in Letter V. Perhaps London seemed so vast and marvelous to Defoe that ordinary superlatives were inadequate. At all events, four pages concerned with the City of London (1: 340–44) supply more than half the book's quota of these phrases; the basic pattern is along the lines "No Accounts in the World are more exactly kept, no Place in the World has so much Business done, with so much Ease . . . nobody is either denied or delayed Payment . . . nothing can be shewn like it in the whole World . . . no Sum is so great, but the *Bank* has been able to raise . . . nor can a Breach be now made on any Terms . . . nothing can be more exact . . . nothing can be more regular. . .we see nothing of this at *Paris,* at *Amsterdam,* at *Hamburgh* . . . " and so on. All these are ways of connoting the *unparalleled* wealth, power, and importance of Britain, a leading strategy of the *Tour.*[17]

A third form of hyperbole resides in the stress laid on sheer multiplicity. There is a whole repertory of words to suggest repletion. They include *numerous, innumerable, not to be numbered, multiplied, crowd,* and *throng,* as well as an odd little group of words *concourse,* and *conflux, confluence,* and *flux,* used of people—generally the gentry or polite society. More important under this aspect are epithets such as *considerable*[18] and *populous,* and the verb *increase,* discussed earlier in this chapter. However, the main work is done by *quantity,* which astonishingly enters the text no less than two hundred times. (By contrast, *quality* appears fewer than half a dozen times). The phrase *vast quantity* accounts for twenty-four of these; *prodigious quantity* for twenty; and *great quantity* for eighty-four. The sheer iterative power of the word, hammering away through the entire book contributes a great deal to the sense of abundance Defoe is seeking.

More than that, its overall density is backed by a few areas of high concentration, where the term is sown through the prose with almost reckless abandon. Usually these areas of the text are concerned with trade under one aspect or another. Thus, the famous description of Stourbridge Fair has fourteen instances of *quantity* in little more than two pages (1: 82–84). An even higher density occurs in the description of Clackmannan: the county produces not merely "the best" coal in Scotland, but also—a far heavier stress—the "greatest Quantity" (2: 801). Other passages showing heavy concentration include that on the Wiltshire wool trade (1: 283–85: thirteen instances); that on the fisheries off the west coast of Scotland (2: 829: six occurrences within three short paragraphs); and that on the Milton/Maidstone district of Kent (1: 113–14: eight uses of *quantity*). In all these sections of the book, other words discussed here are prominent—for example, *prodigious, numbers, inexhaustible, populous,* and so on.

Just now I had recourse to the word "abundance." *Abundant* and *abundance* figure largely in Defoe's own writing: there are almost eighty examples. This is to a great extent explained by his fondness for the construction *abundance of,* meaning "many." The phrase has no article and takes a plural verb as a rule, seemingly by attraction from the noun governed—as, "there are abundance of poor." Defoe places little emphasis on the word, but it does provide further support for the rhetoric of quantity operating throughout the book.[19]

The most distinctive single feature of Defoe's style at large is his fondness for what I have termed elsewhere "approximating" and "alternative" counts.[20] The former is the use of a figure with some expression of vagueness, as in "about a mile," or "not above 22 miles." The latter takes the form "two or three," "60 or 80 barrels," "70, 80, or 100 miles," and so on. Both are ubiquitous in Defoe's writing. I have discussed their employment in *Robinson Crusoe* and *Moll Flanders;* but they occur just as frequently in other long narratives such as *Captain Singleton* and *A New Voyage Round the World.* It will occasion no surprise to discover that both formulas are used hundreds of times in the *Tour.* The simplest kind of usage abounds, for example a reference to "a vast Tract of Land, some of it within Seventeen or Eighteen Miles of the Capital City" (1: 143). Or, much later in the text, a mention of Elgin as being "above 450 measur'd Miles from *London,* and more, if we must go by *Edinburgh*" (2: 816). There are more indirect variants ("not yet of 200 Years standing," 2: 426), and even what might be termed near-approximations: as on the River Trent, which has "a great many (some say thirty, and that thence it had its Name) little Rivulets into it" (2: 544). Sometimes the two manners of counting are combined, as in "above 20 or 30 Foot in Length" (1: 225). The effect may be, as suggested on an earlier occasion, compulsive mensuration even where accurate counting is not possible; but it obviously conveys a kind of honesty and a desire to be as precise as is reliably possible. When Defoe tells the story of the highwayman Nicks (whose ride to York prefigures the legend of Dick Turpin), he describes how the criminal obtained an alibi when he reached York. The mayor consults his watch at the request of Nicks— it was "a quarter before, or a quarter after Eight at Night" (1: 104). This studied vagueness is Defoe's way of telling us that he does not vouch for the exact details, as he has done elsewhere in the story. It is one more means of increasing the plausibility of his account.

Collectively, these devices serve to intensify the reader's sense of size and opulence. By hyperbole and quantification (the latter made more credible by its deliberate vagueness), Defoe suggests that a vast drama is being played out in the physical and social theater which is Britain. The nation is a fluid entity, where things are constantly on the move, and only an alert observer such as the industrious Defoe can keep track of its shifting patterns. Once again there is an ideology behind the rhetoric. Trade is the ultimate engine of this dynamic process, and commercial imperatives underlie the recurrent succession of changes, visible in the social landscape as well as the natural order. *Britannia* had appeared to survey a static world, where the remnants of antiquity still formed the landmarks of the modern nation. In the *Tour* we are presented with a process of unending flux, with which the busy narrator attempts to cope, as around him buildings crumble and bridges suddenly appear, where one town flourishes while another falls into decrepitude, and where gain and loss mingle in a pulsating system of circulation.[21] The *Tour*'s own "circuits" mimic this cycle of flux and reflux, as its author struggles to keep up with the process of growth and decay.[22]

5

The Georgic Element in the *Tour*

DEFOE'S use of *Britannia,* studied in chapter 3, represents mainly the quarrying of information from a convenient source. In this chapter we look at a more inward and even submerged kind of intertextuality, affecting the literary mode rather than the informational content of the *Tour.*

I

It has long been a commonplace that Virgil in general, the *Georgics* in particular, exercised a profound influence on English literature of the Augustan age (something that very epithet converts into a near tautology). John Chalker's book provides a reminder of this pervasive strain in eighteenth-century verse.[1] However, it has not to my knowledge been pointed out that prose of the period also betrays a measure of Georgic influence. Many people might consider Daniel Defoe the least Virgilian of writers, and his *Tour* as embodying his absence of "poetic" qualities. On this reading, the *Tour* would exemplify the forward-looking, confident optimism of the new commercial England; its guidebook form would contrast sharply with the deeply personal imaginative vehicle forged by the Latin poet; and its dry functionalism would stand at the opposite pole from Virgil's rich resources of language and imagery. The *Georgics* and the *Tour* would be literary antitheses.

There is, indeed, no call to invent a straw argument along these lines. The case had been made, in effect. Paul Fussell's remarks focus the line of thinking I have just outlined. We have only to substitute for Johnson (the repository, in Fussell's terms, of humanistic lore and attitudes) the name of that poet whom the eighteenth-century humanists so revered:

> To juxtapose Defoe's *Tour through England and Wales* with Johnson's *Journey to the Western Islands* is to perceive an important difference be-

tween the "modern" and the humanistic in the travel book. Defoe focuses on the benefits of trade and the progress of industry. To him, the merit of a city or town is a function of its manufactures; the idea of progress lurks behind each of his responses and judgments. But Johnson, betraying the natural turn for elegy with which all humanists are afflicted, focuses on the past, and on the enduring, the permanent, and the unchanging. What emerges from Johnson's travel book is not the sense of kinesis and change that Defoe projects: it is instead the colossal and permanent irony of tiny man attempting to defeat time and the elements by works of stone, the ultimate irony of man's attempt to defeat mortality by works of virtue. On the other hand, the road that Defoe chooses to explore is a precursor of Whitman's in *Song of the Open Road* ... Defoe and Whitman are prepared for no complications, and they encounter none.[2]

Fussell has actually invented a book here (or the Everyman edition did it for him).[3] And his account of the *Tour* offers little more than a series of half-truths. On a general basis, it would not be hard to show (1) that for Defoe change is often entropy, the irresistible decline of things, just as often as it is "progress"; (2) that, so far from rejecting complexity, Defoe's attitudes are again and again utterly mixed—his baffled reaction finding rhetorical expression in a constant recourse to paradox and antithesis;[4] or (3) that Defoe, too, fixes insistently on the past, so that both the content and tone of his book are for long stretches authentically "elegiac" in quality. But each of these attri-butes shows up in a more restricted context: what can be identified as the "Georgic" framework of the *Tour*. And rather than follow out the general issues, it will be more economical to stick close to the particular—in other words, to Virgil.

The debt inheres in two modes of parallelism: detailed similarities at a local level, amounting almost to borrowing; and broad thematic analogies. I will consider the first group initially. They provided the most concrete and unarguable links, and they offer the clearest evi-dence that Defoe had in some recess of his mind several portions of Virgil's text.

There is, for example, a definite echo of one famous passage in the first *Georgic*. It is, significantly, in a vein not at all remote from what Fussell identifies as the elegiac.

> Scilicet et tempus veniet, cum finibus illis
> agricola incurvo terram molitus aratro
> exesa inveniet scabra robigine pila,
> aut gravibus rastris galeas pulsabit inanis,
> grandiaque effossis mirabitur ossa sepulcris.
>
> (1: 493–97)[5]

Compare Defoe's reflections on the battlefield of Towton in Yorkshire, where a great and wasteful combat had taken place in 1461, during the Wars of the Roses.

> Tradition guided the Country People, and they us, to the very Spot; but we had only the Story in speculation; for there remains [sic] no Marks, no Monument, no Remembrance of the Action, only that the Ploughmen say, that sometimes they plough up Arrow-heads and Spear-heads, and broken Javelins, and Helmets and the like; so we cou'd only give a short Sigh to the memory of the Dead, and move forward. (2: 634)

Something very similar occurs at Bosworth, the site of "the great Battle which put an End . . . to the long and bloody Contention between the *red* Rose and the *White*,"

> which, as Fame tells us, had cost the Lives of Eleven Princes, Three and Twenty Earls and Dukes, Three Thousand Noblemen, Knights and Gentlemen, and Two Hundred Thousand of the common People: They shew'd us the Spot of Ground where the Battle was fought, and at the Town they shew'd us several Pieces of Swords, Heads of Lances, Barbs of Arrows, Pieces of Pole-Axes, and such like Instruments of Death, which they said were found by the Country People in the several Grounds near the Place of Battle, as they had occasion to dig, or trench, or plough up the Ground. (2: 487)

It is not merely the vocabulary which recalls Virgil—an identical list of military relics—but the precisely caught air of wonder and the sense of incongruity, almost absurdity, when the peaceful activity of ploughing yields such bizarre trophies of the past. Virgil had been describing a civil broil ("ergo inter sese paribus concurre tellis/ Romanas acies interum videre Philippi . . .") and Defoe equally stresses the poignancy of internecine wars:

> I call it [the battle of Towton] most cruel and bloody, because the Animosity of the Parties was so great, that tho' they were Countrymen and *Englishmen,* Neighbours, nay, as History says, Relations; for here Fathers kill'd their Sons, and Sons their Fathers. . . . (2: 634)

He might almost have added with Virgil, as the poet contemplates the breakdown of social and moral decorum that war brings with it, his own solemn, lapidary phrases:

> quippe ubi fas versum atque nefas: tot bella per orbem,
> tam multae scelerum facies; non ullus aratro
> dignus honos, squalent abductis arva colonis
> et curvae rigidum falces conflantur in ensem.
>
> (1: 505–8)[6]

For both writers, agriculture serves as an emblem of peace and rural innocence, something that warfare destroys with its essentially *urban* disruption of the rhythms of nature.

There is a wider congruence here. Virgil of course had written in the aftermath of prolonged civil wars: indeed the *Georgics* are commonly assigned to 30 B.C., just one year after the battle of Actium, which settled the long contentions and initiated the *Pax Romana*. Defoe was born probably in 1660, the year that saw the end of the Commonwealth, which had been initiated by the victory of the Cromwellian parties in the English Civil War. This lengthy contest is now studied mainly for its constitutional implications, but in the generations that immediately followed, the memory of this event simply as a *war* continued to reverberate. Defoe wrote a great deal about the war, but no more than we should expect: *Memoirs of a Cavalier* came out just four years before the first volume of the *Tour* (see also Appendix C).

Predictably, the text of this work is littered with reminscences of the huge upheaval that had struck the nation eighty years before. Defoe still feels obliged to refer in places to "the late unhappy Times" (2: 481): not all the old scores had yet been settled. The phrase quoted relates to the effects of the siege of Lichfield on the cathedral in that city. We must recall that the physical traces of battles still haunted the English landscape; nor were these national memorial parks, carefully sanitized for visitors, but working localities where the scars just survived by chance. It would be a disproportionately long exercise to set out all of Defoe's comments on the war, but a brief summary of the position should illustrate the significance this event had in his mind.

Following, then, the order of the text: we have in the very first letter a fifteen-page journal of the siege of Colchester in 1648 (1: 18–31). This has not seemed very integral to most commentators, and is a target for those who attempt to abridge the *Tour;* but it links up to other passages in the book. Near Devizes, Defoe gives a full account of the battle of Roundway (1643), citing an unnamed historian (1: 287–88). Without any break he passes straight on to the two battles of Newbury (1643, 1644), evoking "a double Scene of Blood" (1: 288–89). In the vicinity of Banbury, Defoe "could not refrain from taking a turn . . . to see the famous spot of Ground" where the battle of Cropredy Bridge took place in 1644. The very next paragraph begins: "From there, being within eight Miles of *Edge-Hill,* where the first Battle in that [Civil] War happen'd, I had the like Pleasure of viewing the Ground about *Keinton,* where that bloody Battle was fought" (2: 428). There are many well-known sights where he would not have traveled eight miles out of his way in order to have the "pleasure" of viewing them. Unmistakably Defoe was interested in the military tactics of these engagements, and replays them as war games; but their location stirs other memories.

The theme recurs at Worcester (2: 442–43); at Newark (2: 490), and more extensively at Marston Moor, where he receives a blow-by-blow of the contest (2: 640–41). The end of this passage is quoted later in this chapter (p. 144). Though "pleased" with the experience, Defoe reflects that "'twas none of our Business to concern our Passions in the Cause, or regret the Misfortunes of that Day; the thing was over beyond our ken; Time had levelled the Victors with the Van-quished. . . ." We are close to the elegiac mood described in chapter 4. But such passages (and I have not had space to list them all) reflect at a simpler level the pervasive memory of the Civil War in the British consciousness. (This is also to leave aside references to battles in the Monmouth rising or the first Jacobite rebellion.) Plainly Defoe inhab-ited an imaginative world not very remote from that of Virgil.

The Civil War served as an emblem of the precariousness of human achievement: its very name bespeaks the breakdown of "civil" society. Contemplating the decaying state of the defenses at Exeter, the author refers to "the late Civil unnatural War" (1: 223). Of course, like all men and women of his time, Defoe was alive to external threats. Britain has not been successfully invaded since 1066, but it has never known the luxury of feeling immune from annexation by foreign pow-ers, in the way that the United States has been able to feel safe. A passage in Letter II describes "the time that the *Dutch* made that memorable Attempt upon the Royal Navy" when they sailed up the Medway in 1667 and destroyed many ships at anchor (1: 109). It was like a penetration of some secret orifice in the nation's body. But more commonly Defoe reverts to internecine contests. Thus, at Shrewsbury, he recalls the battle fought in 1403 which figures in Shakespeare's *1 Henry IV,* and then the support that Charles I received from the local people when he stayed there at the start of the Civil War. There is a characteristic addendum: "But the Fate of the War turning afterward against the King, the Weight of it fell heavy upon this Town also, and almost ruin'd them" (2: 476). Virgil, too, could have reflected the history of Rome through its foreign engagements, most obviously the Punic wars; but here it is the more recent contests that hover most menacingly over his poetry.

II

Another part of the *Georgics* that seems to have particularly caught the imagination of Defoe is the section of Book III dealing with the breeding and schooling of horses. The Roman poet is concerned with chariot-racing, Defoe with horse-racing in its modern form. Yet he takes over several of Virgil's images. For example, there is this advice to the trainer of horses to be used in war-chariots:

> tum cursibus auras,
> tum vocet, ac per aperta volans, ceu liber habensis,
> aequora vix summa vestigia ponat harena:
> qualis Hyperboreis Aquilo cum densus ab oris
> incubuit, Scythiaeque hiemes atque arida differt
> nubila; tum segetes altae campique natantes
> lenibus horrescunt flabris, summaeque sonorem
> dant silvae, longique urgent ad litora fluctus;
> ille volat, simul arva fuga, simul aequora verrens.
>
> (3: 193–201)[7]

Compare Defoe, speaking of horses at Newmarket that were "as light as the Wind, and could fly like a Meteor" (1: 76). When, at Epsom, Defoe sees "the Racers flying over the Course, as if they either touch'd not, or felt not the Ground they run upon" (1: 159), we are reminded of Virgil's picture of the young chariot-racers (*iamque humiles, iamque elati sublime videntur / aera per vacuum ferri atque adsurgere in auras*). And indeed Defoe's whole response to horse-racing seems to be filtered through memories of antiquity:

> Here I fansy'd myself in the *Circus Maximus* at *Rome*, seeing the antient Games, and the Racings of the Chariots and Horsemen; and in this warmth of my Imagination I pleas'd and diverted myself more and in a more Noble manner, than I could possibly do in the Crowds of Gentlemen at the weighing and starting Posts, and at their coming in; or at their Meetings at the Coffee-Houses and Gaming-Tables after the Races were over. . . . (1: 76)

So much for the uncomplicated reporter, bound within the present tense.

Nor, incidentally, is this the only time that Defoe consciously turns away from the contemporary world. Witness the occasion when he comes to speak of Christopher Wren's design for the Sheldonian Theatre at Oxford:

> . . . a Building not to be equall'd by any thing of its kind in the World; no, not in *Italy* itself; Not that the Building of the *Theatre* here is large as *Vespasian's* or that of *Trajan* at *Rome* . . . We see by the remains that those Ampitheatres, as they were for the Exercise of their publick Shews, and to entertain a vast Concourse of People, to see the Fighting of the

Gladiators, the throwing Criminals to the wild Beasts, and the like, were rather great Magnificent *Bear-gardens,* than *Theatres,* for the Actors of such Representations, as entertain'd the Polite part of the World; consequently those were vast Piles of Building proper for the uses for which they were Built.

What Buildings were then made use of in Rome for the fine Performances of —— who acted that of *Terence,* or who Wrote that, we can not be certain of; but I think I have a great deal of reason to say, they have no remains of them, or of any one of them at *Rome;* or if they are, they come not near to this Building. (2: 423–24)

Whatever the motives for this clumsy and inaccurate aside, it is plain that Defoe often found a Roman thought strike him as he compiled the *Tour.*

To return to the direct parallels, we may note that a casual rhetorical formula employed by Virgil takes on greater significance in Defoe's scheme of things.[8] The second *Georgic* has this:

> . . . non hic te carmine ficto
> atque per ambages et longa exorsa tenebo.
>
> (2: 45–46)[9]

Defoe develops this pseudo-realism in a number of ways. As, for instance, at the start of his third letter:

> I shall sing you no Songs here of the River in the first Person of a Water Nymph, a Goddess, (and I know not what) according to the Humour of the ancient Poets. I shall talk nothing of the Marriage of old *Isis,* the Male River, with the beautiful *Thame,* the Female River, a Whimsy as simple as the Subject was empty, but I shall speak of the River as Occasion presents, as it really is *made glorious* by the Splendor of its Shores, gilded with noble Palaces, strong Fortifications, large Hospitals, and publick Buildings. . . . (1: 173: cf. 1: 396)

Similarly, his attitude to the famous "Wonders of the Peak" in the eighth letter:

> And now I am come to this wonderful Place, the *Peak,* where you will expect I should do as some others have, (I think, foolishly) done before me, *viz.* tell you strange long Stories of Wonders as (I must say) they are most weakly call'd . . . (2: 566–67)

This section will be analyzed in detail in chapter 7: here we may simply note the pervasive habit of rejecting the pastoral vision, an attribute the author shares of course with Samuel Johnson.

When Defoe crosses Salisbury Plain, the "vast Flocks of Sheep" once more turn his mind in the same direction:

> Nothing can be like it, the *Arcadians* Plains of which we read so much Pastoral Trumpery in the Poets, could be nothing to them. (1: 218)

Maybe Defoe was thinking of pastoralists of the caliber of Thomas Purney or of Pope's adversary Ambrose Philips. In any event, it is striking how often he returns to this line of thought.

Clearly there is a distinction to be drawn here. Virgil's rejection of pastoral machinery comes with special force from one who had already produced ten eclogues of surpassing beauty and imaginative life. On the other hand, Defoe's antibucolic vein is simply part of his pose as a reliable up-to-date traveler. Both writers affect to distrust the versions of pastoral available to them, and both have good rhetorical reasons for this pose. The *Georgics* finally embody a more convincing realism, in that Virgil is the better able to substitute for false mythology a positive fiction—that is, the human and poetic values of his work offer a richer sustenance to the imagination than Defoe's comparatively literal-minded narrative. However, the similarities are more noteworthy than the differences.

We may pass rapidly over certain casual links between the two works. Defoe's account of the virtues of a Yorkshire-bred horse (2: 629) is remarkably close to Virgil's description of the ideal charger: *illi ardua cervix / argutumque caput* . . . (3: 79ff). But then there can be few ways of expressing the desiderata of equine physique. Again, many of Defoe's remarks on the genius of soils seem to recall Virgil's famous lines (2: 177ff). On occasions Defoe will devote a fairly long paragraph to the topic (e.g., at Bagshot Heath, 1: 143), and quite apart from this his recurrent concern is with the productive nature of the land. The incidence of a number of key terms provides a rough guide in this matter. *Fruitful* occurs over forty times in the text of the *Tour;* *fertile* about half as often. A whole battery of associated terms is deployed through the book *prolifick/luxuriant/flourishing/thriving/ abundan-t,-ce/plent y/nourish/rich/bounty,* and so on. Here again, it is important not to make too much of these facts. One could hardly write about tillage and husbandry as fully as Defoe does without having recourse to such terms, and without overlapping to some degree with the vocabulary of the *Georgics.* Nevertheless, it is interesting that the *Tour* should so often employ epithets straddling agrarian and moral concepts—something seen most directly in the Virgilian epithet *laetus,* as in the opening phrase of the first *Georgic.* Conventionally, this technique is said to enter English literature in poetic diction, with the exploitation of *smiling land* and similar locutions.[10] Yet Defoe performs much the same thing in his prose: *pleasant* occurs almost a hundred times, and its overtones in Defoe are precisely those of *laetus*—a landscape at once delightful and fruitful, peaceful and abundant.

Rather than considering this device along the lines of a simple frequency count, with each word treated as a monad, it will be more revealing to look at a sustained passage where Defoe uses this kind of vocabulary. A representative passage out of many would run as follows:

> ... that which was most surprizing, after such a tiresom and fatiguing Journey, over the unhospitable Mountains of *Merioneth,* and *Carnarvonshire,* was, that descending now from the Hills, we came into a most pleasant, fruitful, populous, and delicious Vale, full of Villages and Towns, the Fields shining with Corn, just ready for the Reapers, the Meadows green and flowery, and a fine River, with a mild and gentle Stream running thro' it: Nor is it a small or casual Intermission, but we had a Prospect of the Country open before us, for above 20 Miles in Length, and from 5 to 7 Miles in Breadth, all smiling with the same Kind of Complexion; which made us think ourselves in *England* again, all on a sudden. (2: 464)

Here we instantly notice how the idea of refreshment mingles with that of agrarian prosperity. In a most characteristic Augustan fashion, personal and aesthetic pleasure is intertwined with social and economic well-being. The key epithets are metaphoric rather than literal (*shining/smiling*). Behind the entire passage lies a half-explicit pathetic fallacy, with the landscape personified both physically (*Complexion*) and morally (*mild and gentle/fine*). The fields are not ripe but—as one would say of a person—"ready." All in all, we may conclude that the underlying drift of this description is poetic and not reportorial in any simple sense. Defoe feels his way into the natural scene, with a sharp response to its visual beauties allied to an unfailing awareness of practical farming considerations. The mountains of Merioneth were "unhospitable" to the picturesque tourist, since they offered little creature comfort and (to a man of Defoe's generation) no aesthetic pleasure. But they are also "inhospitable," inhospitable to profitable tillage, and that is just as important a component in the word. Defoe's choice of language reflects his basic sense of human realities.

III

In discussing this point, we have been moving away from local parallels towards broader similarities in theme or intention. It may be said that these latter, if more elusive, constitute the more profound debts of the *Tour* to Virgil. Contrary to what Fussell and almost every other critic has implied, the *Tour* is suffused by a strong sense of history. Defoe may constantly bring himself up short with the reminder that antiquity is not meant to be his subject, but he cannot stay away for long. He has an acute sensitivity to the vicissitudes of time. With Virgil, he knows that "saevit toto Mars impius orbe" (1: 511). Witness his comments, already briefly touched on, when he reaches the battlefield of Marston Moor, the Civil War engagement that seems to have made most impression on his mind:

> ... 'Twas none of our Business to concern our Passions in the Cause, or regret the Misfortunes of the Day; the thing was over beyond our ken; Time had levelled the Victors with the Vanquished, and the Royal Family being restored, there was no room to say one thing or other to what was pass'd; so we returned to *York* the same Night. (2: 641)

In its slightly angular way, this is as noble a rephrasal of commonplace as Pope's in the *Epistle to Burlington*. In the *Tour,* patriotic sentiment is often wedded to elegy, as in the *Georgics*.

As any reader of *The True-Born Englishman* will know, Defoe was highly conscious of the complex inheritance, racial and cultural, that English nationality brought with it. At the end of the ninth letter, he brings together this idea with his accustomed lament for the decay of the past:

> I cannot but say, that since I entred upon the View of these Northern Counties, I have many times repented that I so early resolved to decline the delightful View of Antiquity, here being so great and so surprizing a Variety, and every Day more and more discovered; and abundance since the *Tour* which the learned Mr. *Cambden* made this Way, nay, many since his Learned Continuator; for as the Trophies, the Buildings, the religious, as well military Remains, as well of the *Britains,* as of the *Romans, Saxons,* and *Normans,* are but, as we may say, like Wounds hastily healed up. . . . The venerable Face of Antiquity has something so pleasing, so surprizing, so satisfactory in it, especially to those who have with any Attention read the Histories of pass'd Ages, that I know nothing renders Travelling more pleasant and more agreeable. (2: 663)

(For a fuller citation see chapter 4, p. 124) Defoe was assuredly one who had so attentively read. As has been said, "Defoe's interest in Roman history is known to all students of his works."[11] He read widely but above all creatively. His antiquarianism was not the pedantic and parochial kind associated with nineteenth-century archeological societies. On the contrary, it is nourished by a lively sense of the way in which traces of the past survive in existing objects: an almost pagan feeling for the historic charge in any human environment. In this passage we hear of the "Wounds" of time, and the "Calous" spread over them. Elsewhere Defoe speaks of the "Injury of Time" (e.g. 1: 309), of ruins eaten up by time (e.g., 2: 796), and similar expressions (see chapter 4, p. 124). There are numerous statements on this pattern: "As you must expect a great Deal of Antiquity in this Country of *Fife,* so you must expect to find all those antient Pieces mourning their own Decay, and drooping and sinking in Ashes" (2: 789). Like many people, Defoe was moved by the past not because of nostalgia, but precisely because he was so acutely aware of the tumultuous present and the ravages it made of what had been.

If, then, he was obsessed by progress, it could not be said that this was in any way a simpleminded concern. His "modernism" is qualified by a corresponding awareness of what Fussell eloquently calls the enduring, the permanent, and the unchanging. The question arises, where did Defoe discover this vein of feeling, so different from those popularly associated with Defoe's work at large? The major translation of the *Georgics* in this era was of course that of Dryden, published in 1697. If anything, the second and third volumes of the *Tour* (1725–26) show more of a Virgilian impress, and it is possible that Defoe had seen William Benson's version published in 1725. This was entitled *Virgil's Husbandry: or an Essay on the Georgics: being the first Book, translated into English Verse.* Benson was an old adversary of Defoe, who accorded him a brief sneering reference in the second volume of the *Tour* (1: 366). Defoe is unlikely to have approved of Benson's feeble literary efforts, but he would not have overlooked their appearance.

For the rest, we know that Defoe had been reading previous anti-quarian and topographic accounts of Britain—as usual, his apparently firsthand account owes much to his quiet industry and oddly bookish disposition. He may have been renewing acquaintance with other Roman authors: a Horatian reminiscence appears in the account of the Protestant martyr Dr. Rowland Taylor:

> The Inhabitants, who have a wonderful Veneration for his Memory, shew the very Place where the Stake which he was bound to, was set up, and they have put a Stone upon it, which no Body will remove; but it is a more lasting Monument to him that he lives in the Hearts of the People; I say more lasting than a Tomb of Marble would be . . . (1: 48)

However, it is a different voice that can be heard for much of the *Tour*. The accents are those of Virgil, and the recurrent theme is

"Time, the great Devourer of the Works of Men" (2: 447). Defoe's picture of England shows the countryside most beautiful when it is most productive. His vision is couched in the familiar terms of agricul-tural prosperity, but ultimately the sense is one of artistic symmetry and cosmic order:

> I cannot but remember, with some Satisfaction, that having two Foreign Gentlemen in my Company, in our passing over this Heath, I say I could not but then observe, and now remember it with Satisfaction, how they were surprized at the Beauty of this Prospect, and how they look'd at one another, and then again turning their Eyes every way in a kind of Wonder, one of them said to the other, That *England* was not like other Country's, but it was all a planted Garden.
>
> They had there on the right Hand, the Town of St. *Albans* in their View; and all the Spaces between, and further beyond it, look'd indeed like a Garden. The inclos'd Corn-Fields made one grand Parterre, the thick planted Hedge Rows, like a Wilderness or Labyrinth, divided in *Espaliers;* the Villages interspers'd, look'd like so many several Noble Seats of Gentlemen at a Distance. In a Word, it was all Nature, and yet look'd all like Art. . . . (1: 388)[12]

Defoe outlines a sort of imaginative *trompe l'oeil* that holds within itself a complex of Augustan ideas regarding the ordering of life. In the face of such writing, it seems unduly harsh to deny the term "humanistic" to Defoe, as Fussell wishes to do. The *Tour* makes agrar-ian health an emblem of that conspiracy between the rhythms of na-ture and the purposes of man that Augustan culture sought to bring about.[13] Equally, the *Tour* sets peace and plenty against the destructive powers of war, famine and the passage of time. The source of these ideas is not Pope or the English pastoralists: they come originally from another age and another country. The irony is that the fullest picture in prose of eighteenth-century England, by a quintessentially English author, owes much of its imaginative depth to four poems of ancient Rome. It may be Virgil filtered through translation, imitation and the cruder processes of anglicization—but Virgil is certainly there. The British landscape is a palimpsest that Defoe scans with the aid of the *Georgics*.

6

Speaking within Compass: The Ground Covered in the *Tour* and *Captain Singleton*

E<small>ARLIER</small>, in the Introduction (pp. 48–53), we saw how Defoe evolved the notion of what he terms "a Circuit, if not a Circle," as a mode of representing his progress. The particular way in which he went on to represent movement across space is the subject of this chapter, as this is brought out in a comparison with a novel Defoe had published just before he began to work on the *Tour*, that is *Captain Singleton* (1720).

In the world of Jane Austen, one has a strong sense of the way distances mark out property and areas of personal familiarity. Going for a walk (a recurrent activity) tends to involve beating certain psy-chological, if not physical, bounds. Characteristic is this exchange in Volume I, Chapter IX of *Mansfield Park*, where Mary Crawford and Edmund Bertram review the peregrination on which they have been engaged. Mary claims that they must have walked "at least a mile" inside a speciality of the Rushworth estate, "a planted wood of about two acres." Edmund demurs:

"Not half a mile," was his sturdy answer; for he was not yet so much in love as to measure distance, or reckon time, with feminine lawlessness.

"Oh! you do not consider how much we have wound about. We have taken such a very serpentine course; and the wood itself must be half a mile long in a straight line, for we have never seen the end of it yet, since we left the first great path."

"But if you remember, before we left that first great path, we saw directly to the end of it. We looked down the whole vista, and saw it closed by iron gates, and it could not have been more than a furlong in length."

"Oh! I know nothing of your furlongs, but I am sure it is a very long wood; and that we have been winding in and out ever since we came into it; and therefore when I say that we have walked a mile in it, I must speak within compass."

"We have been exactly a quarter of an hour here," said Edmund, taking out his watch. "Do you think we are walking four miles an hour?"

"Oh! do not attack me with your watch. A watch is always too fast or too slow. I cannot be dictated to by a watch."[1]

In context, the passage has the effect of revealing Mary's slightly bogus "spontaneity," and dramatizes her combative attitude towards experience. Fanny, though present, is her usual silent self.

Some of the phrasing in this extract, especially that used by Mary, has interesting overtones in an eighteenth-century context. "Within compass" plainly belongs with sense 9 of the noun *compass* in *OED*, that is the meaning "bounds, limits . . . [of] sight, knowledge, power, ability . . . more generally, range, reach, sphere, scope." This sense is preceded historically by a similar notion from which it may have evolved: "circumscribed area or space; in wider sense, space, area, extent." An earlier sense still was the one defined by Samuel Johnson, "moderate space, moderation, due limits." Under this part of the entry *OED* cites a remark from Richardson's *Pamela,* "I must keep within Compass." One could surely say a good deal about the Augustan moral idiom Jane Austen inherited by tracing the movement from physical restriction to behavioral restraint. "Within compass," *OED* tells us, meant "within the bounds of moderation": archaic, it appears, except in dialect.

Defoe uses the word on quite a few occasions, usually within the range of meanings already mentioned—though he was certainly aware of different connotations, for example the meanings grouped in *compass,* sense 11: "circular movement, course, or journey, circuit . . . a roundabout journey, a detour" (this is illustrated from Celia Fiennes). The book where ideas of a "circuit" are most relevant is, of course, the *Tour.* It is central to the rhetorical aims of this work that we embark with the narrator on lingering but finite journeys. There is always the impression that we are wound up on a tight spring, and will be pulled back to the center of things (London most of the time, to a lesser degree Edinburgh in the Scottish sections). We may stray from the orthodox itinerary for a brief while, or to look at it another way the narrator may "digress." But we are confident that we shall get back where we started: the narrative tone is not that of an explorer but of a guide.

In Defoe's fiction we tend to experience rather "voyages," trips into the unknown. This could be said to apply to both parts of Robinson Crusoe's adventures; to *Captain Singleton;* and, explicitly, to *A New Voyage round the World.* But it could also be detected in Moll's outward journeys across the Atlantic, for she has no very definite prospect of return on either occasion. The point about a voyage is not just that it is a sea trip, though that is usually the case. It is instead the sense of traveling to an unknown destination, for a rather vague dura-tion of time: there is no automatic return in view, and there is a good deal of doubt as to whether one will arrive at all. Normally it is a straight-line affair, because there is no scope for agreeable "diversion" along the route. The circuit keeps within compass; that is, tethered and manageable. The voyage is conditioned rather by a pull from the other end, which draws the traveler on through every kind of difficulty.

I

For the purposes of contrast, we can isolate a journey of either kind, to look at the techniques and strategies Defoe adopts according to his immediate needs. The "circuit" in question is in fact the first half only, to be literal, of a circuit that takes Defoe on his *Tour* down to the southwestern tip of Britain and back to his starting place in London. But even if we separate Letter III of the *Tour* in this way, there is never the slightest feeling that the narrator will lose control. He tells us that he had once intended to cover the southwestern counties in one letter; but this would have meant crowding his observations "too close," since so many remarkable spots happen to lie "in a Line, as it were, in one Point of the Compass." His revised plan will "divide the weighty Task" and "make my Progress the more regular" (1: 172).[2] He intends, with a neat symmetry, to take Hampton Court on the way out, in the present letter, and Windsor on the way back, in the succeeding letter. This balances the subject matter of the two letters, and supplies variety of texture in each.

The other case for inspection is the inland "voyage" across southern Africa, performed by Captain Singleton and his shipmates in the first half of that novel. It occupies just over a hundred pages in most editions of *Captain Singleton,* that is to say about a third of the text. This narrative is slightly longer than that of the trip to Land's End in the *Tour,* but not very much: the letter occupies about 120 pages in the first edition of Volume I of the *Tour* (1724), with a much lower number of words per page than is found in modern books. It is, need-less to say, a smaller part of the entire *Tour* than is the overland journey in *Singleton;* but it does occupy a roughly analogous place in the structure, and (a consideration in view of the differences that will emerge) it has not been selected as notably unlike the novel—other sections of the *Tour* would reveal the same points of contrast and comparison.

To begin with a major basis of comparison: in both cases Defoe renders the progress of his journey by means of explicit indications of distance. The main way in which we are invited to apprehend the dynamics of travel is through a running log of each successive stage, marked off in the case of *Singleton* as a day's march (or, briefly, canoe-ing distance). This may seem self-evident, but in fact many travelers do not make much explicit mention of sheer mileage. Picturesque trav-elers, later in the century, seldom deign to give such matters the faint-est attention. Now, it might be argued that Defoe in the *Tour* was providing a sort of national gazetteer, and that the need for basic information explains his readiness to state distances. But this cannot apply to the fictional work *Singleton;* and besides the *Tour* is often rather vague about the directions of a given journey, even as it cites the distance involved (so that mere route-finding cannot be the whole of the story, unless we are to regard Defoe as particularly incompetent).

If this provides an obvious point of comparison, then an equally apparent divergence presents itself. In the one case, Defoe does all he can to suggest leisurely and controlled progress. Distances are not too large, and are generally not cumulated: it is sufficient to record the length of the journey between L and M (Winchester to Salisbury, say) without totting up the running total of A to M. This is because we are moving in chartered territory: there is no expanding frontier, no sense that we may have come along the wrong track and may have to retrace our steps, no impression ever of a receding goal. On the other hand, Singleton's journey emphasizes difficulty, uncertainty, he-roic survival, and the attrition of life in a strange climate when each day may be the last. Singleton begins with the awareness that his party is embarking on a hazardous operation that they "resolved to adventure" out of desperation. They calculate before the start that they must cross "a Continent of Land of at least 1800 Miles; in which Journey we had excessive Heats to support, no Carriages, Camels or Beasts of any kind to carry our Baggage," quite apart from all the dangerous creatures that inhabited the region. They know that they have "the Equinoctial Line to pass under, and consequently were in the very Center of the Torrid Zone."[3] Geography is an expression of personal hardship to be endured: distance becomes an emblem of this laborious manner of living, and the enormity of the undertaking is frequently emphasized by charting the *total*, rather than the intermedi-ary, distance covered. It is this difference in perception of distance that forms the hinge of my discussion. We shall see how Defoe uses rather similar phraseology towards radically different purposes. In one case, distance provides a comforting expression of things as they should be, and were known to be all along. In the other, we have quite another perception of space, in which ground covered is a measurement of the possibilities of survival. One technique—to anticipate my conclusion—is perhaps more effective as a literary instrument.

Within a page of the opening of Letter III in the *Tour,* we come on an expression that typifies Defoe's intent. Hampton Court, he tells us, lies on the north bank of the Thames, "about two small Miles from *Kingston*" (1: 172). This locution had already been used in the preceding letter, in a marginally different form: from Beddington in Surrey "it is but a little Mile to *Cashalton*" (1: 158). For the usage, we must again consult *OED,* that is, the entry *little,* 6b: "Qualifying a s[ubstantive] denoting a definite measure of duration or distance, to emphasize its brevity. Also, in 16–17th c., used for: Bare, scarcely complete." (This latter sense is marked with a dagger to mark its obsolete status.) The examples cited in *OED* show that Defoe was enlisting a perfectly ordinary form of words, and it is one that exactly suits the needs of his narrative. Throughout the *Tour,* Defoe wishes to convey an impression of control. In some regions, notably the parts of the island (Wales, Scotland, the Peak District) that were still in some measure unexplored by civilization, the narrator admits that the country is remote and desolate. But he prefers to lay emphasis on the penetrability of even these arduous tracts of ground. One famous section in Letter VIII describes his laborious passage of the central Pennine hills, with a howling wind and snow in evidence despite the fact that it was August. Defoe's ultimate descent into Halifax has almost the significance of Wordsworth's entry into Italy via the Simplon Pass, except that the earlier writer experiences no sense of anticlimax or loss. Similarly, in Scotland Defoe has recourse to a guide, who leads him "very artfully" through the hills; while in the Highlands he is saved from a circuitous journey around Skye by boat thanks to "the extraordinary Courtesie of some of the Gentlemen of the Country." Such trips are not to be recommended, except to those traveling in a party and those assisted by "very good Guides" (2: 766, 828–29).

The narrative, then, can admit to difficulty: but it is nearly always difficulty overcome. Defoe implies by his very title *Tour* something manageable, perhaps even leisurely. Once again *OED* is useful: the first relevant sense to evolve is the idea of "excursion or journey," first cited from John Denham's *Cooper's Hill* (1643), with the specialized usage Grand Tour not recorded before Richardson and Smollett in the late 1740s. An obsolete sense illustrated from Defoe, among others, is "a short outing taken for exercise, recreation, as a social function, or the like; in 17th c., in London, the drive round Hyde Park." This rather familiar, itsy-bitsy overtone of the word is now entirely lost, but it may hover behind the title of Defoe's book. Last among the relevant entries under *tour* comes the sense "the circuit *of* an island, etc.; a round": the first example is from *Robinson Crusoe*. What this appears to indicate is that Defoe's usage would suggest to a contempo-rary reader that he was embarking on a finite, well-charted route: that the traveler would satisfactorily complete his circuit, and that he would keep safely within the "compass" of the island. A journey may lead us into unexpected territory, but the manifest destiny of a tour is to deposit writer and reader back at their starting point.

It is in this context that the various indications of "progress" along the itinerary should be seen. Much of the trip is undertaken across bare uplands, with few obvious features of interest. Defoe tends to hurry us over these tracts of land: a typical formula would be, "From hence, at the End of seven Miles over the *Downs*, we come to the very ancient City of *Winchester*" (1: 181). The syntax allows us to reach the destination before we are aware of the intervening ground to be covered. It is important that the destination is regularly men-tioned in direct conjunction with the distance, so that the count of miles immediately suggests arrival. Thus: "From *Winchester*, is about 25 Miles, and over the most charming Plains that can any where be seen, (far in my Opinion) excelling the Plains of *Mecca*, we come to *Salisbury*" (1: 187). Nobody believes that Defoe had actually seen Mecca for himself, but his praise of the fairly uneventful region known as Salisbury Plain unabashedly proceeds, in dimensions that are puny by Arabian standards: "This plain Country continues in length from *Winchester* to *Salisbury* 25 Miles, from thence to *Dorchester* 22 Miles, thence to *Weymouth* 6 Miles, so that they [*sic*] lye near 50 Miles in length, and breadth; they reach also in some Places 35 to 40 Miles" (1: 187–88). The purpose of this calculation has little to do with the progress of the tour, or difficulties in travel: Defoe is bent on establish-ing the pattern of husbandry, in particular the density of the sheep population—there are "600000 Sheep fed within 6 Miles" of Dorchester.

After this, we make some small diversions, with a "short Tour to the Hills"—for there are tours within tours—to visit Stonehenge, and an episode where the narrator "stept up into the Country North-West, to see the ancient Town of *Wimburn*," (1: 196, 207). Then the narrator resumes his "first Design," and approaches the coast. The *design* is the purpose of the journey, its goal, but of course the struc-tural basis of the narrative as well. "South of this Town, over a Sandy wild and barren Country, we came to *Pool*, a considerable Sea-Port

. . . . From Hence to *Weymouth,* which is ———— Miles we rode in view of the Sea; the Country is open, and in some respects pleas' ant. . . ." (1: 208–9). This odd lapse is not the only occasion in the *Tour* when Defoe fails to deliver the required information. One might have supposed that he would delete the phrase, which is easily dispen' sable, before he passed the copy to his printer: but he seems almost to think that his standing as a reliable cicerone will be increased by these periodic confessions of ignorance. The tone seems to be, "I can't tell you right now just exactly how far, but it is a nice comfortable distance, not worth any concern on your part."

For Defoe, the sea appears to be a comforting sight; not just a navigational aid that helps to locate the traveler as he proceeds west' ward, but also a kind of emotional guardrail—a confirmation that the tour will not slip away off the island. "From *Dorchester,*" he tells us, "it is six Miles to the Sea Side South, and the Ocean in view almost all the Way" (1: 211). He describes the Isle of Portland, then separate from the mainland, and considered to be worth a mention on the title page of the *Tour* from the second edition onwards. Next comes the "Riffe of Beach" known as Chesil Bank, forming a landlocked inlet that "opens at about two Miles West, and grows very broad, and makes a kind of Lake within the Land of a Mile and a half broad, and near three Miles in length, the Breadth unequal" (1: 214). The specifications tame and domesticize a peculiar natural feature. Then the trip moves along the coast to Bridport and Lyme Regis ("Here we saw Boats all the way on the Shore fishing for *Mackerell* . . . ," 1: 214); and afterwards inland to small towns such as Sherborne and Shaftesbury. Once more we are reminded of the population of sheep:

> *Shaftsbury* is also on the Edge of this Country, adjoyning to *Wiltshire* and *Dorsetshire,* being 14 Miles from *Salisbury,* over that fine Down or Carpet Ground, which they call particularly, or properly *Salisbury Plain.* It has neither House or Town in view all the way, and the Road which often lyes very Broad, and Branches off insensibly, might easily cause a Traveller to loose his Way, but there is a certain never failing Assistance upon all these Downs for telling a Stranger his Way, and that is the Number of Shepherds feeding, or keeping their vast Flocks of Sheep, which are every where in the way, and who, with a very little pains, a Traveller may always speak with. (1: 218)

Apart from the shepherds, there are several "navigating" devices here: (1) the intersection with a former route, (2) the mention of a town recently visited, Salisbury, (3) the county boundaries firmly located on the map, and (4) the confident placing of Shaftesbury itself. By such means the *Tour* establishes its sense of a well-ordered itinerary.

So the journey proceeds, and the same techniques manifest themselves: "From *Honiton* the Country is exceedingly pleasant still, and
on the Road they have a beautiful Prospect almost all the way to
Exeter, which is twelve Miles; on the left Hand of this Road lyes
that Part of the County, which they call the *South Hams*" (1: 222).
Everywhere, of course, has got a name: the frontier mentality, which
goes with the naming of places, would be comically belated in such
an environment. Again there are expressions of future intent: "I shall
take the North Part of this County in my Return from *Cornwall;* so
I must now lean to the South" (1: 224). Still, the lines of visibility
conspire to ease the traveler's progress: "From hence we went still
South about seven Miles, (all in view of this River) to *Dartmouth,* a
Town of note, Seated at the Mouth of the River *Dart*" (1: 225).
Towards the end of the letter, the information is often presented more
curtly: "of which I have little more to say, but that from thence the
Road lyes to *Plymouth,* distance about six Miles" (1: 228: compare
233, 239). Then we finally reach the tip of the island, as the letter
and the road run out together: "I am now at my Journey's End . . . I
must now return *Sur mes pas,* as the *French* call it; tho" not literally
so; for . . . as I have Coasted the South shore to the Land's End, I
shall come back by the North Coast, and my Observations in my
Return will furnish very well Materials for a Fourth Letter" (1: 243).
This Augustan symmetry bespeaks confidence and control. It is possible to plan, to choose routes, to estimate times and distances with
complete assurance. So the organization of the *Tour,* with its neat
home-and-away structure, expresses a sense of space as something
mastered, easily comprehensible, already named and measured.

II

From this we turn to the almost Pascalian vistas of the journey
across Africa made by Captain Singleton and his party. Theirs is the
plainly rash undertaking "to travel over Land through the Heart of
the Country, from the Coast of *Mozambique,* on the East-Ocean to
the Coast of *Angola* or *Guinea,* on the Western or *Atlantick* Ocean,
a Continent of Land of at least 1800 Miles" (58). Singleton himself
faces the prospect with trepidation: "When they came to talk to me
of a March of 2 or 3000 Miles on Foot, of Wandring in Desarts,
among Lions and Tygers, I confess my Blood run chill" (61), and
indeed he argues against the venture. But he is outvoted, and the
travelers consult their charts to calculate their present position, and
to estimate the point at which they should aim. These would of course

be sea-charts, since the interior of the continent was wholly unexplored by Europeans. They decide to head for the coast of Angola, on
a latitude of 8° to 11° South, which would be more feasible if they
could "find Means to cross the great Lake, or Inland Sea, which the
Natives call *Coalmucoa*" (61). This lake was supposed to be the source
of the Nile, a fruitful area for mythology and pseudo-geography over
the centuries. "About the origin of the White Nile there was infinite
surmise," writes J. H. Plumb. "Snow-capped mountains, the mythical
Mountains of the Moon, or a vast inland sea were the most favoured
sources. All geographers endowed the river with enormous length,
placing its source in the heart of South Africa." As late as 1850 the
best authorities were inclined to credit the theory of an inland sea,
"about the size of the Caspian," and it was not until the journeys of
Burton, Speke, Livingstone, and Stanley that greater certainty was
reached. We cannot blame Defoe, still less his party of hardy rogues,
for putting credence in the myth.[4]

So the great journey into the unknown begins. The destination
remains a far-off dream, an alluring phantom. For the most part, Singleton describes a trip up-country, an *Anabasis* with no certain resolution. Time and distance commonly express the scale of difficulty
inherent in such an enterprise: "It was an easy March to the River
Side for us that went by Land, and we came thither in a Piece of a
Day, being . . . not above six *English* Miles; whereas it was no less
than five Days before they came to us by Water, the Wind in the
Bay having failed them, and the Way, by Reason of a great Turn or
Reach in the River being above fifty Miles about" (78). Literally "*English* Miles" is just a way of differentiating one unit of measure among
several in use, but the phrase serves to emphasize the inapplicability
of familiar, tidy concepts in this exotic landscape.

This reminder of the domestic scale is used to different effect when
Singleton observes, "The River was a fair open Channel about as
broad as the *Thames* below *Gravesend,* and a strong Tide of Flood,
which we found held us about 60 Miles" (78). A few lines later, the
comparison surfaces once more: ". . .then it narrowed apace, and was
not above as broad as the *Thames* is at *Windsor,* or thereabouts" (79).
A few pages further on, and we have this: "at the end of these two
Days . . . there was not Water enough to swim a *London* Wherry"
(89). Elsewhere Defoe reverts to the manner of recording distance as
"about 120 English Leagues" (153). The general effect is that of men
trying to accommodate themselves to an alien environment by invok-
ing familiar, but also strained, comparisons.

Two major differences are immediately apparent in the narrative of
the African journey, as contrasted with the English tour. First, Single-

ton often computes his progress by means of a count of days on the march: so we get expressions such as the following—"In our Return of this Day's Journey, our Men that made two Days of it . . ." (101). Or this: "if we found a Supply of Water, we could then travel 21 Days" (98). Or this: "I . . . enquired for the Mouth of the River, which I understood by him was above a Day's March" (76–77). Or, to give one final instance out of many: "he found now, that having marched about 33 Days Northward, we were in 6 Degrees 22 Minutes South Latitude" (129).[5]

Second, the narrator several times tots up the cumulative distance covered, something the tourist in southern England never attempts. Quite a lot of space is taken up with surveys of the ground already covered: "Here, by a moderate Computation, we concluded our selves 700 Miles from the Sea Coast where we began" (96). Again: "I told them we had march'd 700 Miles of our Way" (97). Most fully: "Here, by our Gunner's Account, who kept our Computations, we had marched above 400 Miles over this dismal Place of Horrour, having been four and thirty Days a-doing of it, and consequently were come about 1100 Miles of our Journey" (112). But we also get forward calculations as the journey moves on: "we had but that Morning been calculating, that we must have yet above a 1000 Miles to the Sea-side" (126). The debate as to whether the route should veer north-wards towards the Congo (133) contains a number of such counts. There is more sense of succession than in the *Tour,* and this is rein-forced by locutions of this type: "almost every ten Miles we came to a several Nation, and every several Nation had a different Speech" (87). Canoeing turns out to be much quicker than the slow progress of the march: "we travelled at a considerable Rate, and by our own Account, could not go less than 20 or 25 *English* Miles a Day" (87). Where the tourist had moved at a steady jog trot, the narrative of Singleton's journey displays more of a *rubato* movement: we are re-minded of the daily mileage, and thus we reenact the experience of the traveler rather than simply following a charted itinerary at our own pace.

In the concluding stages of the trek, some of the features come together, as when a group from the party go up in the mountains and observe the feared desert "which, by our Calculation, could not be less than 300 Miles broad, and above 600 Miles in Length" (163). The group is absent for some weeks: "The Journal of their Travels is too long to enter upon here; they stayed out two and fifty Days." The mysterious Englishman encountered in the backlands suggests that the party should perhaps "turn [their] March a little to the South-East, and pitch upon a Place proper for [their] Head Quarters." If they chose to do this, they might extend themselves "over the Country among the Rivers for two or three Year to the Right and Left" (160). But the proposal is rejected, and after further delays the party eventually come through to their journey's end, at "one of the *Dutch* Settlements on the Gold Coast" (167).

There is obvious haste in the concluding paragraph of this narrative, as though Defoe were anxious to move on to the next stage of Singleton's adventures. Following two years' unprofitable loafing in England, this turns out to concern Singleton's adventures in piracy proper, energized by the introduction of the Quaker buccaneer William Walters. The great overland trek is effectively forgotten, so far as the main narrative consciousness is concerned. The intensity of its rendition was very much a matter of charting a gradual progress through a hostile landscape. Defoe uses his rhetoric of distance to keep up suspense: once the goal is reached, and distances no longer convey anything, then the existential urgency drains away. For a guidebook to stick to an annotated route-map is natural enough, and the *Tour* does not suffer on account of its humdrum manner of itemizing geographical data. But a traveler's log needs some support from moral or psychological sources if it is to sustain a serious fictive role: otherwise, as in *Captain Singleton,* we shall be encouraged to identify arduousness with a count of miles or days on the march, and receive only an attenuated sense of any spiritual quest.[6]

Both books are remarkable ones, and characteristic of their author. But Defoe has to invest his statements of distance with a larger significance in the novel: to Singleton and his party, ground covered is the measure of a flight to freedom, with their desperate history of mutiny and piracy. Finally, there is something mechanical about the mode of narration, and the heart of darkness is belittled by the computations. It is rather too easy to see Defoe poring over his maps and geography books at home. With the *Tour* it is different: the stability of the narrative derives from clear, firsthand impressions (except in a very few regions), and the rhetoric of measurement and containment is in key with this ordered motion towards a known goal. To speak within compass is all very well in the closed circuits of a vacation trip, but a voyage into the dark continent needs a more capacious idiom. The lawless roads seem to ask of the language certain evocations of the illimitable, that fine "lawlessness" in computing that Edmund rejected and Mary proudly clung to. The two books are almost contemporary; it is instructive to observe the very different rhetorical strategies they employ for their different ends.

Part III
Context

In every County something of the People is said, as well as of the Place, of their Customs, Speech, Employments, the Product of their Labour, and the Manner of their living, the Circumstances as well as the Situation of the Towns; their Trade and Government; of the Rarities of Art, or Nature; the Rivers, of the Inland, and River Navigation; also of the Lakes and Medicinal Springs, not forgetting the general Dependance of the whole Country upon the City of *London*, as well for the Consumption of its Produce, as the Circulation of its Trade. (1: 3)

7

The Wonderless Wonders of the Peak:
Defoe and the Discourse of Tourism

In the last three chapters, we shift to wider aspects of the world of the *Tour*. An effort will be made to assess the position that the book occupies within contemporary ideological space: in other words, the relation of Defoe's work to some evolving attitudes and social practices as the new Hanoverian dynasty took shape. In the process, we shall look at the author's treatment of "the Rarities of Art, or Nature." The first issue considered is the nature of his response to an emergent practice, tourism, with its attendant discourse.

I

We do not ordinarily think of Defoe in terms of wit or wordplay. Yet his poetry belongs to a recognizable tradition of Restoration and Augustan satire, and his prose works often display much verbal ingenuity. In only one place, however, does he construct a sustained verbal fantasy, using a kind of semantic farce to create a discourse of both mockery and assertion. The passage occurs in Letter VIII in the third volume of his *Tour*, during his passage through Derbyshire. This portion of the text has not gone quite without scholarly commentary: in an important article, P. N. Hartle has discussed the way in which Defoe enlisted satirical as well as laudatory features of Charles Cotton's *Wonders of the Peake* (1681) and consistently "insulted, misrepresented and silently ransacked Cotton."[1] But it remains surprisingly little known, bearing in mind the fact that this is a key section of one of Defoe's greatest works, as well as exploiting wordplay in a manner almost unique within Defoe's oeuvre.

The material in question is confined to little more than twenty pages. It addresses the most conspicuous aspect of the Peak District, as this was known to a growing number of travelers, tourists, and antiquarian sightseers, and as these things had been commemorated

161

by Cotton, by Thomas Hobbes in his poem *De mirabilibis Pecci* (*c*.1636: English version, 1678), and by local historians such as Dr. Charles Leigh's *Natural History of Lancashire, Cheshire, and the Peak in Derbyshire* (1700). Their collective testimony had been to celebrate the marvels of the Peak, and in particular to establish in this district a group of seven modern wonders of the world. It is easy nowadays to read into this a conscious campaign of tourist publicity, such as clearly did exist with the Bath guidebooks of the eighteenth century. However, most travelers seem to have been happy to accept the ascrip-tion of "wonders" without challenge, even if some—like Sir John Per-cival, on his circuit through England with William Byrd II in the opening years of the eighteenth century—seem to have shared Defoe's view that the refurbished mansion and grounds at Chatsworth outdid the other alleged marvels.[2]

It is significant that Defoe alludes to Cotton's poem before he reaches the wonders proper, with a characteristically sharp observa-tion: "I that had read *Cotton's* Wonders of the *Peak*, in which I always wondered more at the Poetry than the *Peak* . . ." (2: 564). One function of such references throughout the *Tour* is to make guilty acknowledgement of the sources that Defoe pillages, not shamelessly but with a bold front.[3] Immediately we see him transferring the notion of "wonder" from one grammatical place to another: that is, from a proper noun, capitalized to indicate its existence as a stock locution as well as a geographical marker, to a sneering verb form reasserting the everyday sense of the root word. Defoe's skepticism is built into his punning redirection of the semantic current. In the phrase "Won-ders of the Peak" we have an unironic assertion of the marvelous, something about which one could genuinely feel awe and amazement. With the verb "wondered at," the sense has become "found incred-ible," "could not stomach."

The truth is that the *Tour* embodies a prolonged effort at demystifi-cation. On its title page we are promised "A Particular and Diverting Account of Whatever is Curious and worth Observation." But this aim includes an important subsidiary function of withholding praise from false curiosities or touristic nonevents. The author looks for "re-markables" (a favorite term), but he constantly adjudicates upon the merits of supposed or *soi-disant* wondrousness. Famously, as we have seen (p. 141), he declares at the start of Letter III, "I shall sing you no Songs here of the River in the first Person of a Water Nymph, a Goddess, (and I know not what) according to the Humour of the ancient Poets. I shall talk nothing of the Marriage of old *Isis*, the Male River, with the beautiful *Thame*, the Female River, a Whimsy as simple as the Subject was empty, but I shall speak of the River as

Occasion presents, as it really is *made glorious* by the Splendor of its Shores, gilded with noble Palaces . . . made famous by the Opulence of its Merchants . . ." (1: 173). In context, the section on the Peak District provides a key segment of Defoe's ideological design, in qualifying the traditional propaganda derived from legend, folk tale, and stock panegyric, to replace it with an alternative genre of realistic appraisal. In part this technique may be seen as downgrading the past and celebrating the present, a feature of the rhetoric apparent to all of Defoe's readers. In part it takes the form of ousting a discourse of enthusiastic encomium and substituting a literary mode of careful description and close specification. These tasks are performed throughout the *Tour,* but nowhere as sustainedly or densely as in the pages on Derbyshire.

We reach the wonders proper a couple of pages later, and Defoe immediately formulates his antiwonder strategy in a sentence blending irony, contempt, and grateful appeal to his ever-present aid, Camden's *Britannia:*

> And now I am come to this wonderful place, the *Peak,* where you will expect I should do as some others have, (I think, foolishly) done before me, *viz.* tell you long strange Stories of Wonders as (I must say) they are most weakly call'd; and that you may not think me arrogant in censuring so many Wise Men, who have wrote of these Wonders, as if they were all Fools, I shall give you four *Latin* Lines out of Mr. *Cambden,* by which you will see there were some Men of my Mind above a hundred Years ago. (2: 566)

The four lines are quoted, first in Latin, then in English. Plainly Defoe does wish to suggest that his predecessors were incompetent; the dark allusion to "some others" may encompass his perpetual antagonist, John Macky, but the general effect is to enlist Camden as an ally against the credulous and naive among earlier travel writers. It was a central part of the narrative role in the *Tour* to establish credence of a particular kind: as the Preface to Volume I expresses it, "to let the Readers know what Reason they will have to be satisfy'd with the Authority of the Relation" (1: 3). Here, characteristically, Defoe envisages his readers in the plural, a mark of the public voice he was striving to create.

The passage continues with a crucial turn on the works, indeed the very titles, of Hobbes and Cotton.

> Now to have so great a Man as Mr. *Hobbes,* and after him, Mr. *Cotton,* celebrate the Trifles here, the first in a fine *Latin* Poem, the last in *English* Verse, as if they were the most exalted Wonders of the World; I cannot

but, after wondering at their making Wonders of them, desire you, my Friend, to travel with me through this houling Wilderness in your Imagination, and you shall soon find all that is wonderful about it. (2: 566–67)

There is the identical sideslip here from the noun *Wonder*, connoting an officially sanctioned marvel, to the verb *wondering*, in the sense of disbelieving. There were special overtones behind the word in this era, for example those caught up in the providential narrative of "wonderful" events (escapes, survivals and the like) that J. Paul Hunter has seen as a major contributory stream to the emergent novel.[4] This in turn had been inflected towards satiric ends in a minor Scriblerian squib, commonly attributed to Swift, *The Wonderful Wonder of Wonders,* followed by another entitled *The Wonder of all the Wonders that ever the World Wondered at.* Both appeared at Dublin in 1721, just five years before the third volume of the *Tour* came out. For that matter, a well-known poem of 1710, *The Age of Wonders,* has been included in the canon of Defoe's own works by John Robert Moore.[5] We need not accept the last ascription to see that such titles reflect a widespread competition among different ideological persuasions for ownership of this concept: the rhetoric of the Peak sections constitutes Defoe's bid to replace a traditional interpretation of the wonderful, as embodied in a reverential and quasi-mystical vocabulary of seventeenth-century enthusiasm, with a more "realistic" and modern sense of what truly invites rational admiration.

In the short span of little more than twenty pages, Defoe employs *wonder* and its derivatives sixty-one times (*wondering, wonderful, wonderless,* etc.) It is not a particularly common word elsewhere in the *Tour,* or in most of his work generally. The sudden density of usage can only be put down to a deliberate attempt to reappraise the marvelous. This function may also involve making sport of Defoe's predecessors, something he never found uncongenial, and there is a degree of gratuitous or ludic fun in the process. Nonetheless, the wordplay has a serious point, not least because the Peak District was precisely the location where modern genteel tourism began in Britain, before it moved on to the Lake District and then the Highlands of Scotland in succeeding generations. It does not seem overingenious, accordingly, to suggest that the physical location of a particular activity with its own distinct ideology (i.e. the Debyshire tourist trade) might supply the textual locus where this ideology could be interrogated, by means of a verbal attack on the associations of "wonder" in a certain kind of touristic discourse.

Before Defoe addresses the seven official wonders of the Peak, he describes at length what he regards as truly remarkable, that is, the way of a life of a poor miner and his family working in a cave in the hillside. This is one of the famous episodes in the entire *Tour*: what has not been observed is the strategy used to introduce it. Defoe's narrative prepares for the genuine miracle by discounting supposed marvels.[6] First he recounts details of the "prodigious" height of a sheer cliff named Matlock Tor, and makes the characteristic addition, "The prodigious heighth of this *Tor* . . . was to me more a wonder than any of the rest in the *Peak*, and, I think, it should be named among them, but it is not. So it must not be called one of the *Wonders*" (2: 567). Having thus set up a feeling of skepticism with regard to the standard itinerary, he proceeds to undermine further any credibility that local folklore might possess:

> The *Peak* People, who are mighty fond of having Strangers shewed every Thing they can, and of calling every thing a Wonder, told us here of another high Mountain, where a Giant was buried, and which they called the *Giant's Tomb*. This tempted our Curiosity, and we presently rod up to the Mountain . . . to see this Giant's Tomb: Here we miss'd the imaginary Wonder, and found a real one. (2: 568)

The true wonder, of course, concerns the miner and his family; Defoe then devotes some five pages to the human interest of such a way of life—something that was highly unusual in standard guidebooks of the day. Noticeably, in this passage of about two thousand words, the expression "wonder" does not occur, although it quickly reemerges when the narrative moves on at the close of the lead-mining episode. Indeed, Defoe makes the point with his customary explicitness:

> If any Reader thinks this, and the past Relation of the Woman and the Cave, too low and trifling for this Work, they must be told, that I think quite otherwise; and especially considering what a Noise is made of Wonders in this Country, which, I must needs say, have nothing in them curious, but much talked of, more trifling a great deal. See *Cotton's Wonders of the Peak, Hobbes's Chatsworth*, and several others. (2: 572)

In this way the narrator distances himself from the mere "curiosities" beloved of antiquarian or dilettante travelers. Defoe's repudiation of imagined wonders has more than a negative function. It is designed also to endorse his own "modern" emphasis on the real England, studied with Baconian rigor and true Royal Society particularity.

II

It is only after this lengthy excursion that the text reaches the seven wonders proper. Naturally, Defoe cannot resist a bout of wordplay when he finally arrives at the first in the series:

> From here ... we had eight Mile smooth Green riding to *Buxton* Bath, which they call one of the *Wonders* of the *Peak;* but is so far from being a Wonder, that to us, who had been at *Bath* in *Somersetshire,* and at *Aix la Chapelle* in *Germany,* it was nothing at all; nor is it any thing but what is frequent in such Mountainous Countries as this is, in many Parts of the World.
>
> That which was more wonderful to me than all of it, was, that so light is made of them as to Use ... (2: 572–73)

The experienced traveler or mountain wallah has come into his own. To deflate the pretended "wonder" of such a location as Buxton baths is to expose the hollowness of local claims to glory, once these are viewed in a national or international setting. The Britain Defoe describes was entering on a phase of greater centralization, and the ancient particularism that had controlled its government and cultural practice was now being threatened by increasing centripetal forces emanating from London. In the same way, the text of the *Tour* enacts a process of centralized planning. Modern travel literature commonly rejoices in finding local oddities and neighborhood customs; Defoe attempts to bring all Britain under the writ of his metropolitan textual authority, and to this end diminishes the claims of the outlying regions to independence or uniqueness.

It is true that in the next paragraph Defoe makes a minor concession, agreeing that some of the claims made for the healing properties of Buxton baths are justified:

> But though I shall not treat this warm Spring as a Wonder, for such it is not; I must nevertheless give it the Praise due to the medicinal Virtue of its Waters; for it is not to be deny'd, but that wonderful Cures have been wrought by them, especially in Rheumatick, Scorbutick and scrofulous Distempers, Aches of the Joints, nervous Pains, and also in scurvy and leprous Maladies. (2: 573)

The rhetoric of plainspoken honesty takes over here, but Defoe carefully limits his approbation to the proven record of medicinal success. In other words, his endorsement of actual physical benefit to be gained by taking the waters allowed the possibility of "wonderful" effects, but it does not extend to any admission that the baths are a "wonder" in themselves, as a natural phenomenon. We might generalize this position to say that Defoe is willing to acknowledge what he would regard as the authentically marvelous; to do this, he makes a point of excluding bogus "miracles" that are readily explicable in nonmysti- cal terms.

Some three pages are devoted to Buxton, mostly in a tone of moder- ate approval. Defoe sums this up by saying, "We saw indeed a Variety of Objects here; some that came purely for the Pleasure of Bathing, taking the Air, and to see the Country, which has many Things rare and valuable to be seen, tho' nothing, as I met with, can be called a Wonder, *Elden-Hole* excepted, of which in its Place" (2: 575). But the note grows more abrasive when the text arrives at the natural curiosities that formed the greater part of the supposed wonders. This is evident when we reach "a great Cave or Hole in the Earth, called *Poole's Hole, another of the Wonderless Wonders of the Peak*" (2: 576). This phrase has a demotic, almost proverbial ring:[7] the "*Wonderless* Wonders*" are to be exposed, as a kind of geographical fraud imposed on the innocent, almost as the South Sea promoters had foisted their project upon the unwary. Defoe contemptuously refers to a tale of the giant Poole who was alleged to have lived in the cave, with the observation, "I say, this I leave to those who such Stories are better suited to, than I expect of my Readers." There follows an especially dizzy piece of playfully tenuous logic: "However, this helps among the People there, to make out the *Wonder;* and indeed such Things are wanting where really Wonder is wanting, else there would be no Wonder at all in it; as indeed there is not" (2: 576). The first *wanting* seems to mean "lacking, therefore necessary," and the second "lacking, because non-existent." But the meaning is not altogether clear, so intent is Defoe on making sport of the local pretensions.

The narrator admits that the cave is impressive in scale. But "that it is very high, is enough to say; for it is so far from a quarter of a Mile [the height proposed by "a late Flaming Author"], that there seems nothing admirable in it." True, the historian Dr. Leigh "spends some time in admiring the spangled Roof, [while] *Cotton* and *Hobbes* are most ridiculously and outrageously witty upon it" (2: 576). But Defoe adopts his usual plain man's caution: if not adopting precisely a strategy of *nil admirari*, he refuses to join in the chorus of rapturous exclamations. His implication is that rational judgment is needed if things are to be appreciated at their true worth, since the fanciful metaphors of previous writers have introduced a kind of false sublime:

For, in short, the Stone is coarse, slimy, *with the constant wet*, dirty and dull; and were the little drops of Water gone, or the Candles gone, there would be none of these fine Sights to be seen for Wonders, or for the learned Authors above to show themselves foolish about. (2: 577)

It is not hard to see why Defoe needed to take this line with Cotton and Hobbes. His own *Tour* was designed to show the remarkable features of Britain, and indeed operates through sustained use of hyperbole and amplification:[8] the strong nationalistic emphasis of the Preface to the first volume makes that explicit. "In Travelling thro' *England,* a luxuriance of Objects presents it self to our View: Where-ever we come, and which way soever we look, we see something New, something Significant, something well worth the Travellers stay, and the Writer's Care" (1: 1). As we can see from the odd capitalization, Defoe seeks the "New" and the "Significant," identified as particularly "worth . . . the Writer's care." An inert posture of wonderment will not suffice. The author must describe, define, and isolate, replacing the poetic flights and facile panegyrics of his competitors with revelations of the authentically remarkable features of the country. Wonders will have to go. Folklore is habitually treated with a good-humored contempt. Defoe would have surely been astounded to know that, nearly three centuries later, readers are commonly more interested in legends than in facts. He himself witnessed, and in a small way helped to bring about, the disappearance of popular tradition in favor of a more sophisticated and "enlightened" array of cultural practices and beliefs. Twentieth-century social historians may regard this process as a loss, but we cannot expect a man of Defoe's generation to see matters in that way.

The narrative quickly disposes of Poole's Hole—"So that, in short, there is nothing . . . to make a Wonder of, any more than as other Things in Nature, which are rare to be seen, however easily accounted for, may be called wonderful." This prepares the way for another blast:

> Having thus accounted for two of the seven Things, called *Wonders* in this Country, I pass by *Elden Hole,* which I shall take notice of by it self, and come to two more of them, as wonderless, and empty of every Thing that may be called rare or strange, as the other; and indeed much more so. (2: 578)

The next sight to be "accounted for" is Mam Tor. This time Defoe adopts a pose of trying to be fair, although the rhetoric instantly turns back on itself, to expose the fraudulence of the claims:

> The Sum of the whole Wonder *is this,* that there is a very high Hill, nay I will add (that I may make the most of the Story, and that it may appear

as much like a Wonder as I can) an exceeding high Hill. But this in a Country which is all over Hills, cannot be much of a Wonder, because also there are several higher Hills in the *Peak* than that, only not just there. (2: 578)

Defoe goes on to an elaborate description of the "pretended Wonder" and the humdrum reality underlying its formation, ending with a typical flourish: "But nothing is more certain than this, that the more Water comes down from it, the less remains in it; and so it certainly is of *Mam Tor,* in spite of all the Poetry of *Mr. Cotton* or *Mr. Hobbes,* and in spight of all the Women's Tales in the *Peak*" (2: 579). "Poetry" has been strategically redefined to convey the sense of "fancy lan'guage." But of course, in its way, Defoe's idiom is just as tricky.

Next we come to "the so famed Wonder call'd, saving our good Manners, *The Devil's A——e in the Peak* ... yet we must search narrowly for any thing in it to make a *Wonder,* or even any thing so strange, or odd, or vulgar, as the Name would seem to import" (2: 579). Defoe makes a show of carrying out this narrow search, with a predictable nil return. Having described the rock formations and water flows, he concludes, "This is the whole Wonder, unless it may be called so, that our Ancestors should give it so homely a Sirname" (2: 579). He stresses the existence of similar geological forms in many parts of England, quite apart from biblical instances such as the Cave of Adullam (from I Samuel). In summary: "If there were no such Vaults and Arches any where but in the *Peak,* or indeed if they were not frequent in such mountainous Countries, as well here, as in other Nations, we might call this a *Wonder.* But as we know they are to be found in many Places of *England,* and that we read of them in the Description of other Countries, and even in Scripture, we cannot think there is any room to call it a Wonder" (2: 580). At such moments Defoe's literalism rises to a kind of poetry of its own; he tells incredu'lously a story of the early mythographers, with this aside, "Indeed, had *Gervaise* of *Tilbury* been credited, this Place had deserved all that Wonder cou'd ascribe to it" (2: 580)—but, of course, the story proves to be incoherent and undependable, like "another of the same kind which *Hudibras* tells of."

With his rhetorical framework now firmly in place, Defoe can afford to be brief at his next stopping-point.

The next Wonder, which makes up Number five, is called *Tideswell.* ... A poor thing indeed to make a Wonder of; and therefore most of the Writers pass it over with little notice; only that they are at a loss to make up the Number seven without it. ... So that all this Wonder is owing only to the Situation of the Place, which is a meer Accident in Nature;

> and if any Person were to dig into the Place ... they would soon see *Tideswell* turned into an ordinary running Stream, and a very little one too. (2: 581)

To turn the extraordinary into the ordinary is not a goal of modern science: but when the scientific revolution was still under way, at least in a phase of consolidation, it may have been necessary for writers to parade their victories over ignorance, jeeringly triumphalist as the tone may now seem. The urge was probably strongest in people like Defoe, who harbored a good many prescientific skeletons in their intellectual closet.

Then comes a shift in direction: "So much for fictitious Wonders, or indeed simple Wonders." What does the last expression mean? Perhaps Defoe has in mind "Sights which provoke an instant but shallow, sense of amazement, until the real explanation is provided." The narrative continues, "The two real Wonders which remain, are first, *Elden Hole,* and secondly, the Duke of *Devonshire*'s fine House at *Chatsworth;* one a Wonder of Nature, the other of Art" (2: 581). By now Defoe is differentiating wonders, by degree or by kind; this is a necessary device in order to clear space for an appreciation of the truly marvelous, which has been waiting in the wings while the five spurious wonders were being dispatched.

The long description of Chatsworth emphasizes (as was usual)[9] the magnificence of the house and gardens, both in conception and execution. It helped Defoe's overall purposes that a major reconstruction had been begun in the 1690s, and thus the grandeur could be imputed first to modern times and second to a human agent, the former Duke, who was "not only capable to design, but to finish" (2: 582). Admittedly, the celebrated Elizabethan noblewoman, Bess of Hardwick, had laid the foundations of Chatsworth's noble appearance:

> The Lady, who it seems, was the mover of the first Design, finish'd the whole in the magnificent Manner which it appeared in, when it was first christen'd a *Wonder,* and ranked among the *Marvelleux* of the *Peak.* But what would the World have called it, or what would Mr. *Cambden* have said of it, had it appeared in those Days in the Glory and Splendor its last great Founder, for so we may justly call him, left it in. (2: 581)

The overall aim of the *Tour* is to supply an up-to-date report, with "the Situation of Things ... given not as they have been, but as they are" (1: 3). Chatsworth is a living example of "improvement" at work, and its status as a wonder is thus endorsed by its capacity—not shared by the natural wonders—to revivify itself under human hands. Defoe finds it surprising only that such a jewel should be set in so unpromising a location, surrounded as the estate was by "a comfortless, barren, and . . . endless Moor." This prompts the reflection, "if there is any Wonder in *Chatsworth*, it is, that any Man . . .who could lay out the Plan for such a House . . . would build it in such a Place where the Mountains insult the Clouds, intercept the Sun, and would threaten, *were Earthquakes frequent here,* to bury the very Towns, much more the House, in their Ruins" (2: 583). The sudden irruption of earth-quakes from nowhere in particular suggests Defoe's strain as he tries to move from a negative idiom of wonderless wonders to one admitting the category of genuine wonders.

The other exception, as we have seen, is made in favor of Eldon Hole. The narrative cites Cotton's experiments with dropping a plumb line down the cavity—Defoe quotes him as saying his rope was eight hundred fathoms in length, which doubles Cotton's actual figure of eight hundred yards. For once Defoe seems to be rounding everything up, instead of down. He continues, "This I allow to be a Wonder, and what the like of is not to be found in the World, that I have heard of, or believe. And would former Writers have been contented with one Wonder instead of seven, it would have done more Honour to the *Peak,* and even to the whole Nation, than the adding five imaginary Miracles to it that had nothing in them, and which really depreciated the whole" (2: 584–85). To a modern reader, the glee with which the text demolishes the false grandeur of numbers one to five comes over more strongly than any real enjoyment in celebrating the true sublimity of the other two wonders. A strategy whose funda-mental purpose lay in the act of demystification proves rather less energizing, from a literary point of view, when it is required to serve a more positive end.

III

Defoe's final gesture is one familiar to readers of all his works—a resumptive passage that goes back over the preceding material with a total lack of any embarrassment concerning redundancy. "Having then viewed those Things with an impartial Mind," he observes in compla-cent tones, "give me leave to reduce the Wonders of the *Peak* to a less Number, and of a quite different Kind" (2: 585). The principal verb is aptly chosen: Defoe's treatment has indeed been reductive in its attitude to the supposed touristic glories of Derbyshire.

The list begins:

1. *Elden Hole* I acknowledge to be a wonderful Place, as I have said, above; but to me the greatest Surprize is, that, after such a real Wonder, any of the Trifles added to it could bear the Name of Wonders.
2. Of *Buxton;* the Wonder to me is, that in a Nation so full of Chronical Diseases as we are . . . there should be such a Fountain of Medicine sent from Heaven, and no more notice taken of it, or care to make it useful.
3. That in a Nation so curious, so inquiring, and so critical as this, any thing so unsatisfying, so foolish, and so weak, should pass for Wonders as those of *Mam Tor, Tideswell, Poole's Hole, &c.* (2: 585)

The narrator saves up for last his most emphatic statement of a true wonder, emphasizing the element of human intervention:

4. As to *Chatsworth,* the Wonder, as I said before, seems to me; not that so noble and magnificent a Palace should be built, but that it should be built in such a Situation, and in such a Country so out of the way, so concealed from the World, that whoever sees it must take a Journey on purpose. (2: 586)

But the palace was built, nature has been overcome by human contriv-ance, Defoe as tourist-guide has made the journey, and the text of the *Tour* has encompassed even this outlying wonder. We may notice how the basic construction by now has turned into "The wonder to me is . . . ," that is to say the quasi-objective roll call of agreed wonders has been supplanted by the textually inscribed wonderment of the narrator. This could be put another way: the root word *wonder* has been moved semantically from the space of the real world to the inner space of the author's mind. At the outset, *wonder* carried its main lexical charge in the area of admiration, awe, reverential and respect-ful gaze. By the end, the primary overtones called up are those of puzzlement, disbelief, and musing self-colloquy. With a Parthian shot, Defoe moves on by alluding to the greater altitudes of the High Peak itself, which lead him to think that "the Mountains of the *Peak,* of which I have been speaking, seem to be but the beginnings of Wonders to this Part of the Country, and but the beginning of Mountains" (2: 586). The great Pennine chain stretches ahead, in geographical terms and inside the text of the *Tour.*

What has happened over the space of these sixty-odd usages seems fairly clear. Defoe has cut the noted tourist spots down to size, to enhance his own touristic ideology. The marvelous has been redefined to exclude inappropriate objects of attention: natural phenomena read-ily explained by scientific means, or readily paralleled in other parts of the world. In this sense "wonders" may be seen as a product of older attitudes of mind—obsolete pieties, genteel assumptions, deference to the past—which a thorough survey, as embodied in the *Tour*, will displace in favor of a more balanced and judicious appraisal. Credulity and enthusiasm will be supplanted by rational investigation.[10] How could Defoe have foreseen that the late twentieth-century would be skeptical regarding his enlightened skepticism, and credulous with regard to the credulities of a folk past? But perhaps more interesting than the ideological messages of the section are the rhetorical means. What most strikes us is Defoe's gusto, his sheer pleasure in running through the changes of the word *wonder*. We have long talked of him in connection with economic man; perhaps it is time we spent more time in thinking of Defoe as *homo ludens*.

8

Defoe's Buildings of England

ARCHITECTURE was one of the remarkably few topics about which Defoe did not write a treatise. Nonetheless, the requirements of his *Tour* were such that he could not ignore the topic. The mania for both building and gardening that overtook landed proprietors; the growth of London, and the rise of provincial centers of culture—what Peter Borsay has called "The English Urban Renaissance"—all these made "taste" in building and the associated arts of design a desirable quality in the genteel. Even if Defoe did not exactly share in this mania— except, perhaps, in the *furor hortensis*—he was well aware of this interest among his readers, and the expectations they would conse' quently bring to his book. Moreover, Defoe was not disabled by a comparative lack of aesthetic awareness. In its place he had a strong sense of the social effects of the "improvement" he saw going on all around him. The Preface to the first volume makes repeated allusions to the way in which "Great Towns decay, and small Towns rise; new Towns, new Palaces, new Seats are built every Day."[1] This was an emphasis equally prominent in the "Addenda" to this volume (1: 250); the Preface to the second volume ("New Foundations are always lay' ing, new Buildings always raising . . . Churches and publick Buildings erecting," 1: 252), and other ancillary portions of the text. Obviously Defoe lays this emphasis partly for marketing purposes, in order to draw attention to the up-to-date state of his book. Nevertheless, his very ambition to document the new made it imperative for him to take account of the building that was occurring around Britain, whether the recently fashionable Palladian vogue in country man' sions, or the squares and town halls of fast-growing urban centers.

There is a second consideration, too. Defoe's relative lack of concern with architecture *per se* did not extend to the issue of town planning. He had a firsthand involvement in schemes to rebuild the area of Whitehall after the fires of the 1690s, an issue raised in the *Tour* (1: 357–64);[2] and he proposed his own visionary project for a kind of new town to be planted in the New Forest—again, details are set out at large in the *Tour* (1: 200–6). And nobody could read Letter V, on London, without sensing that the author was someone with an acute alertness to issues of urban design. He actually begins this section with a surveyor's "line of Measurement," beating the bounds of the city and parceling its circumference up into miles, furlongs and rods (1: 318–23). This is followed by another tabulated passage, enumerating "the New Buildings erected in and about the Cities of *London* and *Westminster* and Borough of *Southwark*, since the Year 1666" (1: 326–332), concluding with three new projects to develop the city as well as to regulate its growth (1: 332).

But what of architecture in the narrow sense? Defoe, as we have seen, did not altogether share the passion for this subject which many of his patrons and readers would (as he knew) exhibit. He did not, after all, possess the background of a dilettante: his formative years had been spent in preparing for the ministry and then in trade, not in viewing the ruins of Rome and galleries of Florence with an officious bear-leader to guide his steps. It may therefore come as a surprise to realize that he described hundreds of buildings in the course of his *Tour*. I exclude from this count items such as ancient earthworks (Old Sarum), ruins such as Stonehenge and Avebury (not yet well known, and not described by that name, 1: 286), Hadrian's Wall and the Antonine Wall, the erections on St. Michael's Mount and Glastonbury Tor, innumerable bridges, and structures such as Lyme Cobb. We can safely ignore also the long descriptions of dockyards at Deptford, Chatham, Portsmouth, Plymouth, and Liverpool, although modern architectural historians might regard these as more clearly belonging to the art of architecture than did Defoe's contemporaries. In the account that follows, I leave aside, too, certain anomalous buildings such as Eddystone lighthouse.

This still leaves a very large group. Defoe pays no attention to ordinarily domestic architecture, except in the oblique sense that he often refers to places as "well built" or "a pretty little Borough Town" (2: 633). In this, he was representative of his age: small individual units of the urban housing stock were invisible to most commentators, and a rustic cottage, however picturesque, did not warrant notice in a serious guidebook. The small, the eccentric, the deviant—categories that cover some of Pevsner's most arresting entries—had not yet surfaced above the architectural horizon. The buildings apparent to the Augustan eye, and therefore treated by Defoe, fall mainly into four types. These are churches and monastic buildings, but above all cathedrals, castles and forts, country seats with their estates, and public buildings. There are very few references to town houses of the wealthy except in passing; the only sustained exception occurs in the coverage of the "very magnificent, large and princely Buildings" oc-cupied by great magnates along Canongate and the High Street in Edinburgh (2: 711–12).

The phrase "Buildings of England" is, of course, a misnomer, in that the *Tour* covers the whole of Britain. But Defoe did not know most of Scotland or Wales well (parts of them scarcely at all), and this is reflected in his treatment of architectural issues. In Letter VI he de-votes most of his physical description to the natural environment, in particular to the mountainous landscape. His entire section on Wales contains scarcely a word on private homes, large or small. There is brief reference to castles such as Harlech and Caernarvon (but no real description); apart from this, attention is focused exclusively on the cathedrals. Indeed, when the narrative begins a long serpentine sweep in this letter with the three choir cities of Gloucester, Worces-ter, and Hereford, the only works of man that receive detailed notice are the cathedrals. Here Defoe was able to supplement his usual sources such as Camden and Dugdale with the works of Browne Willis, including surveys of St. David's, Llandaff, St. Asaph, and Bangor, published between 1717 and 1721. (The evidence is inferen-tial: Defoe makes no reference to Willis in the text.) In all cases the physical description is brief, which argues for a lack of recent firsthand observation. All that Defoe says of Bangor as a structure is, "an old, mean looking, and almost despicable Cathedral Church" (2: 463). On Llandaff, we are told, "Tho' the Church is antient, yet the Building is good, and the Choir neat, and pretty well kept" (2: 454).

With regard to Scotland, the position is a little different. Defoe devotes considerable space to Edinburgh and Glasgow. His material on the other university towns, St. Andrews and Aberdeen, is mostly historical in character. For the rest, we have a few individual secular buildings covered at length: Holyrood Palace, Drumlanrig, Hopton House, Hamilton, Kinross, and Rothes. However, the emphasis is often on the park and grounds rather than the mansion itself. Perhaps the best section is that on Yester (2: 698), where Defoe writes with genuine enthusiasm on the extensive planting of fir trees undertaken by the Earls of Tweedale. Like Samuel Johnson fifty years later, Defoe was preoccupied by the need to encourage planting trees—but where Johnson wishes to see raw nature brought under civilized human con-trol, Defoe has in mind the lasting asset that timber will furnish to the landowner.

In general, it may be said that, with the lone exception of the Edinburgh area, all Defoe's most fresh and vivid memory of particular scenes attaches to English portions of his imaginary journey. As a result, his most interesting architectural commentary is to be found in these sections.

I

It can be no accident that the English cathedral most thoroughly described is St. Paul's, in whose shadow Defoe had grown up. "The Beauty of all the Churches in the City," he observes in his account of London in Letter V, "and of all the Protestant Churches in the World, is the Cathedral of St. *Paul's*; a Building exceeding Beautiful and Magnificent" (1: 334). The author attacks a line of criticism which had been advanced that "the Columns are too gross [and] . . . the Work looks heavy." He retorts that if the columns and panel work were "filled with Pictures, adorned with Carved Work and Gilding, and crowded with adorable Images of the Saints and Angels, the kneeling Crowd would not complain of the Grossness of the Work" (1: 334–35). This "Protestant Plainness" determines the proportions used: "neither by the Rules of Order, or by the Necessity of the Build-ing, to be proportioned and sufficient to the Height and Weight of the Work, could they have been less, or any otherwise than they are." Such comfortable Leibnitzian certainty produces an assured defense of the "Wise Architect" and Defoe is able to conclude, "No man that has the least Judgment in Building, that knows any Thing of the Rules of Proportion, and will judge impartially, can find any Fault in this Church" (1: 336). How impartial the puritan Defoe was in these matters is open to debate. An especially noteworthy word in this passage is "adorable," which Johnson a few years later would define as "That which ought to be adored; that which is worthy of divine honours." The sneer in Defoe's use of the expression is easy enough to detect.

Defoe seems on firmer ground when he can appeal to the rules of classical or baroque architecture in this fashion. His feelings with regard to Gothic were obviously less defined. About Winchester he writes, "The Choir of the Church appears very magnificent; the Roof is very high, and the Gothick Work in the arch'd Part is very fine, tho' very old; the Painting in the Windows is admirably good, and easy to be distinguish'ed by those that understand those Things" (1: 182). At Lichfield he remarks, "The Church . . . is indeed a most beautiful Building; the *West* Prospect of it is charming, the two Spires on the Corner Towers being in themselves perfect Beauties of Archi-tect [sic], in the old *Gothic* way of Building. . . . The Spaces between the Doors are fill'd with carv'd Work and Imagery, no Place being void, where (by the *Rules of Architect*) any Ornament could be plac'd" (2: 480)—another Leibnitzian touch. York Minster prompts this:

> It is a *Gothick* Building, but with all the most modern *Addenda* that Order of Building can admit; and with much more Ornament of a singular kind, than we see any thing of that Way of Building grac'd with. . . . The only deficiency I find at *York* Minster, is the lowness of the great Tower, or its want of a fine Spire upon it, which, doubtless, was designed by the Build- ers. . . . As this Church was so compleatly finished, and that so lately that it is not yet four hundred Years old, it is the less to be wondered that the Work continues so firm and fine, that it is now the beautifullest Church of the old Building that is in *Britain*. (2: 637–38).

Another cathedral that calls out Defoe's admiration, in very similar terms, is Peterborough: "It wants only a fine Tower Steeple, and a Spire on the Top of it . . . to make it the finest Cathedral in *Britain*, except St. *Paul's*, which is quite new, and the Church of St. *Peter* at *York*' (2: 500). But Lincoln elicits a more measured judgment: "The Cathedral is in itself a very noble Structure, and it is counted very fine, though I thought it not equal to some that I have already de- scrib'd. . . . It is much larger than that at *Litchfield*; but the Spires on the Towers at the Angles of the *West* End are mean, small, and low, and not to be nam'd with those at *Litchfield*: The Tower also is very plain, and has only four very ill-proportion'd Spires, or rather Pinna- cles, at the four Corners small and very mean" (2: 491). Plainly Defoe had limited sympathy with Gothic, especially its earlier phases. He has nothing of note to say on Salisbury from an aesthetic standpoint, despite a long recital of monuments and the like: sometimes he takes refuge in platitude—Beverley Minster is "a very fair and neat Struc- ture" (2: 645), which today seems an oddly insensitive formulation. Chichester "is not the finest in *England*, but is far from being the most ordinary" (1: 134)—which looks like mere padding. As for Canter- bury, "The Church is a Noble Pile of building indeed, and looks Vener- able and Majestick at a distance, as well as when we come nearer to it" (1: 117).

In fact, the most vivid apprehension of a cathedral strictly as a building comes when Defoe travels through the Fens in Letter I, and through the mist "the Isle of *Ely* look'd as if wrapp'd up in Blankets, and nothing to be seen, but now and then, the Lanthorn or Cupola of *Ely Minster*" (1: 80). But toward the church itself Defoe is less respectful: "Of the Minster this is the most remarkable thing that I could hear, namely, that some of it is so antient, totters so much with every gust of Wind, looks so much like a Decay, and seems so near it, that when ever it does fall, all that 'tis likely will be thought strange in it, will be, that it did not fall a hundred Years sooner" (1: 74–75). Equally unenthusiastic is the account of Worcester: "The Cathedral of this City is an antient, and indeed, a decay'd Building; the Body of the Church is very mean in its Aspect, nor did I see the least ornament about it, I mean in the out side" (2: 443). Hereford is more sympathetically treated: "The great Church is a magnificent Building, however Antient, the Spire is not high, but handsome, and there is a fine Tower at the West End . . . the Choir is very fine, tho' plain" (2: 449). Much the same terms are used of Gloucester, "an old venerable Pile, with very little Ornament, within or without, yet 'tis well built" (2: 440). Defoe seems unobservant about the finer points of all the medieval architecture he encounters, and his comments suggest that he was unable to educate an eye trained to recognize the ordonnance of classical buildings to perceive the aesthetic intent of Gothic. In this he was representative of many people in his time. We must recall that there were as yet few glimmerings of a Gothic revival, let alone an independent Gothic taste: in Greenwich "Sir *John Vanburg* has built a House Castle-wise" (1: 95), that is Maze Hill, but none of Hawks- moor's Gothic work is mentioned—for that matter, the account of the Queen Anne churches going up in London just as Defoe wrote is perfunctory in the extreme.

The narrative is often seduced from architectural matters, in the narrow sense, by subsidiary issues. The height of Salisbury Cathedral, and the number of windows it possesses; or a range of antiquarian matters such as the contents of the library (easily extractable from authorities such as Browne Willis)—these easily deflect Defoe. He is capable of remarking that the tower of Boston Stump "is not only beautiful by Land, but is very useful at Sea to guide Pilots into that Port" (2: 494), or of debating whether Grantham spire is really crooked (2: 502). What most appalls the prophet of improvement is the sight of decay, something common in Post-Reformation Scotland, but apparent also at many places in England. These include Chester: "'tis built of a red, sandy, ill looking Stone, which takes much of the Beauty of it, and which yielding to the Weather, seems to crumble, and suffer by Time, which much defaces the Building" (2: 469), and Wrexham parish church: "The Work is mean, the Statues seem all mean and in dejected Postures, without any Fancy or Spirit in the Workmanship, and as the Stone is of a reddish crumbling Kind . . . Time has made it look gross and rough" (2: 474). The author's posi- tives emerge from slightly muddled comments such as that on Wells: "One of the neatest, and in some respects, the most beautiful, Cathe- drals in *England,* particularly the *West* Front of it, is One complete Draught of Imagery, very fine, and yet very Antient" (1: 277). Defoe never quite made up his mind how far antiquity got in the way of beauty.

II

"*Tintagel* Castle lies upon this Coast a little farther, a Mark of great Antiquity, and every Writer has mentioned it; but as Antiquity is not my Work, I leave the Ruin of *Tintagel* to those that search into Antiquity" (1: 257). Thus writes Defoe when he journeys along the north coast of Cornwall. The passage continues, "Little or nothing, that I could hear, is to be seen at it; and as for the Story of King *Arthur* being both born and killed there, 'tis a Piece of Tradition, only on *Oral History,* and not any Authority to be produced for it." Leaving aside the surprisingly modern use of the phrase "oral history" (surely one of the earliest recorded), what strikes us here is Defoe's lack of feeling for romantic Arthurian mythology, not just in terms of ideology but also in terms of the sensual impact of picturesque ruins. The same attitudes are visible throughout the text: castles are most commonly ruins, and though these have a certain poetry for Defoe, they more often present themselves as symptoms of decay. Sometimes he evades the issue: the entry for Conway contains not a hint that there is a castle in the town. Naturally, his heart leaps up when he beholds a well-preserved, or better still a renovated castle: the prose begins to flow when he reaches Nottingham and even more Warwick: "The Castle is a fine Building, beautiful both by Situation and its Decoration. . . . The Building is old, but several Times repair'd and beautify'd by its several Owners, and 'tis now a very agreeable Place both within and without: the Apartments are very nicely contrived, and . . . one finds no Irregularity in the whole Place, notwithstanding its ancient Plan, as it was a Castle not a Palace" (2: 484).

The last remark could arguably be applied to Windsor, although by the eighteenth century the primary function of the buildings had long ceased to have any military significance. Defoe's entry (1: 301–12) forms an impressive climax to Letter IV, as the narrative returns to its London base after a long progress through the South West. For once Defoe lets himself go, to dilate with relish on the royal apartments, public rooms, the chapel royal (i.e., St. George's), the terraces, and grounds. The tone is uniformly positive, not to say fulsome: "The Breadth of the Walk is very spacious on the *North* Side, on the *East* Side it is narrower; but neither at *Versailles,* or at any of the Royal Palaces in *France,* or at *Rome,* or *Naples,* have I never seen any thing like it" (1: 304). In sober reality, Defoe probably never saw anything in Rome or Naples, but his rhetorical ends dictate a strong patriotic gesture at this stage of the *Tour*. This is most apparent in lengthy discussion of the Order of the Garter, most filched from Elias Ashmole's history of the order, which had been reprinted with additions in 1715. But the nationalistic imperative shows through, too, in the architectural passages, and even in references to the paintings on show. The narrator describes how Charles II had set up a full length portrait of the Duchess of Portsmouth, of which the King was supposed to say, "'Twas the finest Painting, of the finest Woman in *Christendom;* but our *English* Ladies of Queen *Mary's* Court, were of another Opinion, and the Gallery of Beauties . . . which her Majesty placed in the Water Gallery at *Hampton Court*, shews several as good Faces, and as good Painting" (1: 305).

Defoe seldom lets slip an opportunity to celebrate his patron, William III, or the royal consort. Another chance comes at Kensington Palace, where the author mentions that he had the honor to attend the Queen "when she first viewed the Ground, and directed the doing it [laying out the garden]" (1: 390). Here the text allots one brief paragraph to the house itself, and moves on to historical incidents associated with the place during the time of William and Mary both internally and externally. Defoe had already pointed out that the royal couple had both had a deep influence on English taste, the Queen by introducing callicos and chinaware, the King by promoting the love of both landscape gardening and painting (1: 166–67). Indeed, the impression Defoe leaves is that until William III there was little royal patronage of the visual arts in England, a judgment unfair to both the Tudor and Stuart lines. As it happens, he had a favorable case at Hampton Court, in respect of the Raphael cartoons that had been brought originally by Charles I, but were now more publicly displayed. The section here concludes with a hope that King William's plans for rebuilding Hampton Court might be revived, for "if ever that shall be, I know no Palace in *Europe, Versailles* excepted, which can come up to her, either for Beauty and Magnificence, or of Extent of Building, and the Ornaments attending it" (1: 180).

The royal palaces, then, afford Defoe a chance to display his patriotism, inflected in an unmistakably protestant and Hanoverian direction. With the great country houses of the nation, the aim is not very different: to celebrate the wealth and territorial grandeur of the highest families of the land, most enthusiastically when these represent major Whig dynasties, whether old or new. In line with that purpose, the *Tour* devotes its longest entries under this heading to estates such as Blenheim, seen as a national shrine to the recently dead Marlborough; Cannons, the home of the unscrupulous Duke of Chandos;

Petworth, Chatsworth and Burleigh, all in the possession of families with a solidly Hanoverian record. Robert Walpole's house at Houghton had scarcely risen above the level of its foundations when Defoe made his journey round East Anglia for the opening Letter, but it was well under way by 1724. The result was that Defoe could add an appendix to Letter I describing its progress, and then two years later insert a special addendum to the Preface for Volume III, reporting that the mansion was, "as I am told, now also finished, at least the Outside Work and Figure of the Building is" (2: 536), and incorporating a graceless apology for a small error in his previous account of Houghton (see also p. 108).

It is unclear how close Defoe's acquaintance was with some of these houses. There can be little doubt that scores of bare references in passing indicate the lack of any firsthand knowledge, as when (to take one example from many) Defoe excuses himself from giving a detailed account of Burley on the Hill: "This House would indeed require a Volume of itself, to describe the pleasant Situation, and magnificent Structure, the fine Gardens, the perfectly well-finish'd Apartments, the curious Paintings, and well-stor'd Library: all these merit a particular View, and consequently an exact description; but it is not the work of a few Pages, and it would be to lessen the Fame of this Palace, to say any thing by way of Abstract, where every part calls for a full Account" (2: 503). This is code that can be translated as stating that Defoe has not been inside the recently refurbished home of the Finch family, with whom he had several brushes. He blusters on for a while, "I do not know a House in *Britain,* which excels all the rest in so many Particulars, or that goes so near excelling them all in every thing." But the experienced reader has already come to the conclusion that no detailed description will be emerging.

Even where a much fuller survey is provided, we cannot always be sure if Defoe was writing from his own observation. The long entry for Wilton, the seat of the Earls of Pembroke, contains a number of touches meant to suggest that Defoe had a good knowledge of the interior, as when he writes, "On the left of this Court was formerly a large Grotto, and curious Water-Works, and in a House or Shed . . . which open'd with two folding Doors, like a Coach-House, a large Equestrian Statue of one of the Ancestors of the Family in compleat Armour, as also another of a *Roman* Emperor in Brass, but the last time I had the Curiosity to see this House, I mist that Part; so that I suppos'd they were remov'd" (1: 194). All this *may* be above board; but Defoe was fully capable of piecing together this passage from changes in successive guidebooks by others. In terms of the overall rhetoric of the *Tour,* it does not matter whether the claim to knowledge is authentic or not. What the *Tour* aims to do is to establish a general impression of taste and magnificence, especially where the Whig credentials of the owner were unimpeachable. The author is able to do this in speaking of the "magnificent Palace" of the Child family at Wanstead, built by Colen Campbell in very recent years (1715–20). Defoe refers airily to its appearance: "The Building is all of *Portland* Stone in the Front, which makes it look extremely Glori-ous and Magnificent at a distance" (1: 89–90). One does not have to be unduly cynical to suspect that a distance was as near as Defoe got to this house.

His usual methods in describing the great country seats can be discerned in the entry for Wilton. Much attention is given to the general appearance of the house along with its situation. The coverage of the interior is generally patchy, with well-known features isolated such as the Cube Room at Wilton (1: 195). The collection of pictures usually comes in for notice, although Defoe's gaze rarely strays from family portraits viewed as a marker of hereditary position. An enthusi-astic tribute often follows to the taste of the great magnate concerned: "The Genius of the noble Collector may be seen in this glorious Collec-tion, than which, *take them together,* there is not a finer in any private Hand in *Europe,* and in no Hand at all in *Britain,* Private or Publick" (1: 196). The Earl of Pembroke was indeed a great collector, but Defoe is no less enthusiastic about the former Earl of Exeter at Burleigh. Not content with finding "the Rooms spacious, well directed, the Cielings lofty, and the Decorations just, yet the late Earl found Room for Alterations, infinitely to the Advantage of the whole; as particu-larly, a noble Stair Case, a whole Set of fine Apartments, with Rooms of State, fitting for the Entertainment of a Prince, especially those on the Garden Side; tho' at present a little out of Repair again" (2: 506). It is deeply typical of the author that he should admire a house most of all after it has been renovated. In this section, Defoe again praises the owner's taste with regard to painting, though he admits that the private conduct of Antonio Verrio, who had carried out the decora-tive work at Burleigh, left much to be desired.

Other entries display the same qualities. At Cannons, Defoe starts off with the bluster we encountered at Burley on the Hill ("a Pen can but ill describe it, the Pencil not much better," 1: 385), but this time there is a little more detail:

The Fronts are *all of Freestone,* the Columns and Pilasters are lofty and Beautiful, the Windows very high, with all possible Ornaments: The Pilasters running flush up to the Cornish and Architrave, their Capitals seem as so many Supporters to the fine Statues which stand on the Top, and crown the whole; in a word, the whole Structure is built with such a Profusion of Expence, and all finish'd with such a Brightness of Fancy, Goodness of Judgment; that I can assure you, we see many Palaces of Soveign Princes abroad, which do not equal it, which yet may pass for very fine too either within or without (1: 386).

Again, Defoe's praise of "the Beauties of this Building" is articulated by means of an international comparison: "Tho' many of the Palaces in *Italy* are very large fine Buildings, yet I venture to say, not *Italy* it self can show such a Building rais'd from the Common Surface, by one private Hand, and in so little a time as this; For *Cannons* as I was inform'd, was not three Years a building and bringing the Gardens and all, to the most finish'd Beauty we now see it in" (1: 387). The entry ends with the disclaimer, "But I am not writing Panegyrick" (1: 388), recognizing an assumption which a reader could easily make. As with Chatsworth, Defoe emphasizes the sheer scale of Cannons, and his key terms all work towards this impression: "Lofty," "Magnificent," "Glorious," "Splendor," "Noble," "Spacious and Majestick," and so on. The habitual Augustan positive of architectural "convenience" is displaced in favor of pure grandeur.

Once more, there may be a sign that Defoe had not penetrated the inner sanctum of the princely Chandos: he shifts his attention to exterior features, confessing his inability (allegedly on grounds of limited textual space) to deal in detail with the chapel and the library. But it is also true that Defoe seems happier when directing his gaze towards the gardens with their avenues, walks, fountains and "Vista's."[3] Similarly at Chatsworth, the narrator takes care to set the park in its natural setting, so as to bring out the contrast between "the Gardens exquisitely fine" and the "clear Vista or Prospect" of the surrounding country. A sharp antithesis is created between the work of man ("The Gardens, the Waterworks, the Cascades, the Statues, Vasa and Painting," 2: 582), and the work of nature ("a comfortless, barren, and . . . endless Moor," 2: 583: see also chapter 7, p. 170). As everyone will expect, Defoe's elective affinities lie with the ordered creation of man. This is made explicit if we turn back to the Scottish sections:

Drumlanrig, like Chatsworth in Derbyshire, is like a fine Picture in a dirty Grotto, or like an Equestrian Statue set up in a Barn; 'tis environ'd with Mountains, and that of the wildest and most hideous Aspect in all the South of Scotland. (2: 727).

The great estates are for Defoe triumphs of the human will over the barbarous and anarchic forces of nature. He admires their magnificence as a sign of prosperity and social standing, but more than that as a vindication of the Augustan urge to improve, to transform, to *supplant* nature. It is hard to think of any more unfashionable outlook in the 1990s.

III

The last category to be considered, that of public buildings, may be treated more briefly. It is obvious that Defoe rejoices to see a number of town halls springing up in provincial centers like Northampton. This latter was facilitated by the destruction of the town in a major fire—as was the new market-house at Alresford (1: 181). Defoe actually says of Northampton that "the Beauty of it is owing to its own Disasters" (2: 485), and in terms of the overall thematics of the *Tour* this process of phoenixlike restoration of a city from the ashes represents the archetypal act of building. Defoe is pleased to see new churches and meeting houses go up, as well as customhouses, quays, and exchanges. There is a little less warmth when he encounters assembly rooms at resorts and spas like Tunbridge Wells and Bury St Edmunds, since they pose the threat not just of gambling but of loose sexual behavior, with the prospect in store of a marriage-market (see p. 203). Hospitals are welcomed chiefly as an index of public munificence, allied to charitable instincts.

Little time it spent on the buildings of universities and schools, except for what seems a dutiful nod in a couple of places to King's College chapel at Cambridge. And even here Defoe is at least equally impressed by James Gibbs's new building: "for as it [King's] is now Edifying, it is likely to be the most admir'd in a few Years of all the Colleges of the World" (1: 397). A single exception is afforded by the Sheldonian Theatre at Oxford, which is described as "in its Grandeur and Magnificence, infinitely superiour to any thing in the World of its Kind" (2: 424). The Theatre is "a finish'd Peice, as to its Building, the Front is exquisitely fine, the Columns and Pilasters regular, and very beautiful; 'tis all built of Freestone: The Model was approv'd by the best Masters of Architecture at that time, in the Presence of K. *Charles* II. who was himself a very Curious Observer, and a good Judge; Sir *Christopher* Wren was the Director of the Work, as he was the Person that drew the Model." Nothing is said about the architectural aspects of the Bodleian Library, except for a brief preview of the Radcliffe Camera: "I am told 'tis likely to be such a Building as will be a greater Ornament to the Place than any yet

Standing in it" (2: 425). The most devoted modern admirer of Gibbs
might feel abashed by that judgment.

One final contrast will serve to bring out the social attitudes implicit in Defoe's treatment of architecture. On the *"New Liverpool"*
he is wholly positive, celebrating the arrival of a new wet dock, along
with a church to serve growing areas of the city, with the prospect
of two more as the population continues to spread outwards. His
summary is warm with approval:

> This is still an increasing flourishing Town, and if they go on in Trade, as
> they have done for some time, 'tis probable it will in a little time be as big
> as the City of *Dublin.* The Houses here are exceeding well built, the
> Streets strait, clean, and spacious, and they are now well supplied with
> Water. The Merchants here have a very pretty *Exchange,* standing upon
> 12 Free-stone Columns, but it begins to be so much too little, that 'tis
> thought they must remove or enlarge it. (2: 468)

The optimal architectural state has been achieved, that of the need
for more building. There is nothing that inspires Defoe so much as the
prospect of further development. Liverpool represents the landscape of
trade, and its architecture expresses the dynamism of economic
growth.

A striking contrast can be drawn with the treatment of Bath. The
entry here is quite well-known, and has been long cited by social
historians. But it is entirely devoted to the social round, described
with a certain terse irony. As for the physical side of the city, we hear
nothing, as may be foreshadowed by the opening words of the entry:
"My Description of this City would be very short, and indeed it
would have been a very small City, (if at all a City) were it not for
the *Hot Baths* here, which gives both Name and Fame to the Place"
(2: 432). But not a single word is devoted to the natural setting of
Bath, or to its buildings. It is of course true that the major phase of
architectural development under John Wood senior and junior was
still to come. Nonetheless, by 1725 the city was already poised for a
takeoff just as spectacular in its way as that of Liverpool. The original
Pump Room was completed in 1706, and the first Assembly Rooms
by 1708; other rooms were in the course of construction in the mid
1720s.[4] Moreover, numerous domestic and commercial properties in
the city center had gone up in the past few years, including many
that still survive. The characteristic streets of the city were beginning
to take shape; substantial private mansions were just over the horizon,
with Widcombe Manor House complete in 1727 and Prior Park constructed between 1735 and 1750. Defoe shows absolutely no interest
in any of this, with the result that later editions of the *Tour* after his

death had to make some of their most substantial additions in this portion of the text.

The explanation for this difference is not far to seek. Defoe had little feeling for construction sponsored by leisure pursuits; he prob- ably thought (in the long term correctly) that there was a finite limit to the growth of a pleasure resort, whereas an industrial city like Liverpool could expand almost indefinitely. He revels in the architec- ture of commercial growth, imputing an almost moral character to the landscape which evolves. The building of Bath hinged on a growth industry in which Defoe saw less to admire, that of valetudinarian therapy, idle tourism, and vapid socializing, attended by gambling and spouse-hunting. The picture of the nation the *Tour* is striving to estab- lish is one of increasing national well-being, attested alike by the rise of commercial building, the construction and embellishment of ducal estates, and the restoration of urban amenities in places like the City of London, Warwick and Northampton. Bath simply did not fit into this picture. Its architecture ran counter to the main ideology of the work, and so the text observes a total silence. The buildings of En- gland, for Defoe, are beautiful largely in proportion as they tell the right social messages. Cathedrals are generally most admired when most restored: castles are passed over without comment if their pres- ence in the text would signal only an unregenerate medievalism sur- viving in modern Britain. Resorts like Bath and Tunbridge are treated as architectural cities of the plain, their physical structures effaced as the book minutely describes their social activities. Defoe, famous as the keenest of observers, grows suddenly myopic.

Perhaps the *Tour* is all the more interesting as a register of Augustan attitudes just because Defoe was writing, for once, as an amateur when he dealt with architecture. On most of the concerns that per- vade the book—trade, travel, social life—he was a professed expert. What gives his account of the buildings of England such coherence is the very absence of a virtuoso's specialized tastes. For once, he was seeing the country with an almost innocent eye.

9

Transformations: Defoe and the Making of Modern Britain

THE *Tour* is designed to express the fullness and diversity of the nation Defoe saw growing up around him. Again and again he stresses the dynamic pace of change, with commerce as its engine. Not every book fulfills the promise of its introduction (this one, perhaps included), but the *Tour* really does make good what the declaratory periods offered at the start:

> The Fate of Things gives a new Face to Things, produces Changes in *low* Life, and innumerable Incidents; plants and supplants Families, raises and sinks Towns, removes Manufactures, and Trade; Great Towns decay, and small Towns rise; new Towns, new Palaces, new Seats are Built every Day; great Rivers and good Harbours dry up, and grow useless; again, new Ports are open'd, Brooks are made Rivers, small Rivers, navigable Ports and Harbours are made where none were before, and the like. . . .
>
> Even while the Sheets are in the Press, new Beauties appear in several Places, and almost to every Part we are oblig'd to add Appendixes, and Supplemental Accounts of fine Houses, new Undertakings, Buildings, &c. and thus Posterity will be continually adding; every Age will find an Encrease of Glory. (1:2–4)

As we have seen in chapter 4, where the first part of this quotation was utilized, the process of growth and decay obsessed Defoe; and chapter 5 has explored the sense of loss which Defoe felt as he contemplated a cycle of continuous creation. Here we might notice the fact that "Appendixes, and Supplemental Accounts" are the textual signs of a national phenomenon. Defoe believed that he was living at a turning point in history: it is a common delusion, but in his case it happened to be a justified sentiment. He witnessed, but also in a small measure helped to create, what I called earlier "an access of nationhood." He perceived as quickly as anyone the significance of the new arteries of communication—turnpiked and improved roads, navigation schemes that foreshadowed the coming of the canals two generations later—and his own "circuits" carve their way through Britain like textual channels. As Peter Borsay has written in a fine essay on "Urban Development in the Age of Defoe," Defoe is "no Georgian Baedeker. As the pages unfold, it is evident that the author is engaged upon a journey that traverses not only a topographical landscape but also the economic and social contours of the country. Indeed, our *tour* is not so much a travelogue as an anatomy (even a vision) of the nation."[1] What kind of a nation, then, does the *Tour* of Britain reveal?

I

I say "Britain," partly out of deference to the title and partly from a modern terror of narrow chauvinism. It is true that Defoe does allot three of his thirteen sections to Scotland: in the first edition, these made up over two hundred pages, almost half the third volume. But it is also true that Defoe does not cover Ireland, more of an offshore colony in his day than an integrated part of the kingdom; and that he is relatively weak on Scotland and Wales. Most of his generalizations on matters such as trade and transport relate specifically to conditions south of the border. But these latter reservations should not be pressed too far. Defoe had lived in Edinburgh for long periods around the time of the Union of the English and the Scottish Parliaments in 1707, and he had more than negligible business interests in the city.[2] In fact, it was only the more remote Highland areas that he did not know well, and the fact was that these had scarcely been brought under the writ of Westminster by this date—fifty years later, Johnson and Boswell still found what was virtually a foreign country when they made their famous jaunt to the Hebrides. Moreover, Defoe had evidently a much closer acquaintance with Wales than most Londoners had then or—dare I say it—have today. He seems to have encountered the rawer side of the Welsh landscape with horror rather than enthusiasm, but then, wild Wales had not been invented as a stamping ground for aesthetic adventurers. There are, for that matter, aspects of English life where Defoe shows little relish or enjoyment: he was a man of his time, a trueborn Londoner, and natural bourgeois long before the term had entered the English language.

It cannot be denied that Defoe's patchy knowledge of Scotland presented a real problem, although it was one that his close contact with affairs in Edinburgh at the time of the Union did something to alleviate. A key function of the entire work is to incorporate Scotland into his system, as the Union had been designed to incorporate it into the British polity. The significance of this theme is apparent in Defoe's title ("Great Britain" was a relatively new and even a fictional entity at this date: as Linda Colley has shown in her book *Britons: Forging the Nation, 1707–1837* [1992], it took a prolonged effort of will to overcome local resistance to assimilation.) The theme is also declared openly in the special "Introduction" which is supplied for the Scottish sections (2: 689–91). For the most part, the emphasis is on economic imperatives: "Here are but a few Things needful to bring *Scotland* to be (in many Parts of it at least) as rich in Soil, as fruitful, as populous, as full of Trade, Shipping, and Wealth, as most, if not as the best Counties of *England*" (2: 690). The English establishment is blamed for not implementing changes promised before the Union took place, and Defoe leaves Scotland's "Misfortunes, and Want of being improv'd as it might be" to the consideration of those "in whose Power it is to mend it" (2: 691). But it requires rhetorical, as well as political, effort to drag Scotland into a united kingdom.

In the general Introduction to Volume III, Defoe had admitted that before 1707 Scotland had been "considered as a Nation, now she appears no more but as a Province, or at best a Dominion; she has not lost her Name as a Place; but as a State, she may be said to have lost it, and that she is now no more than a Part of *Great Britain* in common with other Parts of it, of which *England* it self is also no more" (2: 541). This resistance to incorporation affects Defoe's own literary plan. The preface to the same volume apologizes in a half-hearted way for leaving out the offshore islands:

> We have been obliged, for want of Room, to leave wholly out the Description of the Islands of *Scotland*, such as those of the *Hebrides*, or Western Islands, the *Orkneys*, or Northern, and the Isles of *Shetland*: But as they are fully, as also the Island of MAN, describ'd by Mr. *Cambden*, and his learned Continuator; and that those remote places have suffered no Alteration in their Trading that merits any Review; the Loss is nothing. (2: 537)

This omission was repaired in later editions of the *Tour*. Defoe's embarrassment about his lack of familiarity with far-flung localities is hard to conceal, for his intention all through had been to suggest that he had a total grasp of the state of the nation. He had after all promised an account of the *whole* island of Great Britain.

Yet he consistently triumphs over his limitations, and the coverage is astonishingly evenhanded, taking into account the wide range of materials with which he had to deal. If he is more at home in Southwark than on Skiddaw, then that reflects the priorities of his culture. The things he was most interested in were, as it happened, the very forces that were shaping the emergent nation. Had any writer in 1725 sought out a Wordsworthian repose in Grasmere (in fact none did), he or she would have been peculiarly ill fitted for understanding what was going on in British society. Thanks to his framework of "tours" (whether or not these were actually undertaken as they are described), Defoe is able to give a superb account of travel and communications at a moment of growing economic pressures. His famous appendix on turnpike roads provides a comprehensive and detailed review of the subject; but most of all a timely one, since many of the acts Defoe mentions were only just passing through parliament in the year he was writing (1725). His unembarrassed curiosity about such matters gives his work a special amplitude of instance. Again, Defoe is keenly alive to that characteristic process of the age by which money gained in trade was turned into landed property, the great symbol of power and social prestige. Very early in the development of a consumer society, he grasped the importance of purchasing power in the community. He is good on the decline of many towns, and observant about the effect on a town's hinterland when it enters a period of sharp prosperity or decline. And if he lacks the knowledge of practical farming which Cobbett or Young possessed, he has much more to tell us when the wheat leaves the fields and barns and reaches the corn-factor's store or the market.

The *Tour* has long been a central reference for students of the period. It is true that its historical evidence has not always been judiciously employed: Sidney and Beatrice Webb, in their famous work on *The King's Highway* (1913), cite as Defoe's own testimony several remarks by others that first appeared in subsequent editions of the *Tour*. The Webbs further neglect the only sustained treatment of roads that ever appeared in the *Tour*—namely, Defoe's appendix on the new turnpikes (2: 517–33). The reason for this is that the editor of the fourth edition (1748) performed an appendectomy, so that all this valuable information on traveling disappeared for good. It is a wonderfully informative section, displaying Defoe's intimate knowledge of the communications system and witnessing to long hours he had spent on the road. For example, he describes the different stones—flint, clay, chalk, gravel, and so on—he had seen beneath the surface of the highway.

Above all he admires the Roman roads: not just the solidity of their construction, but the imaginative feat they represented in stretching out as a network across primitive Britain: "The Memory of the Romans . . . is preserv'd in nothing more visible to common Observation, than in the Remains of those noble Causways and Highways, which they made through all Parts of the Kingdom, and which were found so needful, even then, when there was not the five hundredth Part of the Commerce and Carriage that is now" (2: 519). The system of roads can foster historical understanding and empathy:

> It is a most pleasant Curiosity to observe the Course of these old famous Highways the *Icknild* Way, the *Watling-street,* and the *Foss,* in which one sees so lively a Representation of the ancient *British, Roman* and *Saxon* Governments, that one cannot help reallizing those times to the Imagination; and tho' I avoid meddling with Antiquity as much as possible in this Work, yet in this Case a Circuit or Tour thro' *England* would be very imperfect, if I should take no Notice of these Ways, seeing in tracing them we necessarily come to the principal Towns, either that are or have been in every County. (2: 485)

Just as Defoe navigates modernity along contemporary routes, so he reads the past by "tracing" ancient routes, "reallizing" them in his imagination.

If the Webbs missed a trick, other eminent historians have used the first edition, recognizing in it the liveliest and most complete introduction that exists to Britain at a crucial stage of social and economic change. "When a survey is demanded of Queen Anne's England and its everyday life, our thoughts turn to Daniel Defoe, riding solitary and observant through the countryside." These are the words of G. M. Trevelyan, opening a section called "Defoe's England," which he set at the head of the third part of his *English Social History;* Defoe, continues Trevelyan,

> first perfected the art of the reporter. . . . so then, the account that this man gives of England of Anne's reign is for the historian a treasure indeed. For Defoe was one of the first who saw the old world through a sharp pair of modern eyes. His report . . . occupies the central point of our thought and vision.[3]

Another distinguished historian, Dorothy George, also gives the title "Defoe's England" to a survey confessedly based on the *Tour.* "Far the best authority for early eighteenth-century England is Defoe," she writes, "His famous *Tour through the whole Island of Great Britain* shows us the country as it appeared to a skilled observer with a marvellous eye for significant detail, who was also a man of business as well as a consummate journalist."[4] More recently Peter Mathias has called Defoe "the keenest observer of economic growth of his time in his *Tour of the Whole Island.*"[5] Whole sections of books such as Paul Mantoux's *Industrial Revolution in the Eighteenth Century,* Cole and Postgate's *The Common People* and other works are quarried directly from the pages of Defoe. Economic historians such as Christopher Hill, T. S. Ashton, Sir John Clapham, and the Hammonds have cited the *Tour* extensively as a primary source of information.[6] The leading modern authority on inland navigation bases his map covering this period wholly on what Defoe reports. All this makes an eloquent testimony to the utility of the *Tour:* it has been given the status of an honorary blue book, and one almost expects to find it listed among official reports together with the journals of parliament and *Statutes of the Realm*. A further irony here, that Defoe—whose undertakings were always very private enterprises—should be given this quasi-official standing.

Not of course that he is reliable in every detail. He is always liable to confuse the generations of a particular family, he quite often gets names wrong, and his estimates of population are rarely better than informed guesses. Occasionally, he is very badly off: he computes the figure for Manchester at 50,000 when it was perhaps 10,000, and for London at a million and a half, which is a good 50 percent too high. (See p. 52.) More generally, it could be argued that Defoe's picture in some respects is a partial one. He is visibly stronger on distribution and commerce than on industrial manufacture, perhaps because he himself had been in the wholesale business. The heroes of his book are provincial merchants and City financiers, rather than captains of industry such as Abraham Darby or the ironmaster Ambrose Crowley. Moreover, the constant emphasis Defoe puts on the role of London in the national economy, valuable as it is, grow somewhat repetitive: it may not be without a certain metropolitan chauvinism. Defoe possibly exaggerates for his own rhetorical ends the triumphs of the cit turned gentleman—men like Josiah Child, Robert Clayton, John Lethieullier "and Hundreds more; whose Beginnings were small . . . and who have exceeded even the greatest Part of the Nobility of *England* in Wealth, at their Death, and all of their own getting" (1: 169). Equally, he lays a heavy emphasis on the falls brought about by the South Sea disasters of 1720. As we have seen, this suits his general purpose in underlining the mutability of things, but it is arguable that Defoe makes too much of a few exceptional cases, such as the forfeited estates of the directors of the South Sea Company. This is one of the few instances where the author permits his own private obsessions to color the public theme.

Properly enough, economic historians treat the text with caution, but they generally end up echoing what the distinguished writer T. S. Ashton once observed: "Defoe had an eye for whatever was striking and unusual, and sometimes he ran to hyperbole; but it is impossible to ignore the picture he presents."[7] The book is perhaps most often requisitioned in the search for England on the verge of industrialism, since this critical moment of "take-off" is of such relevance, theoretically and empirically, to anyone tracing the birth of the modern world. Out of six books on my shelf with the phrase "Industrial Revolution" in their title, five list Defoe among their authorities. (The remaining work, savagely statistical, deems hardly any volume predating 1950 worthy of an entry.) It is certainly true that England in the 1720s was just on the point of expanding, in manufacture, distribution, communications, and agriculture. The first true "factory" may be identified with the Lombes' silk-mill in Derby, erected around 1718–19, which Defoe discusses in Volume III (2: 563). But it is another thing to suppose that the author of the *Tour* was anticipating the entire shape of things to come, or that he would have wholeheartedly welcomed the changes that were imminent.

This point has been made by Peter Earle in an excellent book on *The World of Defoe*:

> Most modern writers miss this conservative, anachronistic element in Defoe's writing. They seize on his *Tour* as a superb description of England on the eve of the Industrial Revolution, which of course it is, but then select from it material which seems to predict the unique changes which were about to change the economy of England and ultimately of the world. The truth is . . . that Defoe had no premonition of the Industrial Revolution and that if he had he would almost certainly have disliked what he foresaw. He thought that England was the wealthiest country in the world because of the way things already were in the most advanced parts of the country and he opposed anything which seemed to threaten this *status quo*, including many changes which later writers have seen as harbingers or necessary conditions for industrialization.

There are, in fact, many mixed feelings in the *Tour*, and Earle is again right when he speaks of Defoe's "superb *Tour*, which describes the working England of his day in a mixture of pride at its riches and exasperation as it follies."[8] We should not exaggerate his conservatism. Defoe was hospitable to improvement where this did not threaten other tenacious loyalties to which he clung on. And he was not opposed to interventionism by public-spirited bodies or properly constituted authorities (turnpike trusts, for example). He could mourn over the disappearance of Dunwich into the sea, or lament with the best of the school of sensibility the passage of old civilizations (as with his plangent reflections at Towton, 2: 634: see p. 137). But he did not regret the decay of towns bypassed by history, or wish to preserve as industrial museums places like Queenborough in Kent, which had succumbed to economic change. He was, in the end, much like the rest of us: guiltily attached to remnants, but in another optimistic mood committed to progress and adaptation.[9]

We might instance briefly one extremely characteristic passage that shows Defoe's concerns in miniature. In Letter V, he has described the rebuilding of London after the Great Fire, and has had occasion to mention several later fires that have destroyed property (a form of natural disaster to which he was drawn throughout the *Tour*). Then he comes to laud the new insurance offices that had been set up to guard against loss of property, whether houses or goods, by land or sea (Defoe, in fact, had himself been involved in marine insurance when this business took off in the reign of William III). The tone is fervent as ever: "In all [these] Offices, the *Premio* is so small, and the Recovery, in case of Loss, so easy and certain . . . that nothing can be shewn like it in the whole World; especially that of ensuring Houses from fire, which has now attained such an universal Approbation, that I am told, there are above Seventy thousand Houses thus ensured in *London,* and the Parts adjacent" (1: 341). Here in a few lines together are visible Defoe's pride in London, his delight in growth statistics, and his superstitious fear of seeing everything come tumbling down around him into ruin.[10]

If we needed a single phrase to describe what was going on in the English landscape at this juncture, then "progress and adaptation" might do. It was a period not so much of radical or systematic transformation along planned lines as the gradual evolution of physical places and social institutions to fit changing demands upon them. The nation was still predominantly agricultural, although just beginning to move toward a greater emphasis on manufacturing. Figures express some of these crucial developments.[11] In 1700 only 1 percent of the population of England and Wales (which stood at over five million) lived in towns with over 20,000 inhabitants. By 1800, when the national gross figure was up to almost nine million, 8 percent did so. Both these counts neglect London, which kept pretty well in step with the national increase: at the start of the century, London had about 575,000 residents, and at the end about 950,000. It was the urban population outside London that increased proportionately: in 1700 only 5 percent lived in towns with a size between 20,000 and 100,000, whereas by 1800 fully a quarter of the urban population did so. I stress "urban population" because this still accounted in 1800 for no more than 30 percent of the nation: in 1700 the proportion had been as low as 19 percent. Finally, it is worth noting that the changes embodied in these figures were apparent by midcentury: the graph grows a little steeper after that time, but not very much. Thus, in 1750 there were already twenty towns, including London, with a population above 10,000. In

1700 there had been only seven, while in 1800 there would be almost fifty. Edinburgh was the only town of any real size in Scotland; Wales had no such town at all.

A spate of preindustrial development had seen towns like Birmingham, Manchester and Liverpool begin to make inroads on the long-standing preeminence of Norwich and Bristol among provincial centers, though it was not until the end of the eighteenth century that the new cities finally overtook their ancient rivals. At the same juncture, many of the older localities actually declined, notably small market towns whose economic base had been undermined by new patterns of consumption and expenditure. This included the appearance of something resembling modern shops to replace the older trafficking that had gone on in as many as seven thousand fairs and markets, supplemented by the trade of itinerant pedlars. Defoe is quick to spot the decayed boroughs and redundant ports; his book is as much concerned with spots of economic stagnation as with the more famous areas of dynamism and growth. See for example, the description of Ayr [2: 739], quoted on p. 124: and see his clear-eyed recognition that once thriving Totnes "has more Gentlemen in it than Tradesmen of Note," (1: 224).

Such demographic returns were not, of course, available to Defoe. But he sees with the utmost clarity the forces that helped to bring about the transformation of Britain, and the consequences they had for the people. More and more of the population, and more and more of the provincial life, is sucked into the growing manufacturing towns, while less successful rivals stagnate or even decline. The contrast between economic importance and political standing grows more apparent. Manchester is termed by Defoe "one of the greatest, if not really the greatest meer Village in England. It is neither a wall'd Town, City, or Corporation; they send no Members to Parliament; and the highest Magistrate they have is a Constable or Headborough" (2: 670). Such constitutional anomalies were to arouse the embittered protest of later radicals. Defoe is sometimes quite philosophical about such things, though he does inveigh against closed corporations, and does permit himself the question as to whom the members for the hill-fort constituency of Old Sarum can be said to represent in parliament (see 1: 188). He sees how the map of England has been affected by shifts in patterns of trade and consumption, for example the relative decline in southern textile areas such as Norfolk and Wiltshire, which was just beginning to show forth clearly. At the same time, he is marvelously alert to the effects of new means of communication: he enjoys reporting the latest schemes to improve river navigation, and though the canal age was still in the future, the gleam of a Forth-

Clyde link lights up in Defoe's eyes as he thinks enviously of the Canal du Midi. He celebrates dockyards (an important engine of eighteenth-century growth), spas and resorts—where he is often very cutting in his comments—and county towns, with their new assembly rooms and market halls.

To a twentieth-century eye, the most striking feature of Defoe's treatment of the world he inhabited is his unabashed glee in observing the progress of industry. Nothing delights him more than the signs of productivity, labor-intensive employment, business expansion. His entry for Halifax (2: 600–7) is a hymn to activity, valued seemingly almost for its own sake. He is excited by the sight visible "at the Door of any of the Master Manufacturers," when he would glimpse "a House full of lusty Fellows, some at Dye-fat, some dressing the Cloths, some in the Loom, some one thing, some another, all hard at work, and full employed upon the Manufacture, and all seeming to have sufficient Business." In a touch that now betrays the impress of the age, he speaks of workmen's dwellings where "the Women and Children . . . are always busy Carding, Spinning, &c. so that no Hands being unemploy'd, all can gain their Bread, even from the youngest to the antient; hardly any thing above four Years old, but its Hands are sufficient to itself" (2: 602). This has the accents of the Modest Proposer to us, with its conversion of children to things.

For modern readers, a more attractive aspect of the book is Defoe's revelation of a vanished world. He lived just before the age of the seaside resort: Scarborough was already in existence, but it was rather a spa on the coast (which is how Defoe regarded it) than the later watering place. There was barely a straggling hamlet where Southend now stands; nothing worth speaking of at Bournemouth—so Defoe does not speak of either. Brighton appears as "*Bright Helmstone . . . a Poor fishing Town*" (1: 129). There was no Blackpool, no Morecambe, nothing recognizable as Torquay or Skegness, just the glint of Eastbourne in Defoe's "Bourn." On the other hand, the inland spas were coming into their first great era of prosperity: Bath, above all, after that Tunbridge, but also a number of others, ranging from Buxton and Knaresborough to extinct health resorts such as Epsom. Elsewhere, the pattern of industrial growth has scarred what were delicious landscapes in Defoe's time; in the opposite way, he encountered "great Foundries, or Iron-works" in the Weald, since iron-smelting was still mainly performed with charcoal, and so the well-wooded southeastern counties were the center of activity. Of course, Defoe had no idea that we who come later would find these adventitious facts so intriguing; but at least he has the great merit of describing what is before his own eyes.

Above all, Defoe proclaims the teeming identity of London. He was not just a thoroughly urban creature, but a Londoner born and bred, with a shrewd, confident outlook on life (too smart by half, his adversaries thought him). As we have seen, he greatly exaggerates the size of the capital, but his reiterated view that the heart of the national economy was London can now be regarded as fundamentally sound. He describes how trade pulsates to and from the city, and he glories in every new artery or vein. Almost everything about the metropolis excites him, whether it is the water supply, parliament, prisons, fire fighting, churches (new ones best of all), prizefighting booths, customs houses, insurance offices (he was an early investor), Temple Bar with its traitors' heads, or hospitals—the list is endless. He can even spare time for the old city gates, although his characterization is revealing: "*Cripplegate* and *Bishopsgate* are very Old, and make but a mean Figure" (1: 354). There are few things of which he disapproves, and then he is often reticent: "However, as I cannot in Justice say any thing to recommend them [masquerades at the Haymarket Theater] . . . I choose to say no more; but go on" (1: 371).

Like the rest of us, Defoe makes slips, as already remarked, and he is not invariably to be trusted on details. But his general sense of what was happening was unfailingly accurate, and that proceeds largely from his long involvement in national life: as a trader, a government official, a political agent, a journalist, a soldier (briefly), a hanger-on at the exchange, an inmate of the gaols, or a lobby-correspondent at court. Just as *Moll Flanders* seethes with inner life, so the *Tour* is irradiated by the conviction of its writing: the eloquence that proceeds from having been everywhere and seen everything. At the center of this comprehension lies Defoe's firm grasp on trade, which as he rightly intuited was critical for the social dynamism of his age. The opening words of his remarkable *Plan of the English Commerce* (1728) are these: "Trade, like Religion, is what every Body talks of, but few understand."[12] Defoe, alone among considerable writers of his own day, did understand.

To say that Defoe had been everywhere is a very slight overstatement: as remarked, the Highlands provide one exception. And he had not always been to some places recently. We have seen that much of his traveling had been done on behalf of Robert Harley, fifteen years or more previously. Some of it was even more distant: his recollections of places like Whitehaven, center of coastal shipping, appear to go back to his trading days in the old century. But he supplemented his travels where he could, and it would be quite wrong to suggest that the *Tour* is badly outdated for any long stretches. Besides, he had informants, both live and in the pages of books. Defoe was not one to pass by a good secondhand story if a firsthand version was unavailable. As we have observed earlier in the book, he had perfected a mode of creative plagiarism (see chapter 3 above).

It is clear then that inspired guesswork, cunning pilfering, and abstruse information-retrieval often had to supplement Defoe's capacious memory, especially in the remoter parts of the country. But unless one knows the biographic facts, one would generally be hard pressed to tell which section is which, in respect of Defoe's firsthand acquaintance. He had, after all, been a political news-gatherer and public relations consultant—a spy, perhaps, would be the more honest word for some of his earlier experiences, in trade, in politics, and in the seamier purlieus of Grub Street. We have no idea what system he employed to assemble all the data that went into the book. There was no electronic data bank, no filofax, no word processor or even typewriter, no e-mail, no photocopier, no camera, and no tape recorder. He presumably took notes on the spot, but it is a mystery how he was able to retain so much—not just facts in the raw sense, but impressions and vistas, sights and anecdotes too. He was a lifelong student of geography, with several atlases in his library; for that matter, the maps that were provided by the leading cartographer of the age, Herman Moll, constituted a major selling-point for the volumes. But the author's hold on his material extends well beyond the routine facts of topography, or the skeleton of economic data that supports the ongoing narrative. Defoe was able to *imagine* Britain in its complicated interfused activity as practically nobody else has been able to do.

Indeed, few books have ever rendered the nation in its fullness as does Defoe's *Tour*. There are many notable works that display parts of the country, its coasts, its mountains, its cities or its villages. There are others that convey a strong personal sense of the nation, often based on a highly selective trip around particular localities, whether favorite tourist traps or the gritty industrial heartland. Among these books are some that aspire to the condition of high literature, and here one naturally thinks of twentieth-century classics such as George Orwell's *Road to Wigan Pier* or of J. B. Priestley's *English Journey*. But it is safe to say that the most comprehensive, the most imaginative, and the most timely account ever given of the state of the nation is the one compiled by Daniel Defoe 270 years ago. It is a sort of guidebook, raised a power or two in grasp and interest. It has the density of census returns from the Bureau of Population and the poetry of a Virgilian threnody. It is truly an epic of the English people.

II

The essential fact about Defoe's vision of the nation lies in his capacity to see Britain as a system. In the Preface to Volume I, he sets out the themes of his work:

> In every County[13] something of the People is said, as well as of the Place, of their Customs, Speech, Employments, the Product of their Labour, and the Manner of their living, the Circumstances as well as the Situation of the Towns; their Trade and Government; of the Rarities of Art, or Nature; the Rivers, of the Inland, and River Navigation; also of the Lakes and Medicinal Springs, not forgetting the general Dependance of the whole Country upon the *City* of *London,* as well for the Consumption of its Produce, as the Circulation of its Trade. (1: 3)

However, he had to do more than perceive this network of connecting fibers in the social and economic life of the country. He had to find a mode of composition that would express this sense of Britain. Writers like Macky were no help here. Camden was his most valuable prede-cessor, not just in giving him a huge quarry of information to pick at, but also as providing a coherent structure (even though Gibson's edi-tion, which he used, interrupted the flow of the book with its lengthy additions and appendices.) Most topographical books up to this time were bitty and spasmodic. The central virtue of the *Tour* is that it presents its material as an intelligible pattern. This is partly a result of the formal devices we have examined earlier. It is also a product of a consistent set of interests and concerns, which enable the reader to move from one entry to another, not as flitting through an alphabeti-cal gazetteer, but rather as meeting with successive events in an ongo-ing narrative. The *Tour* becomes a synchronic story of Britain.

In the 1990s it might be expected that we should be able to discern pervasive signs of strain, as Defoe endeavored to create this sense of unified nationhood. In fact, the formal structure hardly ever comes near the point of cracking, and that mainly in the outlying regions where the author was scraping around for firsthand information. Thus, the final letter drifts into inconsequence as Defoe skims across the Highlands with bare geographic details. Elsewhere, the rhetoric is able to achieve a convincing singleness of purpose, despite the flux of real life going on beyond the text. We admittedly encounter isolated lapses in tone or style, but they seldom impair the overall effect. In any case, this study is concerned with the anatomy of the *Tour,* and scattered lesions on its surface may properly be left to the investiga-tions of specialists, since they do not damage the general health of the book.

If, as this book has argued, the *Tour* is finally a more remarkable work than any of its predecessors in topographical literature, then that is partly because of its more comprehensive nature, and partly because of the heightened visibility of social processes when Defoe came to write. But it is also attributable to qualities in the author himself, which he had evolved during his long years as a professional writer: above all, his feeling for the interplay of growth and decay, his eye for telling detail, his perception of subtle gradations and social nuances in behavior, his acute understanding of the way England worked, and his unfailing awareness of the part money plays in human dealings.[14] A typical passage acknowledges that England to the south of the Trent has "the greatest Variety in its passing over," but goes on to promise further riches in northern Britain: "tho' the Country may in some Respects, be called barren, the History of it will not be so" (1: 253). Nor is it.

Conclusion

THROUGH a variety of methods, Defoe was able to give his *Tour* a clear sense of form not always apparent in his other extended narra-tives. (It is significant that the work is divided into sharply defined "circuits," whereas his novels are notoriously bereft of chapters or other fictional punctuation.) This is a matter of artifice: it owes much to stylistic resources, such as we saw in chapter 4 and chapter 7. Defoe's scheme owed a good deal to earlier topographic writing: but he subverted some of the precepts of touristic literature, and his own *Britannia* was less a book of antiquarian lore (couched, as was Cam-den's originally, in a learned language) than a report on the "present state" of Britain. Its form permitted a sense of dynamism and change, just as its prose resounded with images of increase and dissolution. Written, as it were, on the move, it shows an energy and inventive-ness in composition that proceed from the author's desire to express the teeming life he saw around him, as Britain entered a phase of vigorous expansion. No other book embodies quite so fully the shifting contours of the nation in its commerce, industry, and enterprise—nor the changing landscape of its culture and society.

Social diversity is matched by diversity of texture in the writing. When the *Tour* arrives at spas and pleasure resorts, Defoe adopts an offhand and sometimes frisky tone. At Tunbridge Wells, he admits with a glint in his eye, "I left *Tunbridge,* for the same Reason that I give, why others should leave it, when they are in my Condition; namely, that I found my Money almost gone" (1: 128). One feature of the book that often escapes attention is the abundance of jokes; sometimes dry, occasionally bitter, but nonetheless jokes, an aspect of the work not matched in the heavy topographical surveys of the day. At Bath, Defoe describes the routine of the day "supposing you to be a young Lady," a comic transformation for the elderly narrator. "There the Musick plays you into the Bath, and the Women that tend you, present you with a little floating Wooden Dish, like a Bason; in which the Lady puts a Handkerchief, and a Nosegay, of late the Snuff-Box is added, and some Patches; the Bath occasioning a little Perspiration, the Patches do not stick so kindly as they should" (2: 433). This playful tone seldom appears anywhere else: we have only to contrast the equally breezy entry for Epsom (1: 160–2) with the solid factual air of the London sections, the ravished accents describing Thames-side villas and palaces, or the businesslike treatment of industrial towns such as Leeds. In mountainous regions, such as mid-Wales, the Pennines, or the Lake District, a version of the sublime appears, with the narrator daunted by "the wildest, most barren and frightful [country] of any that I have passed over." With a familiar rhetorical ploy, he offers to ignore this fearsome prospect: "But 'tis of no Advantage to represent horror, as the Character of a Country, in the middle of all the frightful Appearances to the right and left" (2: 679). Yet the sense of a wild and desolate landscape is strongly present, as when the traveler has to "mount" the Welsh "Alps" (see p. 49 above), and this is just one of the ways in which Defoe renders the concrete reality of Britain through the use of different linguistic registers.

Few accounts catch so many facets of the life of a nation. As we have just seen, Defoe reflects the jaded feeling of pleasure resorts, and he is just as effective on the busy idleness of Bury St Edmunds. Defoe roguishly pretends that John Macky had insinuated that the unmarried ladies of Suffolk came to the fair simply to be "Pick'd up," and launches into an extended "defense" of their behavior which plainly shows his dislike of the courting rituals of the town (1: 51–52). When the narrative reaches the coast, there is a strong whiff of salt in the air: whether we are paddling up the marshy creeks of Essex along the Thames estuary (1: 11–12), or clambering on the rugged cliffs of Cornwall battered by "the Force and Violence of the mighty Ocean" (1: 247–48). There is quite a different texture to the writing when Defoe is observing the homely domestic industry of strawhats and bone-lace in Bedfordshire (2: 513–14), as compared with the hum and bustle of cloth manufacturing activity of Leeds (2: 611–15). The author notes the presence of special local features, more common in the highly particularized world of the eighteenth century: at Preston, we are told, "Here's no Manufacture; the Town is full of Attorneys, Proctors and Notaries, the Process of Law here being of a different Nature than they are in other places, it being a Dutchy and County Palatine, and having particular Privileges of its own" (2: 678). He has a clear sense of economic regions as geographical units, as with his description of the clothing trade in Gloucestershire, Wiltshire, Somerset, and Dorset, including places such as Frome, Devizes, Trowbridge, and Sherborne. He comments, "These Towns, as they stand thin, and at considerable Distance from one another; for, except the Two Towns of *Bradford* and *Trubridge*, the others stand at an unusual Distance; I say, these Towns are interspers'd with a very great Number of Villages, I had almost said innumerable Villages, Hamlets, and scattered

Houses . . ." (1: 280) Most guidebooks treat such scattered localities as monads: Defoe computes that the area in question "may take in about Fifty Miles in Length where longest, and Twenty in Breadth where narrowest" (1: 280), and it is only his method of almost kinetic observation which supplies an integrating focus on the region. We may also note the habitual rhetoric of abundance (*unusual Distance; very great Number; innumerable*), discussed in chapter 4.

All sorts of mysteries remain. Defoe once wrote to Robert Harley while on a fact-finding mission to King's Lynn in 1712, "Resolveing to be Incognito, I found I had Room for Many Speculations."[1] As he made his way around the primitive road system of Britain, spending countless hours in the saddle, he must have absorbed an enormous number of impressions. The "tourist" whose account we read was a construct, based on all those years of quiet (sometimes secret) observa-tion. And always there is a *mind* at work, as well as an eye on the lookout. Modern tourism is notoriously hasty and shallow. Most guidebooks are intended to provide quick fixes for the lazy: they have little to do with serious "travel literature." Defoe, who practically invented the concept of tourism, remains percipient, reflective and rhetorically inventive. None of us is ever going to visit Hanoverian Britain, even supposing we wanted to do that; but the *Tour* is not one jot less absorbing for that.

Probably the last words the author actually wrote were those con-cluding the Preface to Volume III. Here he speaks of the need to "close the Account of a Tedious and very Expensive five Years Travel" (2: 537). It may be this was meant to suggest, misleadingly, that he had actually pursued in the last five years such a journey as the book describes. As we have seen, it is certain that he had not been near many of the places "visited" for very much longer than that, and perhaps some on the periphery he had never seen at all. But if we take the "five Years Travel" to refer to the composition of the work, then indeed by late 1726 Defoe had been hard at it for something close to five years. Imaginatively, the *Tour* had been a long haul, as Defoe maneuvered himself around the length and breadth of the na-tion, turning up old records of his travels and splicing them into his more recent observations, as well as poring over maps and ransacking the literature of topography. The outcome was truly a mirror of Brit-ain, but also a verbal enactment of a journey up and down almost every creek and cranny of the whole island.

Appendix A: Samuel Richardson and Later Editions of the *Tour*

Many of the five hundred or so works by Defoe await full bibliographic description. Even in the case of such a popular and influential work as the *Tour*, this is true: the changes in the text of successive editions have been explored,[1] but no adequate account of the publishing history has been given.[2] Among unsolved questions comes the responsibility for later editions of the *Tour*. It has long been known that Samuel Richardson was connected with the third, fourth, and fifth editions (1742, 1748, 1753). It is likely that this was also the case with the sixth edition (dated 1762–61), though this did not appear until November 1761, four months after Richardson's death. The major uncertainty, however, concerns the second edition of October 1738. B. W. Downs and Paul Dottin thought that Richardson was involved in the revisions here too. William M. Sale Jr., relying on statements in the 1742 preface concluded that Richardson did not take over as editor until the third edition.[3] Recently, in the standard biography, T. C. Duncan Eaves and Ben D. Kimpel have revived the earlier claim. They write, "It seems to us almost certain that Richardson's connection with the *Tour* began in 1738." This conclusion is based on revisions and editorial interpolations in the text of that year.[4]

A small bibliographic anomaly permits us to add further corroborative evidence. We know that Richardson's firm printed Volumes I and II of the second edition;[5] and it is an error in this area—more specifically binding—that supplies the clue. All copies of the work I have examined contain the same oddity in the entry for Eton College, at the end of the first letter in Volume II. The cause of the confusion is easily located. And although the exact sequence of events can only be conjectured, a strong circumstantial case builds up pointing at Richardson's involvement.

When the second volume of the *Tour* originally came out in 1725, Defoe had referred briefly to repairs carried out on the college buildings. He also named the then Provost, Henry Godolphin.[6] In 1738 the editor added a mention of a new library, and continued:

In the great Court a fine Statue is also erected to the Honour of Dr. *Godolphin,* Dean of St. *Paul's,* and Provost of this College, who was a Benefactor to it.

This occurs on p. 71, the recto of the last leaf in gathering D (D12). However, all copies then follow with another leaf (E1) paginated 71–72, and signed E. Thereafter the register proceeds in the normal fashion. The new leaf has the first paragraph of the recto, just cited, amended thus:

In the great Court a fine Statue is also erected to the Honour of the Founder, by Dr. *Godolphin,* late Dean of St. *Pauls's,* and Provost of this College, and the Library has receiv'd several considerable Benefactions of late Years.

To make room for this change, the second paragraph from the foot of the page is reset to fit two, instead of three, lines. Otherwise the page is identical (apart from the addition of "VOL. II E" prior to the catchword), and the verso is wholly undisturbed.[7] In fact, the bulk of the type was left standing.

The reason for making the textual change is easy to find. In its original wording, the paragraph described the statue as that of Godol-phin, rather than of Henry VI. But it is here that the oddity appears. Instead of simply canceling the erroneous leaf, the book presents a mosaic of both versions. In turn we have pp. 71–72 in an uncorrected state, making the ordinary D12; then the same pages, making E1, and starting off a perfectly ordinary gathering. The second letter of this volume begins at E2^r, p. 73.

It is obvious that the presence of both cancelland and cancel leaves arose from a technical slip-up: perhaps, faulty instructions to the binder. However, it is also apparent that the mistake was noted too late for correction for press but before the imposition of the first form of sheet E. While the type of signature D was still undistributed, the change was made in time to reimpose the standing type of D12 recto (corrected) and verso (unaltered) in the two forms of sheet E. The rest of the book went on unaffected.

This was undoubtedly a printing-house alteration, concerned with an error missed at proof stage. It is incidentally the kind of adjustment made throughout, though normally it is Defoe's text that is being revamped, and the aim is updating rather than correction of a mistake.[8] Significantly, there was someone directly involved in the printing of the book who could authorize and compile a new paragraph of this sort. The reworking of the entire sentence forbids the possibility that a compositor simply missed out a few words from his copy. The passage has indeed been rewritten, and this occurred (as we have seen) on the spot during the printing of the sheets.

Only one other name has ever been tentatively associated with revisions of the *Tour,* and this on dubious evidence. A manuscript note in the British Library copy of the 1742 edition states that supplementary material was furnished (for this occasion?) "by Mess^r. Richardson, Kimber & others."[9] Whatever the plausibility of Isaac Kimber on general grounds, he would be an unlikely man to find in a printinghouse during the production of a book: conceivably his son Edward is meant. That either of the Kimbers, or anyone else apart from Richardson, could have been in a position to find the error so quickly, and correct it so confidently in the midst of printing, is surely highly improbable. The "reviser" here was practically certain to be Samuel Richardson. And this strengthens the already powerful case of Eaves and Kimpel, dating Richardson's share in the enterprise back to 1738.

As remarked, it had already been established that Richardson was responsible for editing (as well as printing) the third, fourth, fifth, and sixth editions of the *Tour.*[10] There is thus a reliable account of the third edition (1742) in W. M. Sale's *Bibliographical Record* of Richardson.[11] All copies of this edition that I have encountered or have seen described correspond with Sale's specification, except for some latitude in a small variant mentioned by Sale that concerns booksellers' advertisements at the close of the work. In all previously recorded copies, the imprint includes seven London booksellers, listed identically in all four volumes.

Early in 1982 a set of the third edition that displays a surprising anomaly came into my possession. The departure from the standard pattern as described by Sale concerns the title page of Volume I only. The two lines in the imprint listing the seven booksellers have been replaced by a quite different formula, which reads : "Printed for THOMAS HARRIS, at the *Looking-Glass* and | *Bible,* on *LondonBridge.*" The preceding line "L O N D O N:" and the following line (separated by a short rule) "M.DCC.XLII." remain in the same form. This is the only substantive difference, but a few small changes in layout were made when the type was unlocked for the major alteration to be performed. Measurements indicate that this is the same setting of type, but the Harris version differs from the booksellers' title page in a few small particulars.[12]

As stated, the remaining volumes in this set are normal, with the usual corps of booksellers recorded in the imprint. With the exception of this cancelled title page, the rest of Volume I in the Harris text is identical with that of copies previously described. The question there-fore arises, why should Harris apparently have sold Volume I, but no others? And why did booksellers as well established as Osborn and Millar permit the arrangement? There is no doubt that this group held the rights to the work, and Harris was not in a large enough way of business to challenge by piracy these giants of the trade.

The clue may lie in one of the few firm items of knowledge concern-ing Harris.[13] He was chiefly active in the early 1740s, always from the London Bridge address, and according to Plomer went bankrupt in 1745. The same authority suggests that he was still living in 1763. "Like all the London Bridge booksellers, Harris dealt in chapbooks, ballads, and penny histories," Plomer adds. To this brief account of his career we can add a relevant fact, for which I am indebted to Michael Treadwell. Harris had been apprenticed to James Hodges, the only new name among the booksellers listed in 1742: all the others had been involved in the second edition of the *Tour*, published in 1738. Hodges had bought presumably the share formerly owned by Francis Cogan.[14] Hodges operated from precisely the same address as Harris, that is the sign of the Looking Glass on London Bridge: and he, too, dealt largely (though by no means exclusively) in chapbook literature. Now Harris had been bound to Hodges in 1732 and freed as recently as March 1741. It looks likely that Hodges and Harris had come to some sort of private arrangement, perhaps to dispose of sur-plus copies of the first volume that lay on Hodges's hands.

It would be rash to suggest a very precise explanation of these circumstances, in the absence of definite evidence. Several possibilities open up. But it is worth noting that the London Bridge dealers chiefly supplied hawkers who went round the counties south of the river—whereas the Midlands and the North were supplied from a warehous-ing center in West Smithfield.[15] It is fair to deduce that chapmen supplied by Hodges or Harris would find their readiest market for the portion of Defoe's *Tour* which dealt with the southeastern counties. Letter III in the first volume is mainly concerned with Kent; Letter IV contains "A Description of the County of Sussex, other Parts of Kent, and Parts of Hants, Surrey, &c."[16] In Letter V the *Tour* proceeds through Hampton Court (Middlesex: the running head on p. 241, "Surrey," is mistaken) and then crosses the Thames at Chertsey, *en route* for Berkshire and northern Hampshire, then ultimately to the southwest of England. The return journey is made in the next letter, which occurs at the head of Volume II: but there the route is more northerly, skirting the left bank of the Thames from Reading down-wards. London is reserved for a letter by itself in Volume II. There-after the *Tour* moves farther afield.

It is immediately apparent that all the material bearing directly on the southeast is to be found in this first volume of the *Tour*. (I mean by this expression the counties of Kent, Sussex, and Surrey, with possible extensions into Hampshire and Berkshire: some of this area would be part of London by modern definitions, but not by those of 1742.) Harris presumably had clients who might be able to find customers for the single volume within the counties named. There is no deception about the title page: Harris acknowledges that this is the first of four parts, that many of the contents have to do with remoter parts of Britain, including offshore islands, and that this is after all a tour "of the whole island." What price might have been asked for a single volume, thus bereft of its proper accompaniment, I have not discovered. The full set sold for 12s. bound—a price that, in those times of inflationary innocence, remained in force for the three succeeding editions, up to 1761. It should perhaps be mentioned, first, that Letters I and II in this volume concern East Anglia, and occupy about a third of the whole text: and second, that an index is supplied for each separate volume, which does bestow on them a more selfcontained effect.

It is possible, but unlikely, that other booksellers made parallel arrangements with distributors to market the work "in parts" north of the Thames, in Wales, or in Scotland. What does emerge is that Defoe's *Tour* appears to have been the subject of an interesting and unusual selling operation in 1742: the work scarcely corresponded with the normal run of chapbook material, though other books by Defoe—*Robinson Crusoe* and *Moll Flanders*—were classics in this sphere of publishing. It should be noted that R. C. Alston has challenged one of the assumptions made here, namely that Harris was primarily a chapbook publisher.[17] He demonstrates from the *Eighteenth-Century Short Title Catalogue* files that Harris issued a number of "important books by well-known writers." This is a consideration of some weight. However, Alston concedes that there is "something odd" in a cancel title page appearing in only one of a fourvolume set; and of course the oddity is greater than that, since it resides in a publisher apparently involving himself in a single volume. Whatever Harris's other activities, he seems to have been associated only with a lone volume of the *Tour*, and that the one dealing with the area in which Harris had the largest number of trade contacts. There is no indication that he bought into the rights of the work held by a group of prominent booksellers. Even a single volume of the *Tour* would be too large to market as a chapbook, but this does not preclude the possibility that Harris enlisted the distribution network in the

southeast built up by the London Bridge booksellers. Certainly the
volume seems to have been marketed by methods outside those generally operating in the trade, such as the copyright owners of the *Tour*
would utilize. If that is the case, it is an interesting fact about the
kind of appeal the work might possess in given localities.

Appendix B: Defoe's Antiquarian Library

THE sale catalog of Defoe's books (together with those of the obscure clergyman Philipps Farewell) contains an interesting collection of books disposed of by Olive Payne in November 1731.[1] The most immediately relevant items for this book include item 186, "Gibson's Camden's Britannia, fine Cuts and Maps 1695," and Macky's *Journey through England* in two volumes, 1722. Most of the topographical works may safely be allotted to Defoe's share in the collection; some of the antiquarian works conceivably belonged to Farewell, but this would be an unlikely supposition in the case of some books explicitly cited in the *Tour*. These include the 1723 edition of Carew's *Survey of Cornwall* (see for example, 1: 232; 236); and Sir Thomas Browne's *Antiquities of Norwich Cathedral* in an edition of 1712 (see 1: 63). It can hardly be doubted that a source for the *Tour* (1: 443–45) was *Antiquities of the Cathedral of Worcester* (1723), possibly by Browne Willis. Some other relevant works listed in the catalog were John Norden's *Delineation of Northamptonshire,* first published in 1720 and here in an edition of 1723; and the same writer's *Description of Middlesex and Hertfordshire* in the edition by John Senex (1723). There are road-books and guides such as *Names of all the Parishes, Market Towns, Villages,* and *Hamlets and Small Places in England* (1668), as well as the historian Robert Brady's *English Cities and Boroughs* (1722 edition). County histories are represented by Sampson Erdeswicke's *Antiquities of Staffordshire,* which was first published by Edmund Curll in 1717. A final book brings us back to where we started: this is item 467, "Brook's Errors in Camden's Britannia, and Camden's Answers, 1723," that is the controversy between Camden and his rival Ralph Brooke, as published by the herald John Anstis in 1723.

It will be noticed how many of the items were books published in the years leading up to the composition of the *Tour;* often these were works originally dating from the seventeenth century and reedited in Defoe's lifetime. In this sense the *Tour* obviously benefited from the surge of interest in antiquarian and topographical literature (see pp. 24, 37).

Appendix C: Parallels in the *Tour* and *Memoirs of a Cavalier*

As indicated in chapter 5 (pp. 138–39), the English Civil War lies heavily over many sections of the *Tour*. Only four years before the first volume of the work appeared, Defoe had produced his *Memoirs of a Cavalier*, which describes in detail the hero's experiences during the Civil War. Not surprisingly, there are several passages where the two texts overlap. Some of the direct parallels are listed below. MC refers to *Memoirs of a Cavalier*, ed. J. T. Boulton (London: Oxford University Press, 1972).

subject	MC	*Tour*
[Battle of Leipzig	60–63	2:641]
King's reception at Shrewsbury	146–47	2:475–76
Battle of Edgehill	155–62	2:428–29
Battle of Roundway Down	177–78	2:287–88
1st Battle of Newbury	189–90	1:288–89
Battle of Marston Moor	199–206	2:640–41
Battle of Cropredy Bridge	220–21	2:428
2nd Battle of Newbury	224–25	2:288–89
Treaty of Uxbridge	227–28	1:393
Siege of Leicester	241–42	3:489
Siege of Newark raised	267	2:490
King at Holmby House	269	2:486

There are many brief references in the *Tour* to episodes treated more fully in *Memoirs of a Cavalier*.

NOTES

INTRODUCTION

1. Backscheider, pp. 3–4.

2. See J. H. Plumb, *The Growth of Political Stability, 1675–1725* (London: Macmillan, 1967); and P. G. M. Dickson, *The Financial Revolution in England* (London: Macmillan, 1967). An important discussion of the former concept will be found in Geoffrey Holmes, "The Achievement of Stability," with colloquy by H. T. Dickinson, in *The Whig Ascendancy: Colloquies on Hanoverian England*, ed. J. Cannon (London: Arnold, 1981), pp. 1–27: see also J. V. Beckett, "Introduction: Stability in Politics and Society, 1680–1750," in *Britain in the First Age of Party*, ed. C. Jones (London: Hambledon, 1987), pp. 1–18.

3. See Appendix B.

4. Daniel Defoe, *The Great Law of Subordination Consider'd* (London: Harding, 1724), pp. 47–48.

5. *The Great Law of Subordination*, pp. 49–51.

6. Backscheider, p. 30.

7. *Letters*, pp. 108–13, 115–18.

8. See chapters 1 and 2, especially sections dealing with the West and Wales.

9. See Appendix B.

10. *A Plan of the English Commerce* (Oxford: Blackwell, 1928), pp. 15–21. Compare also the treatment of the sheep around Dorchester (*Plan*, p. 121: *Tour*, 1: 210, as well as *Complete English Tradesman*, 2: ii. 57).

11. See *Moll Flanders*, ed. G. A. Starr (London: Oxford University Press, 1976), pp. 262–68.

12. Backscheider, pp. 466–70.

13. *Moll Flanders*, ed. Starr, p. 106. We might note that when Moll's Lancashire husband, Jemy, decides to "take a Tour" (p. 280), he is going out on the road for booty: a sense apparently unrecognized in *OED*. It is possible that Jemy's account of his daring escapade on the road (p. 300) is a deliberate echo of the story of "Mr Nicks" (*Tour*, 1: 104–5).

Other senses of *tour* which *OED* does list include "the circuit of an island etc."; "the course or compass of anything"; and "a circuitous journey embracing the principal places of the country or region mentioned." See also p. 148.

14. For the widespread interest at this juncture in geographical matters, exemplified by such items as educational playing cards showing different nations and counties, see Backscheider, p. 472.

15. Backscheider, p. 476.

16. The pamphlet is used in my essay "Blacks and Poetry and Pope," in *Eighteenth Century Encounters* (Brighton: Harvester, 1985), pp. 75–92. See generally Lincoln B. Faller, *Crime and Defoe: A New Kind of Writing* (Cambridge: Cambridge University Press, 1993).

17. For one such reference, see Applebee's *Weekly Journal* for 21 April 1722, reprinted in Lee, 2: 512–13. See chapter 1, p. 70.

18. See "An Essay on [sic] Projects," in Henry Morley, *The Earlier Life and the Chief Earlier Works of Daniel Defoe* (London: Routledge, 1889), pp. 59–76.

19. Morley, *Life and Earlier Works*, p. 59.

20. Morley, *Life and Earlier Works*, p. 59.

21. For Digby's dealings with Kettlewell, and his seat in Coleshill, see Howard Erskine-Hill, *The Social Milieu of Alexander Pope* (New Haven: Yale University Press, 1975), pp. 132–65.

22. *Letters*, p. 112. For other references in the *Review*, see 5 June 1705 and 17 August 1706.

23. See *Letters*, p. 105.

24. Romney Sedgwick, *The House of Commons 1715–1754* (London: History of Parliament Trust, 1970), 1: 339–40.

25. See Lee, 2: 511–14. This is the same piece that refers to the Arundel Coke affair (see note 17).

26. Compare the passage commending the Petre family at Ingatestone in Essex, who "by a constant Series of Beneficent Actions to the Poor, and Bounty upon all charitable Occasions, have gain'd an affectionate Esteem thro' all that Part of the Country, such as no prejudice of Religion could wear out, or perhaps ever may; and I must confess, I think, need not; for Good and Great Actions command our Respect, let the Opinions of the Persons be otherwise what they will" (1: 89). This of course was the family at the center of events in *The Rape of the Lock*, and indeed the act of "rape" may itself have taken place at Ingatestone.

The *Tour* does not comment on the number of Catholics in northern Lancashire, as Colonel Jacque does when he lives near Lancaster. There is perhaps a very oblique reference in Defoe's remarks about the effects on the local gentry of the battle with the Pretender in 1715 (2: 678).

27. See "'This Calamitous Year': *A Journal of the Plague Year* and the South Sea Bubble" in *Eighteenth Century Encounters*, pp. 151–67. For the treatment of the Bubble in *The Complete English Tradesman*, see "Merchants and Ministers," *Eighteenth Century Encounters*, pp. 105–9.

28. Alistair M. Duckworth, "'Whig' Landscapes in Defoe's *Tour*," *PQ*, 61 (1982): 453–65.

29. Esther Moir, *The Discovery of Britain: The English Tourists, 1540 to 1840* (London: Routledge, 1964).

30. Moir, p. 24.

31. Moir, p. 35.

32. Moir, p. 36.

33. See Camden, col. 745: and *The English Travels of Sir John Percival and William Byrd II*, ed. Mark R. Wenger (Columbia, Missouri: University of Missouri Press, 1989), p. 103. For Fiennes' reference to the fisherman, see Moir, p. 45.

34. See the edition of Harrison's *Description* (1577; rev. ed. 1587) by Georges Edelen (Ithaca: Cornell University Press, 1968). This excludes the directly topographical sections, but by common consent these are less noteworthy than the social analysis and human detail. Harrison does give a list of fairs (pp. 392–97), which might have been of some use to Defoe though it no longer corresponded to the exact state of things. Similarly, there are lists of parliamentary counties and boroughs (pp. 154–62), and of the colleges at Oxford and Cambridge (pp. 77–78): but Defoe does not describe the Cambridge colleges, and is fuller than Harrison on Oxford— he had better sources here.

35. The best short survey of Camden's achievement will be found in Stuart Pig-gott, "William Camden and the *Britannia*," in Camden, pp. 5–13.

36. *The Journeys of Celia Fiennes*, ed. C. Morris (London: Cresset, 1949), p. xxv.

37. There is a useful entry for Celia Fiennes by Janet Todd in *A Dictionary of British and American Women Writers 1660–1800*, ed. J. Todd (London: Methuen, 1984), 126–27. See also Moir, pp. 35–46. There are chapters on Fiennes and Defoe in a recent popular treatment, that is Richard Trench, *Travellers in Britain: Three Centuries of Discovery* (London: Aurum, 1990), pp. 75–137, but they are seriously inaccurate. Trench claims (p. 102) that Defoe witnessed Fiennes's will. I do not know if that is true.

38. See J. H. Andrews, "Defoe's *Tour* and Macky's *Journey*," *N&Q*, 205 (1960): 290–92. See also comments by G. D. H. Cole in *Tour*, 1: xxiii: "In short, Macky's volumes are a guide-book, whereas De Foe's are not."

39. See Backscheider, p. 470.

40. G. M. Trevelyan, *England Under Queen Anne: Ramillies and the Union with Scotland* (London: Collins, 1965), p. 216.

41. See Martin Price, "The Picturesque Moment," in *From Sensibility of Romanti-cism*, ed. F. W. Hilles and H. Bloom (New York: Oxford University Press, 1965), pp. 259–92 (quotation from p. 277). For intelligent comments on Gilpin in the context of the wider movement, see Malcolm Andrews, *The Search for the Picturesque: Land-scape Aesthetics and Tourism in Britain 1760–1800* (Stanford, Calif.: Stanford Univer-sity Press, 1989), pp. 56–58 and *passim*.

42. Quoted by A. R. Humphreys, *The Augustan World* (London: Methuen, 1954), p. 248, from Gilpin's *Observations on the River Wye and Several Parts of South Wales* (1782).

43. See Stuart Piggott, *William Stukeley* (London: Thames and Hudson, 1985).

44. The most thorough, if ponderous, treatment of Young is John G. Gazley, *The Life of Arthur Young 1741–1820* (Philadelphia: American Philosophical Society, 1973).

45. *The Itinerary of John Leland*, ed. L. Toulmin Smith (London: Bell, 1907–10), 1: 7.

46. Camden, col. 433.

47. *Journeys of Celia Fiennes*, p. 117.

48. William Cobbett, *Rural Rides*, ed. G. D. H. Cole and Margaret Cole (London: Peter Davies, 1930), 1: 109.

49. This is the title of the first two volumes (1714–22). The third volume appeared as *A Journey through Scotland* (1723). This latter book is allotted to Defoe in the Everyman edition of the *Tour* (London: Dent, 1962), p. xvii.

50. See Macky, *Journey*, 2: 223ff, 231ff, 236ff.

51. For similar usages, see *Tour*, 1: 249; 2: 682. Lincoln B. Faller picks up the very same word in discussing a section of Letter II, where Defoe comments on the road over the "Hogback" ridge between Farnham and Guildford (1: 146). "This passage," writes Faller, "takes pains to orient its reader in space and then gives that space an affective quality.... Then, moving the reader through its space, up the hill to the crest, it looks back to Guildford where citizens ... can look up the mile and a half to the gallows that reader (and text) have just passed by." He concludes, "This passage (it is indeed a passage) *conducts* us from Guildford to Farnham, makes us feel a progress; should we ever walk that road again, we'd know it" (Faller, *Crime and Defoe*, p. 38). Compare chapter 6, pp. 150–54.

52. Other occurrences of "excursion" are at *Tour*, 2: 467, 539, 765, 802.

53. Cf. the following: "As I am now at *Chester*, 'tis proper to say something. . ." (*Tour*, 2: 468).

54. Cf. the very first words of the book: "If this Work is not both Pleasant and Profitable to the Reader, the Author most freely and openly declares the Fault must be in his Performance, and cannot be any Deficiency in the Subject" (1: 1).

55. Depending on how one establishes the bounds of London, and whose figures one trusts, one can arrive at different population figures from three quarters of a million upward. In 1725 the total for greater London, i.e., the City and Westminster with the outparishes, plus Southwark, may have been approaching the million mark. Defoe's estimate is "at least, Fifteen Hundred Thousand" (1: 324). This is certainly too high, even if one included the immediately adjacent suburbs; but it is worth remembering that Defoe would organize his *Tour* according to his belief. See E. A. Wrigley, "A Simple Model of London's Importance in Changing English Society and Economy 1650–1750," in *People, Cities and Wealth* (Oxford: Blackwell, 1987), pp. 133–56; and H. J. Habakkuk, "English Population in the Eighteenth Century," *Economic History Review,* 6 (1953): 117–33.

56. Other rhetorical formulae are suggested by these quotations: "*Harwich* is a Town so well known, and so perfectly describ'd by many Writers, I need say little of it" (1: 34); "I could say much more to this Point, if it were needful, and in few Words could easily prove . . ." (1: 44); "I can't omit, however little it may seem. . ." (1: 59); "To all this I must add, without Compliment to the Town, or to the People, that the Merchants . . . of *Yarmouth* have a very good Reputation in Trade" (1: 68); "At the entrance of a little nameless River, scarce indeed worth a Name, stands *Whitby*" (2: 656).

57. Paul Theroux, *The Kingdom by the Sea* (New York: Washington Square, 1984), p. 6.

58. Jonathan Raban, *For Love & Money* (New York: Harper & Row, 1989), pp. 264–65.

59. Paul Fussell, *Abroad: British Literary Traveling Between the Wars* (New York: Oxford University Press, 1980), pp. 37–50 (quotation from p. 38).

60. See chapter 5.

61. For the background, see Andrews, *Search for the Picturesque;* and Ian Ousby, *The Englishman's England: Taste, Travel and the Rise of Tourism* (Cambridge: Cambridge University Press, 1990). Both these books deal with the motives for tourism, the aesthetic contexts and the sociocultural role of travel, rather than with the poetics of travel writing. The most suggestive and provocative treatment of latent ideologies within the fashion for travel is that of Carole Fabricant, "The Literature of Domestic Tourism and the Public Consumption of Private Property," in *The New Eighteenth Century: Theory, Politics, English Literature,* ed. Felicity Nussbaum and Laura Brown (New York: Methuen, 1987), pp. 254–75.

All three studies deal with the rise of a touristic discourse starting around, or slightly after, 1750. Later editions of Defoe's book may have a place in this story. If we are to fit his pioneering exploitation of the "tour" in the 1720s into the narrative, we shall have to rewrite the plot. For Defoe's introduction of the term, see also p. 151.

62. "Tour writing is the very rage of the times," wrote John Byng in 1782, adding with surprise, "It is selldom that I am in the fashion." See *The Torrington Diaries: A Selection from the Tours of Hon. John Byng,* ed. C. B. Andrews and F. Andrews (London: Eyre & Spottiswoode, 1954), p. 65. How much successive editions of Defoe's *Tour* up to the 1770s had helped to inspire the fashion can only be conjecture.

CHAPTER 1. THE MAKING OF VOLUME I

1. The count is based on *Letters*.
2. Calculations refer to *Checklist*.

3. The 1708 tally is followed, although the *Checklist* needs to be corrected at #156 in the light of research by Professor H. L. Snyder. See also the reservations of P.N. Furbank and W. R. Owens, *Defoe De-Attributions* (London: Hambledon Press, 1994).

4. Lee, 1: 377. Lee adds, "No doubt some of these journeys had been made, and materials collected, on former occasions, when travelling on government or other business." See also A. W. Secord, *Studies in the Narrative Method of Defoe* (Urbana: University of Illinois Press, 1924), p. 79.

5. Thomas Wright, *The Life of Daniel Defoe* (London: Cassell, 1894), pp. 307–8: see 33–34.

6. James Sutherland, *Defoe* (London: Methuen, 1950), pp. 29–30, 263. For more recent comments, see the same author's *Daniel Defoe* (Cambridge, Mass.: Harvard University Press, 1971) pp. 221–27.

7. G. D. H. Cole ed., *A Tour through the Whole Island of Great Britain* (London: Dent, 1962) 1: xv. This is the Everyman, modernized text. Similar comments by Cole to those cited appear in *Tour* (1: vii). F. Bastian has attempted to identify a number of Defoe's early travels (real or presumed) from references in the *Tour*: for example his travels in Sussex and Hampshire in the mid 1690s, investigating the timber business with a friend: see *Defoe's Early Life* (Totowa, N.J.: Barnes and Noble, 1981), p. 183. It is certain that Defoe did use early memories (e.g., his boyhood experiences around Dorking), and many are quite openly exploited. But it seems rash to chart Defoe's supposed journey north in 1703, for example, as Bastian does (284), and to specify an exact route through Lincoln, Beverley and other places.

8. G. M. Trevelyan, *Blenheim* (London: Collins, 1965) p. 14 n. This statement, which first appeared in 1930, was repeated in the author's subsequent *English Social History* (London: Longmans Green, 1942); see for instance the Pelican edition (Harmondsworth: Penguin, 1964), 3: 18 n. In any case Defoe's tours for Harley covered the later years of Anne also: e.g., *Letters*, pp. 385–92. See also Defoe's statement in the *Review* of 22 February 1711 concerning his travels.

9. See *Checklist*, p. 184.

10. Lee, 2: 508–14. See in particular the issue for 21 April, mentioned below in connection with Coventry and Bury St Edmunds.

11. Biographic details are dependent on standard works of reference. Sources are not stated unless some more inaccessible material (such as a contemporary newspaper) has been used, or unless there is a conflict of evidence.

12. See for example Lee, 1: 362–64: Backscheider, pp. 467–70, 503–4.

13. In 1712 Defoe was at Cambridge in September (*Letters*, p. 385), but by October he was in Newcastle, having reached Lincoln by 20 September. If he returned quickly from Newcastle by the route he had followed northwards, he might just have attended a race meeting at Newmarket by the end of the month: but this seems unlikely. J. R. Moore allots to September 1712 the incident at Aylesbury races involving the Duke of Marlborough, described in the *Tour* (1: 394). See Moore's *Daniel Defoe, Citizen of the Modern World* (Chicago: University of Chicago, 1958), p. 352; henceforth cited as *Citizen*. Godolphin was an early patron of racing; his son imported the three Arab stallions who are the ancestors of every thoroughbred racehorse since then.

14. See for instance John Ashton, *Social Life in the Reign of Queen Anne* (London: Chatto & Windus, 1897), p. 231. Ashton mentions Frampton's horse Dragon running on 30 October 1712.

15. *Letters*, p. 58. As regards Bury St Edmunds, it is noteworthy that Defoe refers to ladies attending the "Comedy" (1: 52) : the first theatrical performances recorded

in the town date from 1721 and 1722. See *Moll Flanders*, ed. G. A. Starr (London: Oxford University Press, 1971), p. 398.

16. *The Complete Baronetage* supplies contradictory information regarding the death of the second baronet's wife. Her husband died on 1 October and was buried 7 October; that would place Defoe's visit between the two dates. But it is not clear whether Lady Davers died on 5 October and was buried along with her husband; or on 11 October and was buried on 14 October. If the latter, Defoe's ignorance of the matter is more accountable. For reports in the press of her death, see e.g. *London Journal* (10 November 1722).

17. Information derived from various sources. James Henry Monk, in what remains the standard biography, *The Life of Richard Bentley, D. D.* (London: [Rivington], 1830), is infuriatingly vague on dates.

18. At 1: 89 the reference is to Simon Lydiatt (d. 1712) and his successor, Hugh Hutchin, who held office until his death in March 1725. At 1: 86, to the mayor, who was a certain James Fletcher. Healey provides a cross reference to a letter of 1705 (*Letters*, p. 105), and this is undoubtedly the origin of the story retailed in the *Tour*. However, unknown to Healey, Defoe got the facts slightly wrong. Daniel Love, although a leading abettor of the mayor, was not actually subject to the University's punishment of discommoning. For the true story, see Charles Henry Cooper, *Annals of Cambridge* (Cambridge: Warwick, 1852), 4: 73–75.

19. As mentioned above (p. 25), Moll Flanders was brought up in Colchester, and later in the book reverses Defoe's circuit by traveling from Stourbridge Fair to Bury St Edmunds, Harwich, Ipswich, Colchester, and so back to London. This is an indication of the marked interest Defoe took in East Anglia round 1722, perhaps as a result of his business ventures. But it should also be remembered that Defoe had covered practically the same route for Harley in 1705 (*Letters*, p. 113), and some of it during the previous year (pp. 58–62).

20. For some dealings between Barrington and Defoe, see *Letters*, pp. 256–59.

21. Lee, 2: 512. The attempted murder had taken place on the night of 1 January 1722; the criminals were condemned on 13 March and executed at the end of the month. The matter was a notorious one for long after; as late as 30 March 1723, the *London Journal* was arguing that the would-be murderer was innocent beside Atterbury. Defoe could have made use of profuse pamphlet literature on the topic (if he did not contribute to that); e.g., *An Exact and Particular Account of a Cruel and Inhumane Murder*, issued by James Roberts on 20 February 1722, which includes all the salient facts mentioned by Defoe. See introduction, p. 26.

22. That Walpole was building at Houghton, was revealed by the *London Journal* (which Defoe assuredly read) on 5 January 1723. Defoe's allusion to the mode of election for a master at Colchester Grammar School may have been called out by the occurrence of such an election in March 1723 on the death of the incumbent, Mr. Allen (*London Journal*, 23 March; 1: 33).

23. One fact that came too late to be taken into account was the death of Sir Basil Firebrace on 7 May 1724, two weeks before Volume I came out. Defoe's reference to the family (1: 49) is not wholly unambiguous but, as one would expect, it appears to suggest that Firebrace was still alive. More disconcerting is Defoe's apparent ignorance that Firebrace's daughter-in-law, heiress of the Cordell family, had herself died in 1712.

24. Other explicit references include the following: 1) Mention of "Sir *William Scawen*, lately Deceased" and "Sir *John Fellows*, late Sub-Governor of the *South-Sea* Company" (1: 159). Fellowes was removed from his subgovernorship in February 1721 and was heavily fined, but as Defoe implies was allowed to keep his house at

Carshalton: see John Carswell, *The South Sea Bubble* (London: Cresset, 1960), p. 253. It was here that he died on 26 July 1724—just too late for this fact to figure in the *Tour*. On the other hand Scawen's death is recorded in the *London Journal* of 27 October 1722. Defoe says that Scawen left his heir £9,000 a year; the *Journal* for 15 December 1722 gives the sum £6,000 per annum. 2) A list of prominent City men who had risen from small beginnings to great affluence at the time of their death (2: 169). These include Scawen, Sir James Bateman (d. 10 November 1718), Lethieullier (d. 4 January 1719) as well as earlier figures, Child and Clayton. 3) On the same page Defoe mentions those who "have sunk under the Misfortune of Business." These include Sir Joseph Hodges, a young profligate who died on 1 April 1722, and Sir Justus Beck, who died on 15 December 1722 after a great reverse in his fortunes (see Carswell, p. 202). 4) Immediately prior to this, Defoe has listed the large estates still flourishing around London. "Mr *Howland*'s, now the Dutchess of Bedford's [house]" visibly antedates the death of the Duchess in July 1724. More curious is the anachro-nistic "Sir *Richard Temple*'s House," in view of Cobham's elevation to the peerage in 1714.

25. Defoe appears to have been at Tunbridge around 1720, when the Prince and Princess of Wales would have given the place a better tone than the South Sea financier, Sir John Blunt, who was there that summer (1: 126). Defoe had been in Kent at the end of 1703 (see *Citizen*, 152) and his experiences at Sheerness (1: 112) and Queensborough (1: 110–11) perhaps date from that time. His observations at Tilbury Fort (1: 102) were almost certainly made when he had his brick factory there around the turn of the century. Finally, two small indications: the weekly bills for the year 1722 are quoted at 1: 170; while the reference to an election at Win-chelsea (1: 131), as ancient an event in truth as the 1678 poll, is paralleled in *Applebee's Weekly Journal* for 7 April 1722 (Lee, 2: 507). See pp. 31–34 for the South Sea theme.

26. The Duchess died on 23 November 1722, her daughter four days later, in childbirth according to *GEC*'s *Complete Peerage*.

27. *Letters*, pp. 97–98.

28. See note 18.

29. *Letters*, p. 100.

30. *Letters*, pp. 94, 109.

31. *Citizen*, pp. 303–4. See also p. 24.

32. Sir Peter King was Lord Chief Justice until 1725 (1: 224) and Defoe's reference here is accurate.

33. For the link with Macky, see pp. 38–39; and for the use of Camden, see chapter 3.

34. See chapter 4.

CHAPTER 2. THE MAKING OF VOLUMES II AND III

1. See chapter 1.

2. This was in fact the practice with all eighteenth-century editions of the *Tour*, as produced by Samuel Richardson and others. The standard pattern in four volumes was that laid down in the fourth edition of 1748, edited and printed by Richardson: the volumes contain respectively six, seven, six, and six letters. It should be noted that the "facsimile" edition published by Peter Davies (London, 1927) and reissued by Frank Cass (London, 1968), that is *Tour*, introduced a sophistication of the text by printing the letters as one continuous sequence.

3. The existence of separate pagination and signature does not necessarily mean that the text was set up at intervals, as Defoe supplied the printer with each letter in turn, but it does point strongly in that direction.

4. George Strahan and William Mears seem to have been the leading agents in promoting the *Tour*, though the booksellers were conventionally named in the order of their "freedom" in the London guild. Strahan was admitted to the livery in 1704 and Mears in 1708. By this date Mears had acquired a share in *Robinson Crusoe* following the death of its original publisher, William Taylor. In all three volumes, the author appears as simply "a Gentleman," the invariable practice until the seventh edition in 1769.

5. *Letters,* pp. 109–10. For Moll's maps, see *Tour,* opp. 1: 224, 240.

6. *Letters,* pp. 108–12.

7. *Letters,* p. 99: *Review,* 25 August 1705.

8. Another apparent production of this trip was a story concerning Okehampton in the *Review* of 21 February 1706.

9. *Letters,* p. 116.

10. *Calendar of State Papers: Domestic Series 1686–87* (London: Stationery Office, 1964), p. 440. The speculation by James Sutherland, *Defoe* (London: Methuen, [1937] 1950), p. 31, that Defoe "remained on the fringe" of the campaign can no longer be sustained.

11. The foundation stone had been laid on 19 March 1724; see the *London Journal* for 24 March.

12. See the edition of Letter V (with a small part of VI), brought out by Sir Mayson Beeton and E. B. Chancellor as *A Tour thro' London about the Year 1725* (London: Batsford, 1929). This work supplies helpful annotation on topographical matters, but little on other issues: it provides no guide to the process of composition. Henceforward "Beeton/Chancellor."

13. The *London Journal* for 5 January 1723 reports that the governors of Bedlam have given directions for building an hospital for incurables "as soon as the Weather permits." According to the *Journal,* the bequest by "Colonel" Withers stipulated that the hospital should be founded within a year and a day of his death, otherwise the money would revert to his heirs. That deadline had already been reached, unless Withers really died in January 1721/2.

14. Captain G. A. Raikes, *The History of the Honourable Artillery Company* (London, 1878), 1: 272.

15. *Selections from the Journals & Papers of John Byrom,* ed. H. Talon (London: Rockcliff, 1950), p. 65.

16. I have collated a number of sources, including *New Remarks on London* (1732), John Summerson, *Georgian London* (Harmondsworth: Penguin Books, 1962), and Kerry Downes, *Hawksmoor* (London: Thames and Hudson, 1959).

17. It should be stressed that many of the "new" buildings and institutions date from the 1680s, 1690s, and early 1700s. See Beeton/Chancellor for documentation of this point. It is clear that Defoe had been a careful observer of the London scene for more than half a century. I confine myself to recent developments, not because Defoe so confined himself, but because these alone supply a guide to the writing of the *Tour.*

18. Information in this paragraph is based on C. H. Collins Baker and Muriel I. Baker, *The Life and Circumstances of James Brydges, First Duke of Chandos* (Oxford: Clarendon, 1949), pp. 265–95.

19. [Macky], *A Journey through England* (London, 1722), 2: 5.

20. This account largely follows J. J. Park, *The Topography and Natural History of Hampstead* (London, 1818), pp. 246–49. As early as July 1722 the *London Journal*

was reporting "a remarkable Alteration for the better"; but highwaymen were always active in the district, and in June 1723 Howell was forced to hire "twenty stout laboring men" to guard patrons on their return to the City (*London Journal*, 5 June). The proprietor had taken a coffeehouse in the City in the previous winter, and Belsize had lain empty after being "strip'd." See *London Journal* for 12 January, 9 March 1723.

21. The presentation of broadcloth to the Elector of Hanover, mentioned at Stroud (2: 441–42), obviously took place in the last few years of Anne's reign.

22. J. R. Moore, *Daniel Defoe, Citizen of the Modern World* (Chicago: University of Chicago Press, 1958), p. 346, allots the former visit to 1682. Henceforth cited as *Citizen*.

23. *Review*, 8: 136, 152.

24. *Letters*, p. 116.

25. The story is retailed by Thomas Wright, *The Life of Daniel Defoe* (London: Cassell, 1894), pp. 38–39. For doubts concerning alleged Bristol connections, see my article "Daniel Defoe, John Oldmixon and the Bristol Riot of 1714," *Transactions of the Bristol & Gloucestershire Archaeological Society*, 92 (1973): 147–56. Moore, *Citizen*, pp. 171–72, takes the affirmative view.

26. See for instance W. A. Speck, *Tory & Whig: The Struggle in the Constituencies 1701–1715* (London: Macmillan, 1970), pp. 27, 130.

27. *Letters*, pp. 105–8: Lee, 2: 511–14. Defoe was at Coventry in 1708, another election year: *Letters*, p. 255.

28. Sutherland, pp. 251–53; Backscheider, pp. 467–70. For Carte's affair, see also *London Journal*, 18 August 1723 and *Daily Journal*, 3 November 1722, where the price on his head is announced. See also p. 29.

29. The *London Journal* announced on 14 April 1722, "The Directors of the South-Sea Company have lately taken some new Resolutions in Favour of the Greenland Fishery," and implied that the Company was only waiting for new accommodation to be built. However, on 28 April the same newspaper reported the deferment of these plans. See David Macpherson, *Annals of Commerce* (London, 1805), 3: 130 ff, where parliamentary activity in support of the project is dated from 1724, and the fishing itself from 1725.

30. This is a suitable place to mention one small clue: in a number of places Defoe drops the first person singular and conducts the narrative in the plural. Some of these sections correspond to journeys that Defoe had demonstrably made in company—the South West of Scotland with Pierce (whoever he was), *Letters*, p. 163 & n; the West Country, with an unnamed minister, and perhaps with his brother-in-law Robert Davis; and with Christopher Hurt around Norwich and King's Lynn (compare 1: 73–75 with *Letters*, p. 59 & n. 3). Moore, *Citizen*, p. 179, suggests that Davis is the "Navigator" mentioned at 1: 254. Whether Defoe slipped into the "we" form consciously or unconsciously, it does seem that the usage is not random, but directly related to the actual circumstances in which he visited a given part of the country.

31. Tallard was allowed to return to France after the fall of Marlborough at the end of 1711.

32. *Records of the Borough of Nottingham, 1702–60* (Nottingham, 1914), 6: 85, 90.

33. *Letters*, p. 117: Wright, pp. 176–77. In case it seems that the Halifax story has been written off too blithely, it should be pointed out that Wright has Defoe living in Yorkshire at a time when his extant letters to Harley show him moving through eastern England to Scotland, with a stay at Newcastle.

34. *Letters*, pp. 381, 384.

35. See chapter 3.

36. See for instance *Letters*, pp. 130–31, 291, 332, 369, 388, 427–28: cf. *Citizen*, p. 217, and *Checklist*, p. 122.

37. D. C. Browning, in the new Everyman edition of the *Tour* (London: Dent, 1962), strangely attributes this book to Defoe himself (1: xvii). F. Bastian indicates that Defoe made long visits to Scotland in 1698 and 1703, and indeed may have visited the Orkneys and Shetland around 1693/4: see *Defoe's Early Life* (Totowa, N.J.: Barnes and Noble, 1981), pp. 179, 211–14, 284. Like Bastian's other claims to trace the writer's movements, these are mainly conjectural, and can be neither proved nor disproved.

38. Note, too, the comment on the Duke of Roxburgh's seat in Teviotdale: "His House call'd *Floors* is an antient Seat, but begins to wear a new Face; and those who view'd it fifteen or sixteen Years ago, will scarce know it again, if they should come again a few Years hence, when the present Duke may have finished the Additions and Embellishments which he is now making, and has been a considerable Time upon" (2: 764). It is not wholly clear whether Defoe has been a recent visitor; but his phrasing suggests that he was assuredly there fifteen years before.

39. For Defoe's contacts with Queensberry around the time of the Union, see *Citizen*, p. 160, and Backscheider, pp. 224–25 228–30, as well as *Letters*.

40. I follow here *Letters*, pp. 180–81, as against Moore, *Citizen*, p. 374 n. 2, where the supposition is made that Defoe himself witnessed Hepburn's open-air meetings.

41. *Letters*, p. 218–19. Defoe's claim is likely to be accurate: the murderer was a kinsman of the Earl of Leven, with whom Defoe had close contacts. The murderer escaped from the Tolbooth, and was never brought to justice (*Letters*, p. 247).

42. *Citizen*, pp. 179–80, is based on full and convincing documentation. Defoe was certainly willing to go north in 1707 in order to check on Jacobite activities (*Letters*, p. 230). He was at this time "on Fife side."

43. In 1706 Defoe helped to settle his brother-in-law Robert Davis in a shipbuilding business in Leith: see Backscheider, 277, and see also *Letters*, pp. 182, 283–84, for comments on Leith, Queensferry and the Forth estuary. Defoe had traveled with Davis on fact-finding missions for Harley in 1705 (Backscheider, p. 186).

44. The first Earl of Stair, Hew Dalrymple, David Dalrymple and the second Duke of Queensberry all subscribed to Defoe's *Caledonia* in 1707; so did Gilbert Eliot the elder. Ormistoun was one of the more surprising omissions.

45. Defoe's comment on Yester is hard to reconcile with the known facts: "Tho' there is the Design of a noble House or Palace, and great Part of it built; yet, as it is not yet, and perhaps will not soon be finished, there is no giving a compleat Description of it" (2: 697). All the authorities available to me date the rebuilding of Yester to the period 1740–46. Defoe may simply have heard from a distance that a new house was planned, and attempted to hide behind a studied vagueness.

46. Summerson, pp. 105–11.

CHAPTER 3. THE USES OF PLAGIARISM

1. *PQ*, 8 (1929): 187–88. Davies's subsequent study appeared in *MP*, 48 (1950): 21–36. An article by J. H. Andrews, "Defoe and the Sources of his *Tour*," *Geographical Journal*, 136 (1960): 268–77, is of some interest. See also F. Bastian, "Defoe's *Tour* and the Historian," *History Today*, 17 (1967): 845–51.

2. See p. 24.

3. Macky, *Journey through England* (1714–23), 2: 5 ff.; 1: 386. Both Macky and

Defoe are cited in Otto Erich Deutsch, *Handel: A Documentary Biography* (London: Black, 1955), pp. 144–45, 190–91.

4. The 1722 edition of *Britannia* was published prior to the appearance of the *Tour*, but it can be shown that Defoe used the 1695 version. This was the copy listed in *Librorum ex Bibliothecis Philippi Farewell, D. D., et Danielis De Foe, Gen.* (London, 1731), p. 5. Defoe first cited Gibson's edition in *An Essay upon Projects* (1697). See also Appendix B.

5. Similarly Defoe allots a paragraph of 159 words to the Peverell line (1: 38–39). Camden provides exactly the same facts in 85 words (col. 346). The discrepancy is caused by Defoe's fondness for arch asides and genteel evasions: Camden's blunt "Concubine" becomes "Mistress, or what else you please to call it." Always the movement is extensive, rather than intensive.

6. See also the account of Salisbury Cathedral in Camden, col. 92, and Defoe, 1: 190.

7. Equally, it would be a mistake to imagine that Defoe's life history of Bishop Herbert (1: 68) demonstrates a wide-ranging familiarity with medieval sources. Defoe has simply put together an abridgement of Camden's dispersed references to the bishop (cols. 383, 386–87, 400). The account is based on adroit mental indexing rather than deep learning.

8. See J. H. Andrews, "A Case of Plagiarism in Defoe's *Tour*," *N&Q*, 6.10 (1959): 399.

9. It should be noted that Defoe will use an innocent-looking phrase such as "They boast that . . ." as a prelude to a borrowing. Such a formula, as at 1: 34, points not to local gossip, but to *Britannia*—here, Gibson's note (col. 359).

10. At one point Defoe conducts a cross-argument with "our Friend" Gervaise of Tilbury (1: 580), safe in the undisclosed knowledge that Camden had quoted the story in order to dismiss it (col. 495). For what are obviously direct borrowings from Carew, see *Tour*, 1:234–36, 257; compare Richard Carew, *The Survey of Cornwall*, ed., F. E. Halliday (London: Andrew Melrose, 1953), pp. 136, 203, 210, and 212.

11. Compare the rather similar finding of Arthur W. Secord, that Bulstrode Whitelocke may be almost the only source for the Civil War sections of *Memoirs of a Cavalier*, despite the alleged similarities with other historians. Secord's essay, "The Origins of Defoe's *Memoirs of a Cavalier*," appears in *Robert Drury's Journal and Other Studies* (Urbana: University of Illinois Press, 1961), pp. 72–133. His conclusion that "The *Memoirs* is essentially a compilation based on previously printed biographies, memoirs, and histories" (p. 130) is suggestive with regard to the *Tour*.

12. Secord wrote earlier that "Defoe's invention begins where history leaves off, embroidering fictions round the facts." See his *Studies in the Narrative Method of Defoe* (Urbana: University of Illinois Press, 1924), p. 236. It is possible that, in addition to antiquarian works, Defoe had recourse to contemporary manuals to glean facts on matters such as parliament and the peerage: these would include John Chamberlayne's *Anglicana Notitiae* or Guy Miège's *Present State of England*, both of which appeared in numerous editions. But I have not found conclusive evidence to this effect. On Windsor, as noted elsewhere (p. 181), Defoe applied to Elias Ashmole's history of the Order of the Garter.

13. Defoe has at least one amusing dig at Camden. His passage abjuring epithalamia when he comes to the meeting of the Thames and Isis (1: 173) relates to Camden's section on the marriage of these rivers, beginning, "Near this place Tame and Isis with mutual consent joyn as it were in wedlock, and mix their names as well as their waters" (Camden, col. 264). Verses on the subject follow in Latin and English: for an extensive citation, see my essay, "*Windsor-Forest, Britannia*, and River Poetry,"

Essays on Pope (Cambridge: Cambridge University Press, 1993), pp. 54–69. For Defoe's passage in response, see p. 141.

Another facetious reference occurs at Coventry, when Defoe alludes to the story of Lady Godiva as she rode naked through the streets: "But Mr. *Cambden* says positively no body look'd at her at all" (2: 483).

CHAPTER 4. THE RHETORIC OF GROWTH AND DECAY

1. G D. H. Cole, introduction to the Everyman edition of *A Tour through the Whole Island of Great Britain* (London: Dent, 1962), 1: vii. (This is a different introduction to the one Cole supplied for *Tour*.) For a similar judgment, see the Everyman introduction: "It is, then, primarily as a guide to social and economic conditions that DeFoe's *Tour* is important" (1: ix).

2. Cole, introduction to Everyman edition, 1: vi–vii.

3. Cole, introduction to Everyman edition, 1: v.

4. See chapter 5. Surprisingly, *improve(ment)* is not especially widespread in the text.

5. Cole enunciates the traditional view well enough: "Here then I leave the *Tour*, making for it no extravagant claim as a work of exceptional genius, but rather suggesting that its very plainness and the humble purpose it was designed to serve give it a special value as a work of historical record. It is well written, in clear quickly-moving sentences that make it easy and pleasant reading. That is all De Foe tried to make it" (1: xxiv). The same notion of Defoe's plain and artless style appears in Esther Moir's account: "Defoe in contrast [to Celia Fiennes] writes a straight-forward narrative prose, cold, critical and measured, scorning to indulge in the hyperboles with which her work is adorned" (*The Discovery of Britain* [London: Routledge, 1964], p. 36). My own analysis prompts an opposite conclusion on all the issues raised here, as regards Defoe; even the word "critical" may need some qualifications.

6. Other relevant items of "growth" vocabulary are *glut, overgrown, throng,* and *multiply*.

7. *Increase* does figure in *A Journal of the Plague Year,* but by no means so prominently. (*Innumerable* and its variants also appear.) *Spread,* on the other hand, appears to be relatively more common in the *Journal* than in the *Tour*.

8. A representative context for *sink* is this: "But now things infinitely modern . . . are become Marks of Antiquity; for even the Castle of *York* . . . is not only become antient and decayed, but even sunk into Time, and almost lost and forgotten; Fires, Sieges, Plunderings and Devastations, have often been the Fate of *York;* so that one should wonder there should be any thing of a City left" (2: 636).

9. Esther Moir writes, "Defoe's determination not to be led astray from his avowed purpose of studying the present day into the delightful view of antiquity, has deprived us of what would undoubtedly have been refreshingly sane and balanced descriptions" (p. 45). This is to take Defoe's protestations too literally; his need to *resolve* and *mortify himself* arises from his inability to stick to his declared objectives. Actually the *Tour* never holds to this self-denying ordinance for longer than a page or two at a time. The book is full of passages like this: "I was tempted greatly here to trace the famous *Picts* Wall, built by the *Romans* . . . of the Particulars of which, and the Remains of Antiquity seen upon it, all our Histories are so full; and I did go to several Places in the Fields thro' which I passed, where I saw the Remains of it, some almost lost, some plain to be seen. But Antiquity not being my Business in this

Work, I omitted the Journey, and went on for the North" (2: 661). Thus, Defoe has his cake and eats it.

10. A well-known instance occurs in the description of Bushey Heath: "It was all Nature, and yet look'd all like Art" (1: 388). See also 2: 581.

11. Defoe speaks of "the Corps of the old *English* Grandeur laid in State" (1: 365), by which he means the "ruin'd Antiquity" of the Palace of Westminster.

12. *Abate* and *decline* also figure on a number of occasions, e.g., 2: 449. *Depredated* occurs at 1: 187.

13. See 1: 37, 356: and for Defoe's obsession with the Bubble, see Introduction, pp. 31–34. There are also references to the ruin occasioned by the stop of the Exchequer in 1672 (e.g., 1: 153).

14. Hyperbole of an orthodox cast—"almost every Gentleman's House is a Castle" (2: 682)—is quite common also. Cf. 1: 384 (Hampstead Heath is "so near Heaven" that only a race of "Mountaineers" could live there!), as well as 1: 391; 2: 807.

15. *Utmost* appears in one way or another on at least ten occasions, generally in combination with a word like *extent*. A strange phrase employed is "so every where" (1: 162). Superlatives come in bundles: *the best and fattest, and the largest veal*.

16. Variants are *to an extreme,* and *to perfection*. Another mode of emphatic super-lative is attained simply by accumulation: "the first, and best, if not the only Haven" (1: 256).

17. Cf. also 2: 427: "Nor can any Nation in *Europe* show the like Munificence to any General, no nor the greatest in the World; and not to go back to antient times, not the French Nation to the great *Luxemberg,* or the yet great *Turenne*: Nor the Emperor to the great *Eugene,* or to the yet greater Duke of *Lorrain* . . . I say none of these ever receiv'd so glorious a Mark of their Country's Favour," as did Marlborough when the nation bestowed Blenheim Palace on him.

18. The word *considerable* appears over seventy times. Defoe maybe thought that it was not an impressive term without a modifier; *very considerable* is the com-monest usage.

19. *Abound* is employed in a few places, normally in proximity to "growth" clusters involving *flourishing* and the like. The "Abundance" of citizens making a "glorious show of Wealth and Plenty" provide a view of "the Luxuriant Age in which we live" (1: 169).

20. See my book on *Robinson Crusoe* (London: Allen and Unwin, 1979), pp. 122–3; and "Moll's Memory," *English,* 24 (1975): 69–72.

21. For an interesting discussion of relevant issues, see David Trotter, *Circulation: Defoe, Dickens and the Economies of the Novel* (New York: St Martin's, 1988). Trotter has a brief but suggestive passage on images of circulation in the *Tour* (pp. 1–6).

22. Hence the need for perpetual adjustments: "Addenda" to Volume I, "Appen-dix" to Letter I and Volume II: Prefaces to each volume, two Introductions (one for Scotland) in Volume III. Almost all of these contain updating of what has gone and what has sprung up in its place.

CHAPTER 5. THE GEORGIC ELEMENT IN THE *TOUR*

1. John Chalker, *The English Georgic* (London: Routledge, 1969). An earlier and still valuable study is Dwight L. Durling, *Georgic Tradition in English Poetry* (New York: Columbia University Press, 1935).

2. Paul Fussell, *The Rhetorical World of Augustan Humanism* (Oxford:

Clarendon, 1965), p. 264. I should perhaps add my opinion that Fussell's book is in general an exemplary work of criticism.

3. Earlier Everyman reprints of the *Tour* omitted the Scottish sections and were retitled in the form Fussell employs. After 1962 the entire text was made available and the original title substituted.

4. Phrases such as "an innumerable Number," "full Perfection of Decay" and so on, are discussed more fully in chapter 4. See 1: 54 for a central passage on Dunwich in Suffolk: "This Town is a Testimony of the decay of Publick Things, Things of the most durable Nature . ." (cited p. 120). Virgil is quoted from the Loeb edition (Cambridge, Mass.: Harvard University Press, 1946), of which vol. 1 contains the *Georgics.* Translations by Dryden are taken from *The Poems of John Dryden,* ed. J. Kinsley (Oxford: Clarendon, 1958), 2: 935–66.

5. Dryden translates:

> Then, after length of Time, the lab'ring Swains,
> Who turn the Turf of those unhappy Plains,
> Shall rusty Piles form the plough'd Furrows take,
> And over empty Helmets pass the Rake,
> Amaz'd at Antick Titles on the Stones,
> And mighty Relicks of Gygantick Bones.

6. Dryden's version is this:

> Where Fraud and Rapine, Right and Wrong confound,
> Where impious Arms from ev'ry part resound,
> And monstrous Crimes in ev'ry Shape are crown'd.
> The peaceful Peasant to the Wars is prest;
> The Fields lye fallow in inglorious Rest.
> The Plain no Pasture to the Flock affords,
> The crooked Scythes are streightned into Swords.

7. Here is the corresponding passage in Dryden:

> Thus, form'd for speed, he challenges the wind;
> And leaves the *Scythian* Arrow far behind;
> He scours the Field, with loosen'd Reins,
> And treads so light, he scarcely prints the plains.
> Like *Boreas* in his race, when rushing forth,
> He sweeps the Skies, and clears the cloudy North:
> The waving Harvest bends beneath his blast;
> The Forest shakes, the Groves their Honours cast;
> He flies aloft, and with impetuous roar
> Pursues the foaming Surges to the Shoar.
> Thus o're th' *Elean* Plains, thy well-breath'd Horse
> Impels the flying Carr, and wins the Course.

8. It might be noted that the ending to the second *Georgic* is echoed by Defoe's own use of the self-conscious metaphor to describe his own progress: e.g., "But I must land, lest this Part of the Account seems to smell of the Tarr, and I should tire the Gentlemen with leading them out of their Knowledge" (1: 351).

9. In Dryden's translation:

> Nor will I tire thy Patience with a train
> Of Preface, or what ancient Poets feign.

10. See for example Reuben A. Brower, *Alexander Pope: The Poetry of Allusion* (Oxford: Clarendon, 1959), pp. 40–41.

11. J. R. Moore, *Defoe in the Pillory and other Studies* (Bloomington: Indiana University Press, 1939), p. 156. It should be noted that Defoe wrote just too early to benefit from a new wave of work on the archeology of Roman Britain, instituted by John Horsley's *Britannia Romana* (1732), as well as by the published journeys of William Stukeley. On Horsley, see Joseph M. Levine, *The Battle of the Books: History and Literature in the Augustan Age* (Ithaca: Cornell University Press, 1991), pp. 389–402.

12. Compare 1: 167–69, for a similar alignment of nature and art in the "shining" seats by the Thames in this "luxuriant" age. For an interesting gloss on the passage quoted in the text, see A. R. Humphreys, *The Augustan World* (London: Methuen, 1954), pp. 26–27.

13. Defoe characteristically speaks of "gleaning" a rich "Harvest" of information when he begins his *Tour* (1: 2): see p. 56.

CHAPTER 6. SPEAKING WITHIN COMPASS

1. Jane Austen, *Mansfield Park*, ed. John Lucas (London: Oxford University Press, 1970), p. 85.

2. See pp. 49–50. The passage shows that Defoe had roughly sketched the plan of Letter VI, in Volume II, at least a year in advance.

3. *The Life, Adventures and Piracies of the Famous Captain Singleton*, ed. James Sutherland (London: Dent, 1963), p. 58. Future references to this edition are supplied in the text.

4. J. H. Plumb, "The Search for the Nile," in *Men and Places* (Harmondsworth: Penguin, 1966), pp. 213–23; quotations are from pp. 213–14.

5. Other examples to add to those cited in the text would include "the next Day, which was the tenth from our setting out" (105); "we found none till after twenty Days Travel, including eight Days Rest" (141); and "On the thirteenth Day we set forward . . . after a Day's March upon this River . . . we followed it about three days" (158).

6. Lincoln B. Faller remarks that "Singleton finds—and makes—Africa impenetrable even as he succeeds in traversing it": see *Crime and Defoe: A New Kind of Writing* (Cambridge: Cambridge University Press, 1993), p. 97. By contrast the *Tour's* methods make Britain "penetrable" by author/traveler and reader/?nontraveler alike.

CHAPTER 7. THE WONDERLESS WONDERS OF THE PEAK

1. P. N. Hartle, "Defoe and *The Wonders of the Peake*: The Place of Cotton's Poem in *A Tour thro' the Whole Island of Great Britain*," *English Studies*, 67 (1986): 420–31. Hartle points out that Defoe had probably not been to the Peak since 1712, and may have experienced bad weather on his earlier visits (p. 425). He also shows that Charles Leigh was the main source, and that John Macky (who quoted Cotton's poem at length) was not a principal aid to Defoe (p. 423).

2. See *The English Travels of Sir John Percival and William Byrd II*, ed. Mark R. Wenger (Columbia: University of Missouri Press, 1989), pp. 144–50.

For the way in which antiquarian surveys, like that of Charles Leigh for the Peak district, gradually took more notice of geological issues, see the chapter on "The

Natural History of the Earth" in Roy Porter, *The Making of Geology* (Cambridge: Cambridge University Press, 1977), esp. pp. 53–58. Porter's book supplies an excellent intellectual context for the discussion of natural "wonders" in Defoe.

3. For Defoe's habits in this regard, see chapter 3.

4. See J. Paul Hunter, *Before Novels* (New York: Norton, 1990), pp. 208–17.

5. See *Checklist*, p. 70.

6. He has already suggested that the capacity of the local Barmoot Court to sort out the wrangles of the notoriously quarrelsome Peak inhabitants "may be called the greatest of all the Wonders of the *Peak*" (2: 566).

7. As well as proverbs such as "Wonder is the daughter of ignorance." We might recall titles such as Susannah Centlivre's *The Wonder: A Woman Keeps a Secret* (1714), one of the most popular stage plays in the period.

8. For the use of hyperbole in the *Tour*, see pp. 129–34.

9. See for example *Travels of Percival*, p. 15ff.

10. Hartle (p. 425) says that it is hard to determine "the reasons for Defoe's antipathy to the Peak." The analysis here suggests that his major antipathy was to the credulous and hyperbolic descriptions which topographic writers had given of the region. It is less an attack on the Peak *per se* than a rebuke to fanciful antiquarians, poets, and mythographers of this emerging tourist area.

A classic instance of the demythologizing urge in Defoe occurs elsewhere in the *Tour* at Stonehenge, when the narrator describes as "*a meer Country Fiction, and a ridiculous one too*" a story that it was impossible to count the number of stones twice and get the same answer each time (1: 197). Defoe performs the experiment and finds that on four tests the score is always 72—a nicely round, almost geometrical, result.

For the later development of the cult of the Wonders of the Peak, as promoted by the tourist industry of the later eighteenth century, see Ian Ousby, *The Englishman's England: Taste, Travel and the Rise of Tourism* (Cambridge: Cambridge University Press, 1990), pp. 131–37. It needs scarcely to be said that Defoe's skepticism did not prevail.

CHAPTER 8. DEFOE'S BUILDINGS OF ENGLAND

1. *Tour*, I, 2. The work referred to is Peter Borsay, *The English Urban Renaissance* (Oxford: Clarendon, 1989).

2. See Spiro Peterson, "Defoe and Westminster, 1676–1706," ECS, 12 (1979): 306–38.

3. The use of this same vocabulary in describing (often identical) estates is noted by Mark R. Wenger ed., *The English Travels of Sir John Percival and William Byrd II* (Columbia: University of Missouri Press, 1989), pp. 28–29. Percival was sometimes more sympathetic and expressive on certain styles of architecture, notably Perpendicular (Wenger, p. 30). Defoe usually admires the situation as well as the architecture of the great houses, but Petworth is an exception (1: 133).

4. See for example Bryan Little, *The Building of Bath* (London: Collins, 1948), p. 62.

CHAPTER 9. TRANSFORMATIONS

1. Peter Borsay, "Urban Development in the Age of Defoe," in *Britain in the First Age of Party, 1660–1750*, ed. C. Jones (London: Hambledon Press, 1987), pp.

195–219. See also the same author's important study, *The English Urban Renaissance* (Oxford: Clarendon, 1989).

2. For Defoe's business interests in Scotland, see Backsheider, pp. 300–12.

3. G. M. Trevelyan, *Illustrated English Social History* (Harmondsworth: Pelican, 1964), pp. 17–83; quotations from pp. 17–18.

4. M. Dorothy George, *England in Transition: Life and Work in the Eighteenth Century* (Harmondsworth: Penguin, 1953), pp. 29–42; quotation from p. 29. Four extracts from the *Tour* are printed in George's anthology *England in Johnson's Day* (London: Methuen, 1928).

5. Peter Mathias, *The First Industrial Nation* (London: Methuen, 1969), p. 161.

6. Clapham, for example, quotes Defoe seventeen times in fifty pages on industrialism, and seven times in nine pages: see *A Concise Economic History of Britain: From the Earliest Times to 1750* (Cambridge: Cambridge University Press, 1963).

Defoe's continuing centrality in this area of study is evidenced by the opening words of a recent work: "This is a book about the middle classes in the period between 1660 and 1730. The period was chosen because of the availability of sources and also because it was the lifetime of Daniel Defoe . . . whose views on a wide range of subjects will be found scattered through the pages." Chapter 1 of the same work begins, "This is a book about the men and women who occupied what Daniel Defoe called the middle station." See Peter Earle, *The Making of the Middle Class: Business, Society and Family Life in London, 1660–1730* (Berkeley: University of California Press, 1989), pp. xi, 3. The *Tour* is of course not the only text by Defoe cited, but it is drawn on regularly, along with a battery of up-to-date statistical and computer-based findings. Particularly relevant to the present book is Earle's discussion of London's role in the national economy, where he cites Defoe's account of Stourbridge Fair (pp. 40–44).

7. T. S. Ashton, *An Economic History of England: The Eighteenth Century* (London: Methuen, 1955), p. 33.

Defoe was not engaging in hyperbole when he stressed the prosperity of the nation. It was generally agreed that "by 1700 Englishmen enjoyed a higher level of material welfare than the inhabitants of any other country in the world, save Holland." See Keith Thomas, *Religion and the Decline of Magic* (Harmondsworth: Penguin, 1991), p. 778.

8. Peter Earle, *The World of Defoe* (London: Weidenfeld, 1976), pp. 107–8. One of the surprising omissions in the *Tour* is noted by Earle: "Birmingham, the most rapidly developing industrial town in the country, is hardly mentioned" (p. 126). In defense of the author, it could be said that the population of Birmingham (a market town in previous centuries) was still only 7,000 in 1700; when Defoe wrote his book, the population had not yet risen beyond 12,000. By the midcentury, twenty years after Defoe's death, it reached almost 25,000; but the main period of takeoff came in the second half of the century.

9. It is fair to observe that stability as well as change characterized some aspects of economic life, as it did social and political life. To take a single example, inflation was amazingly low by modern standards. A cost of living index based on the year 1700 (as 100) had reached only 133 by 1790, and in several decades it actually fell. (The index used is that of E. W. Gilboy.) Equally, the population grew only slightly in Defoe's day; it actually declined in the late 1720s, when the birthrate dropped and the death rate surged.

10. For a convenient summary of developments in insurance and fire fighting in the period, see Thomas, *Religion and Magic*, pp. 779–83. For Defoe's losses in shipping and marine insurance, see Backscheider, pp. 52–62.

11. These figures are drawn from a variety of sources, including the following major authorities: E. A. Wrigley and R. S. Schofield, *The Population History of England, 1541 to 1871: A Reconstruction* (Cambridge: Cambridge University Press, 1981), especially pp. 192–284; E. A. Wrigley, *People, Cities and Wealth: The Transformation of Traditional Society* (Oxford: Blackwell, 1987); P. J. Corfield, *The Impact of English Towns* (Oxford: Oxford University Press, 1982); C. W. Chalklin, *The Provincial Towns of Georgian England* (London: Edward Arnold, 1974); Peter Mathias, *The Transformation of England: Essays in the Economic and Social History of England in the Eighteenth Century* (London: Methuen, 1979); Peter Clark, ed., *The Transformation of English Provincial Towns 1600–1800* (London: Hutchinson, 1984); as well as Borsay's book, cited in note 1 above.

Broadly speaking, it was with Britain as with the rest of Europe. In the century prior to Defoe's lifetime, larger cities had grown more rapidly than smaller cities (say, those with less than 50,000 inhabitants). It was not until 1750 that the process was reversed, and towns like Birmingham and Glasgow started to grow quicker than London. For a statistical demonstration, see Jan de Vries, *European Urbanization 1500–1800* (Cambridge, Mass: Harvard University Press, 1984), pp. 104–7. It is noteworthy that even in Scotland a full 17 percent of the population were urban livers by 1800, taking the threshold as communities above 10,000 people (de Vries, p. 44). This is a figure well above the European norm, and represents a process of deruralization which had started to become apparent in Defoe's time.

12. *A Plan of the English Commerce* (1728, reprint, Oxford: Blackwell, 1928), p. 1.

13. In the *Review* in 1711 Defoe claimed that he had tracked through "every Nook and Corner" of England, adding, "I have been in every County, one excepted. . . ." We do not know which was the single county that had escaped his attention at this date. Possibilities might be Herefordshire or Monmouthshire. In any case, the gap was probably filled by 1724.

14. See Earle, *Middle Class,* for confirmation of this point. To cite only statements from the opening pages of Earle's book: he argues that "in this period, London . . . totally dominated English urban culture and indeed invented it" (p. xi), an emphasis Defoe repeatedly lays in the *Tour.* We are reminded that "this was still a pre-industrial society in which most capital was engaged in agriculture, commerce and distribution" (p. 4); Defoe was observant about the first, though not expert, and thoroughly knowledgeable about the second and third of these areas. Earle further charts the rise of "active merchants who considered themselves and were considered by others to be gentlemen" (p. 8). The *Tour* mentions several such men.

Another recent historian to cite Defoe on the growth of London is L. D. Schwarz, *London in the Age of Industrialization* (Cambridge: Cambridge University Press, 1992), pp. 8, 79. For a general survey which makes extensive use of Defoe, see Jack Lindsay, *The Monster City: Defoe's London, 1688–1730* (London: Granada, 1978).

CONCLUSION

1. *Letters,* p. 385.

APPENDIX A

1. Godfrey Davies, "Daniel Defoe's *A Tour thro' the whole Island of Great Britain*," *MP,* 48 (1950): 21–36.

2. For a summary of the history, see my note "Later Editions of Defoe's *Tour*," *The Book Collector*, 25 (1976): 390–92.

3. For various views, see William M. Sale, Jr., *Samuel Richardson: A Bibliographical Record* (New Haven, 1936; reprint, Hamden, Conn.: Archon, 1969), pp. 39–44.

4. T. C. Duncan Eaves and Ben D. Kimpel, *Samuel Richardson: A Biography* (Oxford: Clarendon, 1971), pp. 72–76. Quotation from p. 73^n.

5. William M. Sale, Jr., *Samuel Richardson: Master Printer* (Ithaca: Cornell University Press, 1950), p. 163.

6. The repairs mentioned seem to be those begun in the 1690s. The hall was repaired in 1720, and there were already plans for a new Library in 1725—but these had to be deferred. See H. C. Maxwell Lyte, *A History of Eton College* (1911), p. 289.

7. The catchword at the foot of p. 72 is "LET-," leading to Letter II on the next recto. It is likely that the original intention was to start the next gathering with another letter, but the alteration made this impossible.

8. For example, two paragraphs earlier, the reviser had turned a reference to the ownership of a lodge at Windsor from the present to the past tense. One paragraph back, he had cut out a parenthesis to the effect that all bridges over the Thames were of timber.

9. See Sale, *A Bibliographical Record*, p. 41. The note is possibly by William Musgrave.

10. Richardson had also printed a portion of the first edition (1724–26). See items 30, 232, 295, 352, 406 and 514 in Sale, *Richardson: Master Printer*.

11. See items 28–32 in Sale, *Richardson: A Bibliographical Record*.

12. A detailed description of the changes is given in my note, "Defoe's *Tour* (1742) and the Chapbook Trade," *The Library*, 6.6. (1984): 275–79.

13. Information on Harris and Hodges comes initially from H. R. Plomer, *A Dictionary of the Printers and Booksellers . . . from 1726 to 1775* (Oxford: Oxford University Press, 1932), pp. 116, 127–28. There is a little more on Hodges in Victor E. Neuburg, *Popular Education in Eighteenth Century England* (London: Woburn, 1971), p. 161: see also Neuburg, *Chapbooks: A Guide to Reference Material*, 2nd ed. (London, 1972), p. 52. More pertinent information came from Professor Michael Treadwell, who offered many valuable suggestions.

14. I do not know the price of a share in the rights in 1740. Twenty years later, Thomas Lowndes bought one thirty-second share in the *Tour* for five guineas: this would indicate the full rights were worth £168. Then in 1772 Lowndes bought one ninety-sixth share, which cost him £1.11.6: this would mean that the full rights were worth £151.4.0. For the purposes of comparison, it may be added that a job lot including *Moll Flanders* and *Roxana* (one-eighth shares of each) cost Lowndes one guinea only in 1770. See British Library, Add. MS. 38730, ff. 39, 168, 200.

15. Professor Treadwell points out to me that this meant the chapmen need not penetrate the City directly: many of them would have confined their activities to the north or south of the urban center. This would obviate territorial disputes, economize on time and effort, and simplify distribution. See also Cyprian Blagden, "Notes on the Ballad Market in the Second Half of the Seventeenth Century," *SB*, 6 (1954): 161–80.

16. *A Tour* (3rd ed. London, 1742), 1: 173 (typographically normalized).

17. R. C. Alston, correspondence in *The Library*, 6.7 (1985): 63.

APPENDIX B

1. *Librorum ex Bibliothecis Philippi Farewell, D. D. et Danielis De Foe, Gent.* [1731]. There is an edition by Helmut Heidenreich (Berlin: Hildebrand, 1970).

Bibliography

EDITIONS OF DANIEL DEFOE'S *TOUR*

A *Tour Thro' the whole Island of Great Britain, Divided into Circuits or Journies* . . . (By a Gentleman). London: Strahan, 1724-"27" [26]. 3 vols.

A *Tour thro' the Whole Island of Great Britain* . . . *by Daniel Defoe, Gent*. With an Introduction by G.D.H. Cole. London: Peter Davies, 1927; Reprint, London: Frank Cass, 1968. 2 vols. This is the text used in the present book.

A *Tour Through the Whole Island of Great Britain*. With an introduction by G. D. H. Cole. London: Everyman, 1962. 2 vols. This edition was originally published in 1927 without the Scottish sections as A *Tour through England and Wales*.

A *Tour through the Whole Island of Great Britain*. Abridged and edited with an introduction and notes by Pat Rogers. Harmondsworth: Penguin, 1971.

A *Tour through the Whole Island of Great Britain*. With an introduction by Pat Rogers. London: Folio Society, 1983. 3 vols.

A *Tour Through the Whole Island of Great Britain*. Abridged and edited by Pat Rogers, with photographs by Simon McBride. Exeter: Webb and Bower, 1989.

A *Tour Through the Whole Island of Great Britain*. Abridged and edited by P. N. Furbank and W. R. Owens: picture research by A. J. Coulson. New Haven and London: Yale University Press, 1991.

For the later eighteenth-century editions of the *Tour*, see Appendix A above.

ANCILLARY WORKS

The Letters of Daniel Defoe. Edited by G. H. Healey. Oxford: Clarendon, 1955.

The Libraries of Daniel Defoe and Phillips Farewell. Edited by H. Heidenreich. Berlin: Hildebrand, 1970.

Moore, J. R. A *Checklist of the Writings of Daniel Defoe*. Bloomington: Indiana University Press, 1960. See also P. N. Furbank and W. R. Owens. *Defoe De-Attributions: A Critique of J.R. Moore's Checklist*. London: Hambledon Press, 1994.

SECONDARY WORKS

Andrews, J. H. "A Case of Plagiarism in Defoe's *Tour*," *N&Q*, n.s. 6 (1959): 399.

——. "Defoe and the Sources of his *Tour*," *Geographical Journal*, 126 (1960): 268-70.

——. "Defoe's *Tour* and Macky's *Journey*," *N&Q*, n.s. 7 (1960): 290–92.

Backscheider, Paula R. *Daniel Defoe: His Life*. Baltimore: Johns Hopkins Press, 1989.

Bastian, F. "Defoe's *Tour* and the Historian." *History Today,* 17 (1967): 845–51.

Borsay, Peter. "Urban Development in the Age of Defoe," in *Britain in the First Age of Party, 1680–1750.* Edited by C. Jones. London: Hambledon Press, 1987, 195–219.

———.*The English Urban Renaissance.* Oxford: Clarendon, 1985.

Camden, William. *Britannia,* ed. Edmund Gibson (1695; reprint, Newton Abbot, Devon: David & Charles, 1971.

Davies, Godfrey. "Daniel Defoe's A *Tour thro' the whole Island of Great Britain.*" *MP,* 48 (1951): 21–36.

Duckworth, Alistair M. "Whig Landscapes in Defoe's *Tour.*" *PQ,* 61 (1982): 453–65.

Earle, Peter. *The Making of the English Middle Class: Business, Society and Family Life in London, 1660–1730.* Berkeley: University of California Press, 1989.

———. *The World of Defoe.* London: Weidenfeld, 1976.

Hartle, P. N. "Defoe and *The Wonders of the Peake.*" *English Studies,* 67 (1986): 420–31.

Lee, William. *Daniel Defoe: His Life and Recently Discovered Writings.* 3 vols. 1869; Reprint, Hildesheim: Georg Olms, 1968.

Moir, Esther. *The Discovery of Britain.* London: Routledge, 1964.

Ousby, Ian. *The Englishman's England: Taste, Travel and the Rise of Tourism.* Cambridge: Cambridge University Press, 1990.

Sill, Geoffrey M. "Defoe's *Tour:* Literary Art or Moral Imperative?" *ECS,* 11 (1977): 79–83.

Index

The index is divided into three sections: (1) Persons, (2) Places, and (3) Topics. For matters that receive extensive coverage in the *Tour*, see Index 1 under "Defoe." For general references within the present book, see Index 3.

Main entries are in bold face.

DD = Daniel Defoe

(1) PERSONS

(2) Places

The place-name in each entry is allocated to counties according to their boundaries in Defoe's time, not to the modern location.

(3) Topics

See also Index 1 under Defoe, Daniel